Scientific-Technological Change and the Role of Women in Development

Also of Interest

Science and Technology in a Changing International Order, edited by Volker Rittberger

† *From Dependency to Development: Strategies to Overcome Underdevelopment and Inequality*, edited by Heraldo Muñoz

Women and Technological Change in Developing Countries, edited by Roslyn Dauber and Melinda L. Cain

Transnational Enterprises: Their Impact on Third World Societies and Cultures, edited by Krishna Kumar

Women and the Social Costs of Economic Development: Two Colorado Case Studies, Elizabeth Moen, Elise Boulding, Jane Lillydahl, and Risa Palm

Technological Progress in Latin America: The Prospects for Overcoming Dependency, edited by James H. Street and Dilmus D. James

† *The Underside of History: A View of Women Through Time*, Elise Boulding

† *The Theory and Structures of International Political Economy*, edited by Todd Sandler

Economic Development, Poverty, and Income Distribution, edited by William Loehr and John P. Powelson

A Select Bibliography on Economic Development, with Annotations, John P. Powelson

Appropriate Technology for Development: A Discussion and Case Histories, edited by Donald D. Evans and Laurie Nogg Adler

† *The Challenge of the New International Economic Order*, edited by Edwin P. Reubens

† Available in hardcover and paperback.

Westview Special Studies on Social, Political, and Economic Development

*Scientific-Technological Change
and the Role of Women in Development*
edited by Pamela M. D'Onofrio-Flores
and Sheila M. Pfafflin

This critique by women of male-generated and male-dominated technologies grows out of a consciousness of women as essential, yet unsalaried, participants in production processes. The authors document the ways in which women suffer from technological development in industrialized and developing countries and assess how technological developments perpetuate inequalities between nations, regions, classes, and sexes. They discuss the implementation of modern technology in agriculture and its effects on rural women, look at the position of women in the basic and applied sciences and in science policymaking, and analyze the place of women in selected technology-based industries.

Pamela M. D'Onofrio-Flores is a researcher and writer at the United Nations Institute for Training and Research (UNITAR) and was a member of the UNITAR delegation to the 1979 United Nations Conference on Science and Technology for Development (UNCSTD). She was a drafter of the resolution "Women, Science, and Technology" adopted at that Conference. **Sheila M. Pfafflin** is president of the Association for Women in Science. After receiving her doctorate from Johns Hopkins University she worked for Bell Laboratories doing research in human behavior and learning; she is now at the American Telephone and Telegraph Company in the Human Resources Department.

Published for

UNITED NATIONS INSTITUTE
FOR TRAINING AND RESEARCH
(UNITAR)

INSTITUT DES NATIONS UNIES
POUR LA FORMATION ET LA RECHERCHE
(UNITAR)

Scientific-Technological Change and the Role of Women in Development

edited by
Pamela M. D'Onofrio-Flores
and Sheila M. Pfafflin

Westview Press / Boulder, Colorado

Westview Special Studies in Social, Political, and Economic Development

Published in 1982 in the United States of America by
Westview Press, Inc.
5500 Central Avenue
Boulder, Colorado 80301
Frederick A. Praeger, Publisher

UNITAR RR/27

Library of Congress Cataloging in Publication Data
Main entry under title:
Scientific-technological change and the role of women in development.
 (Westview's special studies in social, political, and economic development)
 Includes edited papers presented at the 1979 United Nations Conference on Science and Technology for Development.
 Includes index.
 Contents: Technology, economic development, and the division of labour by sex/Pamela M. D'Onofrio-Flores – Women and technology in the industrialized countries/Maria Bergom-Larsson – Women and technology in peripheral countries: an overview/Zenebeworke Tadesse – [etc.]
 1. Women – Social conditions – Congresses. 2. Rural women – Social conditions – Congresses. 3. Underdeveloped areas – Women – Congresses. 4. Underdeveloped areas – Technology – Social aspects – Congresses. 5. Women in science – Congresses. I. D'Onofrio-Flores, Pamela M. II. Pfafflin, Sheila M. III. United Nations Institute for Training and Research. IV. United Nations Conference on Science and Technology for Development (1979: Vienna, Austria) V. Series: Westview special study in social, political, and economic development.
HQ1154.S33   305.4′2   81-10463
ISBN: 0-86531-145-5   AACR2

Printed and bound in the United States of America

Contents

Preface

As part of its contribution to the 1979 United Nations Conference on Science and Technology for Development (UNCSTD) and the follow-up thereto, the United Nations Institute for Training and Research (UNITAR) organized an informal research group to assess various aspects of applying science and technology to development through the United Nations system. One of the activities of this group is the production and dissemination of a series of Working Papers on Science and Technology. These papers seek to provide preliminary analysis rather than definitive conclusions. Their purpose is to facilitate the access of others to the ongoing work of the group and to stimulate critical comments and reactions leading to further improvement of this work.

As UNITAR endeavours to include in its work, whenever possible, an integral component on the situation and role of women in connection with the subject under study, this series of papers on science and technology includes several papers written by women and relevant to the role of women. The production of the papers on women, science, and technology was made possible with the aid of a generous grant from the government of Norway. Revised versions of these papers make up this volume.

That the issue of the impact of scientific-technological change on the role of women in development has attained importance as an international issue may be gathered from the considerable attention it has received at the Conference of the International Women's Year, the World Population Conference, the World Food Conference, the World Conference on Agrarian Reform and Rural Development, the United Nations Conference on Technical Co-operation Among Developing Countries, the United Nations Conference on Science and Technology for Development, and the World Conference of the United Nations Decade for Women.

In response to this demonstrated interest, UNITAR, the Training and Research Centre for Women of the Economic Commission for Africa, the Economic and Social Commission for Asia and the Pacific, the United Nations Conference on Trade and Development, the United Nations Children's Fund, the International Labour Organisation, the United Nations Development Programme, the Food and Agricultural Organization of the United Nations, and the United Nations Educational, Scientific and Cultural Organization, among others, have all planned activities and studies concerning technological development in order to enhance women's economic, political, and societal efficacy.

Within the contexts of most countries, the choice and implantation of technology aggravates the existing disparities in earnings and in sociopolitical efficacy between men and women. Changes in technology that accompany "modernization" have, for the most part, led to a female concentration in domestic-related roles, nonmarket productive roles, and labour-intensive activities.

Men appear universally to assume "women's work" when production changes from a subsistence to a market economy. It also seems a universal trend that as soon as a working operation becomes mechanized it becomes a male preserve. For women this translates into the loss of control over the means of production and over economic resources as well as reduced possibilities for the provision of food and care for their families. Often it means harder work for longer hours with less appropriation of the economic returns to their own labour.

Internationally, the unequal distribution and use of scientific-technological resources, of innovative capacity (research), and of power have severe implications for women's access to technology or lack thereof. The transfer of technology in many cases has worsened the employment and health conditions of women; displacement of labour occurs, and foreign models of consumption accompany such transfer. In certain large industries operated by transnational corporations, new discriminatory labour practices have appeared in both rural and urban areas; increases in the employment of women, particularly in the urban context, have been due in great measure to an increase in the exploitation of the cheap, semiskilled labour of young and unmarried women.

The purpose of this volume is to contribute to a greater understanding of the linkages between science, technology, development, equality, and political and economic power. The UNITAR working papers written by women constitute a significant step toward positive action in the actualization of this goal by sensitizing the international community to the negative impacts suffered by women as a result of contemporary patterns of scientific-technological development and implementation.

UNITAR hopes that the ideas put forward in this book will act as a catalyst for the active and equal participation of women in the decision-making process related to science and technology, including planning and setting priorities for research and development, and in the choice, acquisition, adaptation, innovation, and application of science and technology for development.

In keeping with UNITAR policy, the opinions expressed in the chapters that make up this volume are the responsibility of the individual authors and do not necessarily reflect the views of the Institute, its Board of Trustees, or the organizations with which the authors are associated.

Davidson Nicol
Under-Secretary-General, United Nations
Executive Director, UNITAR

The Contributors

Maria Bergom-Larsson received a Ph.D. in Scandinavian literature from the University of Stockholm. She is currently a free-lance writer and literary critic, mainly in Sweden's principal morning paper, *Dagens Nyheter*. In the early 1970s she was very involved in the student and left-wing movements and published several books with a Marxist and psychoanalytical approach to literature. During the 1970s, she became active in the feminist movement and has written two books concerning family, class, and the suppression of women. For the past two years she has devoted her energies to the Women for Peace movement against nuclear power and the arms race. Her book, *Ingmar Bergman and Society*, has been translated into English.

Pamela M. D'Onofrio-Flores is currently a research assistant, Office of the Executive Director, UNITAR. She has been a consultant on science and technology for development to the International Science and Technology Affairs Programme of the Council on International and Public Affairs (New York), the United Nations Office for Science and Technology, and the Research Policy Programme, the University of Lund (Sweden). In addition she has provided expertise in the area of science and technology to such organizations as the United Nations Interim Fund for Science and Technology for Development and the Secretariat of the World Conference of the United Nations Decade for Women. She was a UNITAR delegate to the 1979 United Nations Conference on Science and Technology for Development (UNCSTD) and has officially represented the Institute at such meetings as the United Nations Intergovernmental Committee on Science and Technology for Development and the United Nations Advisory Committee on Science and Technology for Development. Among her recent publications is *Science and Technology for Development: International Conflict or Cooperation. A Bibliography of Studies and Documents Related to the 1979 United Nations Conference on Science and Technology for Development.*

Mildred Robbins Leet is a consultant on women in development and a partner, Leet and Leet Consultants. She is also a United Nations representative of the International Society for Community Development. She has been chairperson of the Non-Governmental Organization Task Force on the Roles of Women in Science and Technology for Development and was a member of the U.S. delegation to the United Nations Conference on Science and Technology for Development, Vienna, 1979. She was also a member of the U.S. delegation to the United Nations Commission on the Status of Women, President of the National Council of Women (U.S.A.), and Vice-President of the International Council of Women.

Davidson Nicol is currently an Under-Secretary-General of the United Nations and Executive Director of the United Nations Institute for Training and Research (UNITAR). Dr. Nicol was previously Vice-Chancellor and Head of the University of Sierra Leone in Freetown, a Danforth Fellowship lecturer in African affairs at the Association of American Colleges, Permanent Representative of Sierra Leone to the United Nations, High Commissioner of Sierra Leone to the United Kingdom, and Ambassador of Sierra Leone to Sweden, Norway, and Denmark. He gained first class honours and doctorates in natural science and medicine from Cambridge University, and was elected a Fellow of Christ's College. Dr. Nicol has published numerous articles and books on scientific, literary, and political subjects. He is the author of *Africa: A Subjective View* (1964) and the coeditor of *The United Nations and Decision-Making: The Role of Women* (1978). With L.F. Smith at Cambridge, England, in 1959 he elucidated the structure of human insulin.

Sheila M. Pfafflin is the President of the Association for Women in Science. She received her doctorate in psychology from the Johns Hopkins University, worked for Bell Laboratories doing research in human learning and training, and is now with the American Telephone and Telegraph Company in the Human Resources Department. She is a Fellow of the New York Academy of Sciences and has been involved in various programs concerned with the status of women in science. She was one of the organizers of the New York Academy of Sciences' Conference on Expanding the Roles of Women in the Sciences. She was also a member of the NGO Task Force on the Roles of Women in Science and Technology for Development and has served as Treasurer and Board Member for the Federation of Organizations for Professional Women. She is also a member of the

National Science Foundation Committee on Equal Opportunities in Science and Technology.

Mangalam Srinivasan is the Director of the Technology Policy Council of the Center for International Technical Co-operation, the American University. She is also an adjunct technology Assistant Professor at the American University and a Consultant for the Organization of American States, the United States Department of Energy, and the United Nations. She is a Fellow of Harvard University.

Zenebeworke Tadesse is currently a doctoral candidate at the State University of New York, Binghamton. She has been a consultant on socioeconomic change and its impacts on women of the East African region, at the United Nations Institute for Namibia, the United Nations Educational and Scientific Organization (UNESCO) in Paris, and the United Nations Research Institute for Social Development (UNRISD). Her work on women in Ethiopia has recently been published by the Scandinavian Institute of African Studies (1978).

Abbreviations

ACAST	Advisory Committee on the Application of Science and Technology to Development
CONACYT	National Council of Science and Technology (Consejo Nacional de Ciencia y Tecnología) (Mexico)
ECA	Economic Commission for Africa
ECLA	Economic Commission for Latin America
ECOSOC	Economic and Social Council
ICSTD	Intergovernmental Committee on Science and Technology for Development
ILO	International Labour Organisation
IWY	International Women's Year
NGO	Nongovernmental organization
NIEO	New international economic order
UNCSTD	United Nations Conference on Science and Technology for Development
UNCTAD	United Nations Conference on Trade and Development
UNESCO	United Nations Educational, Scientific and Cultural Organization
UNITAR	United Nations Institute for Training and Research

Introduction

Davidson Nicol

UNITAR activities related to scientific-technological change, of which this volume on the role of women in development forms part, constitute an important aspect of its Programme of Work. The UNITAR mandate is to enhance the effectiveness of the United Nations by the performance of its functions in the maintenance of peace and security and in the promotion of economic and social development. In light of the provisions of the United Nations Charter and the interest of the United Nations General Assembly in the promotion of equality between women and men, their equal integration in development, and increasing their contribution to peace, UNITAR has always striven to include women professionals on its staff; the proportion of women on its professional staff reached 25 percent in 1980.

The Institute's Training Department conducts training programmes on the work and organization of the United Nations and on special aspects of the work of the Organization for members of permanent missions in New York and Geneva, for international officials, and for national officials having international responsibilities. UNITAR also conducts special training programmes at the request of Member States and assists in strengthening collaboration among training officers at the interagency level in the United Nations system.

All UNITAR training activities are open to women, and women are both discussion leaders and participants on a basis of equality with men. Many of the UNITAR training programmes are directly or indirectly relevant to the themes of the United Nations Decade for Women, namely, equality, development, and peace. For example, during 1979 and 1980 the Institute, among other things, conducted a seminar on the drafting of plurilingual instruments, treaties, and resolutions and a seminar on the structure of the world economy and prospects for the new international economic order and organized a series of activities as part of the United Nations Programme of

Fellowships on Disarmament.

Since 1975, in response to the policies adopted by the General Assembly and supported by the UNITAR Board of Trustees, the UNITAR Programme of Work has emphasized issues concerning the establishment of the new international economic order (NIEO). In this regard, the problem of the application of science and technology to development remains one of the main concerns of the United Nations and its affiliated organizations. The accelerated rate of technological advance and the uneven distribution of its benefits make the situation complex and some problems more acute than anticipated. In particular, it is obvious that the new international economic order will require new mechanisms and modalities for the transfer of technology.

UNITAR has a rich history of interest and involvement in studying the impact of technological development on world affairs, specifically on the study of the access of developing countries to technological innovation. Ten years ago the Institute published a series of research reports detailing problems and prospects in the transfer of technology from developed to developing countries on both an industry-specific and a country-specific basis. Subsequently, the Institute also conducted extensive empirical investigation into the causes and conditions of the "brain drain" from developing to developed countries. In addition, the UNITAR Project on the Future has since 1976 been deeply engaged in assessing the physical limits and supply possibilities of energy and natural resources, concentrating on new technologies and new energy resources, and to date has organized six major conferences on this important subject.

A subproject, "Technology, Domestic Distribution and North-South Relations," explores the reasons why the result of past policies of national development and international cooperation are now so widely judged to be unsatisfactory. The International Development Strategy for the 1970s set forth a series of objectives that have to be analytically related to one another as well as to measures designed to achieve them. One feature explicit in the strategy has been overlooked, namely, that a more equitable distribution should not be viewed solely as a normative objective, superimposed on a number of others, nor as an automatic by-product of growth. Rather, present distribution must be seen as one of the elements responsible for the malfunctioning of the economies of many countries and of the world economy as a whole. Although the analytical tools worked out are of very general application, in the North and in the South, they are particularly relevant to the conditions of unequal exchange, demographic pressures, high elasticity of labour supply, and technological dependency.

The early work on the project was based on extensive scenario analyses and "explanatory" mathematical models that seek to identify causal relationships involved in different types of interaction in national economies and the international system. "Delinking" (from the North) and "relinking" (with the South and also differently with the North) are inherent in policies of self-reliance. They require a substantial change in the output mix of an economy – a change effected through the orientation of new investments and the recognition that an initial redistribution, even at a low level of income, substantially facilitates industrial development.

Technology choices are seen as crucial instruments in the pursuance of such policies, as technological preferences not adequately related to social objectives may generate situations that are difficult to reverse. Intensive work, both empirical and analytical, has explored a great number of industrial activities from this point of view, elaborating criteria for choice and articulating a conceptual framework within which optimum packages of very advanced technologies with more simple, labour-intensive processes can be worked out.

The project concentrates on the creation of an indigenous capacity for scientific-technological research and development, the availability of local skills, and greater participation in the control of production systems and the social organizations that support them, with a view to more self-reliant patterns of development for the developing countries. The more recent work has focused on the construction of the global model, describing the dynamics of the world economy through the operation of six international markets (food, energy, minerals, capital goods, armaments, manufactured goods) and their impact on six different types of economies.

Similarly, a UNITAR research team has studied the preparatory process of and the issues before the 1979 United Nations Conference on Science and Technology for Development (UNCSTD). The team has produced a series of working papers on science and technology. In these papers a large number of topics, including the financial and institutional aspects of United Nations policymaking in this field, have been discussed.

Several papers focusing on the role of women in scientific-technological development were made possible by a grant from the government of Norway and are reproduced in this volume. These papers, produced by women and relevant to the roles of women, were distributed to all delegations of the United Nations Conference on Science and Technology for Development. By providing a substantive and conceptual framework within which the issue found acceptance with both the developing and industrially developed countries, these papers contributed significantly to the unanimous passage of the resolution entitled "Women, Science and Technology" at the conference.

The resolution invites Member States of the United Nations to promote an equal distribution of the benefits of scientific-technological development, equal participation of women in the decision-making process in the area of science and technology, and equal education, training, and access to professional careers in science and technology. The resolution also recommends that all organs, organizations, and other bodies of the United Nations system review the impact of their programmes on women and promote the full participation of women in the planning and implementation of programmes. In addition, the resolution calls for the newly established Intergovernmental Committee on Science and Technology for Development to give due regard to the perspectives and interests of women in its activities and to review the progress made in implementing the resolution in its annual report.

The Nordic delegation to UNCSTD and the Norwegian delegation in particular commended the special effort of UNITAR in providing valuable background material and direct assistance to this initiative. Pamela D'Onofrio-Flores of UNITAR joined a panel consisting of the members of the Norwegian delegation and Ambassador W.K. Chagula of Tanzania (who had introduced the resolution) in answering questions at an international press conference held immediately following the passage of the resolution.

In addition, the UNITAR papers on women, science, and technology were utilized by the Secretariat of the 1980 World Conference of the United Nations Decade for Women in the preparation of conference documentation on the same subject (e.g., Conference Document A/CONF.94/29, *The Effects of Science and Technology on the Employment of Women*, and Conference Document A/CONF.94/26, *Technological Change and Women Workers: The Development of Microelectronics*).

In the context of this UNITAR project on UNCSTD, a seminar on "Financial Arrangements for the Promotion of Science and Technology for Development" was held at Schloss Hernstein, Austria, in July 1979. A preliminary report on the proceedings of the seminar was unofficially circulated among a cross-section of the delegates from all regions at the UNCSTD. The general thrust of the deliberations of the seminar was fully reflected in the conference outcome on the subject of financial arrangements.

Following UNCSTD and the adoption of the Vienna Programme of

Action, the research team is now moving into the second phase of the project, which focuses on the responses to and the implementation of the Vienna Programme of Action by governmental, nongovernmental, and intergovernmental actors. UNCSTD and its outcome represent a new element in the involvement of the United Nations in promoting science and technology for development. At the institutional level, a considerable amount of restructuring of the decision-making process has been initiated by establishing new intergovernmental, secretariat, and consultative organs or entities. Moreover, new financial arrangements for an interim period have been established, and a negotiating process for new long-term financial arrangements has been launched. The UNITAR research team will attempt to assess whether, how, and to what extent these new arrangements will contribute to strengthening the role of the United Nations in the promotion of science and technology for development. This research will result in various studies to be published in the working paper series. Among topics to be addressed are the impact of new technologies on the development prospects of developing countries and the institutional and financial implications of the Vienna Programme of Action.

UNITAR has increased the effective participation of developing countries in international organizations concerned with the application of science and technology to development by holding interregional meetings on science and technology, in accordance with their established procedures and practices. The Institute held a briefing seminar on UNCSTD in Geneva on 20 March 1980, with thirty-five participants from twenty-seven permanent missions in attendance. The programme began with an overview of the United Nations Conference on Science and Technology for Development and a discussion of follow-up action. Other presentations concerned the financial implications of and arrangements for science and technology for development, the state of negotiations within the United Nations Conference on Trade and Development (UNCTAD) on a code of conduct for the transfer of technology, and the revision of the Paris Convention for the Protection of Industrial Property under the auspices of the World Intellectual Property Organization (WIPO).

The recently held UNITAR seminar on "Multilateral Diplomacy and the New International Economic Order" explained the historical background of the call for the new international economic order and studied key issues such as the role of science and technology for development. For the third consecutive year, UNITAR and the Economic Development Institute of the World Bank held a seminar on economic development in its international setting, designed for those senior diplomats in permanent missions to the United Nations who have responsibilities related to economic and social development matters. Development issues, including the international monetary system and the transfer of capital and technology, were discussed.

In response to a request from the Permanent Mission of Ethiopia, the Training Department organized a briefing late in November 1979 for new delegates from Ethiopia. Topics included science and technology in the context of the new international economic order.

The sociocultural implications of science and technology for development have always been an integral component of UNITAR's approach and work in this field. For example, a project on the "Evaluation of the Liability of States for Damage Caused Through Scientific and Technological Innovations," consists of a comprehensive study of the impact of scientific-technological change on the international legal responsibilities of states for injuries arising from their misuse or negligent control of technologically advanced instruments, materials, or fuels. Considerable research has been completed by an international team of scholars.

It should also be noted that since 1970 UNITAR has been concerned with the role of women in the United Nations system as well as in development and has done pioneering work on the status of women in the United Nations. The Executive Director of UNITAR has written and spoken extensively on improvement of the status of women at conferences of the United Nations, at United Nations Association gatherings, United States federal agencies, and colleges and universities around the world.

The first initiative of UNITAR was the Colloquium of Senior United Nations Officials at which the situation of women in the United Nations was discussed, held at Schloss Hernstein in July 1972. In May of the following year UNITAR published a report (Research Report No. 18) based on the proceedings of the colloquium and containing additional research data and factual information not discussed at the colloquium.

Together with the American Association for the Advancement of Science (AAAS), the Overseas Development Council (ODC), and the Mexican National Council of Science and Technology (CONACYT), UNITAR cosponsored the Seminar on Women in Development that took place in Mexico City in 1975, just prior to the World Conference of the International Women's Year (IWY). The Institute presented a paper to the seminar on "Women and Development: The Role of the United Nations System," written by Fadia Nasr of Egypt and Marcel Nguema-Mba of Gabon. The Institute was represented at the seminar by several staff members and Special Fellows. The Executive Director and three members of the staff represented UNITAR at the following IWY Conference. A background paper, "The Situation of Women in the Light of Contemporary Time-Budget Research," was prepared for the World Conference of the IWY by Professor Alexander Szalai, a UNITAR special fellow.

The UNITAR contribution to the world conference was the publication of a special issue of *UNITAR News* on the subject of "Women and the UN," which contains an updating of the earlier report on "The Situation of Women in the United Nations" written after the 1972 conference at Schloss Hernstein. The issue also contains a number of other articles on women in the international civil service and women as diplomats and national officials having responsibilities in the international sphere. This special issue of the *UNITAR News* was distributed to the participants of the World Conference of the IWY and given wide circulation within the international community.

The World Plan of Action adopted by the Conference gave high priority to national, regional, and international research activities and to data collection and analysis on all aspects of the situation of women. It called for promotion of a wide exchange of information and research findings and for maximum use to be made of existing research institutes of the United Nations, including UNITAR.

In the World Plan of Action it was noted that the Decade for Women and the plan itself called for a clear commitment on the part of the international community to accord importance and priority to measures to improve the situation of women. The plan envisaged that all organizations in the United Nations system, including the relevant United Nations organs and bodies and especially, *inter alia*, UNITAR, should take separate and joint action to implement its recommendations.

The World Plan of Action called for international action to support existing programmes and expand their scope in the following areas among others: research, data collection and analysis, training and advisory services, including coordination with national and regional activities of organizations within the United Nations system, elaboration and ongoing review of international standards, dissemination and exchange of information, and review and appraisal, including monitoring of progress made in achieving the aims and objectives of the plan.

The plan also called on international organizations, both governmental and nongovernmental, to strengthen their efforts to distribute information on women and related matters. The Programme of the Decade for Women adopted by the Commission on the Status of

Women in September 1976 also called on all organizations in the United Nations system to participate in implementing the Programme of the Decade. The 1977 UNITAR Colloquium on Women and Decision-Making in the United Nations was part of this effort. Following the colloquium a two-volume study entitled *The UN and Decision-Making: The Role of Women* was published. These studies show that although progress has been made at the United Nations, the long process toward equal opportunity and participation for both sexes is far from complete.

The World Conference of the International Women's Year also adopted a number of resolutions specifically addressed to the role of women in development. These resolutions were later endorsed by the United Nations General Assembly. One of the resolutions requested the Secretary-General, in close consultation with the appropriate agencies and institutions within the United Nations system, to establish a system-wide United Nations research programme on the position and role of women in development in order to obtain quantitive and qualitative data needed for the formulation of policies to promote the full integration of women in development in the various regions of the world.

Another resolution adopted by the world conference and later endorsed by the General Assembly recommended that all organs of the United Nations development system, specialized agencies, and other technical and financial assistance programmes and agencies:

1. Give sustained attention to those initiatives that integrate women in the development process;

2. Incorporate in their development plans, programme and sector analyses, and programme documents an impact statement of how such proposed programmes will affect women as participants and beneficiaries, in consultation with the United Nations Commission on the Status of Women;

3. Establish a review and appraisal system and undertake to serve in the design, implementation, and evaluation of programmes and to use social and economic indicators as a means of measuring progress in the integration of women in the development process; and

4. Ensure that women participate on an equitable basis with men on all levels of decision making that govern the planning and implementation of these programmes, keeping in mind the principle of geographical distribution.

As a continuation of its efforts to give prominence to the role of women in development and as its major contribution to the 1980 World Conference of the United Nations Decade for Women,

UNITAR held a seminar entitled "Creative Women in Changing Societies" in Oslo, Norway, during July 1980. The seminar brought together women from all regions and focused on ways in which creative women have succeeded in overcoming obstacles to advancement in their respective professions. The major goals were (1) to identify the psychological and structural determinants that both allow and prevent creativity in women and to explore the similarities and differences among women within the same profession; (2) to examine alternative perspectives and structures for the advancement of women; and (3) to discuss and encourage the formation of regional follow-up meetings, seminars, and networks. The findings and recommendations of the seminar will be published in a forthcoming volume together with a number of background papers prepared for the seminar by its participants.

A UNITAR project on "Intra-Regional Migration in the Commonwealth Caribbean and its Implications for Population Policies and Development Planning" is expected perforce to include exploration of the interactions between population growth, migration, social and economic change, and the role of women in the development process.

In May of 1980 UNITAR hosted a conference on "Regionalism and the New International Economic Order" organized in cooperation with the Club of Rome and the Centre for Economic and Social Studies of the Third World (CEESTEM) in Mexico. The question of women and regionalism was addressed, and a paper on the same subject was prepared by a woman.

The UNITAR research team dealing with issues related to the situation of women supports the thesis that the new international economic order is unlikely to be achieved unless the inequality between men and women is eliminated—hence the need for new strategies and data. UNITAR is organizing a Task Force on International Development in cooperation with major research institutes worldwide to examine the policies required at all levels to implement the objectives of the International Development Strategy for the Third United Nations Development Decade, for the achievement of which the Programme of Action of the World Conference of the United Nations Decade for Women considers the NIEO integral.

The UNITAR project on progress in the establishment of the new international economic order, implemented in close collaboration with CEESTEM, focuses on the critical areas and factors relating to the NIEO where rectification and adjustment are in order, with special attention to the obstacles to achieving development goals and strategies for promoting a nontraumatic path for the creation of a more univer-

sally equitable international economic order. The results of all phases
of this project are being issued in a seventeen-volume series jointly
edited by UNITAR and CEESTEM. A number of these studies are being written by women on such subjects as the condition of women and
the exercise of political power in the context of the NIEO.

UNITAR attempts to involve men in the process of attitudinal
change relevant to increasing the participation of women in international decision making and in study of the impacts and implications of
specific strategies or research findings for women. Change in attitudes
can be brought about only by linking the integration of women into
national life with the relevant international questions of our time,
such as poverty, unemployment, peace, and liberation.

The objectives and the goals of the second half of the United Nations
Decade for Women cannot be dissociated from the current world
political economic system. One of the central issues is that a minority
of the world exists by the underdevelopment and starvation of the majority. The low prices paid for commodities from developing countries
and the high prices they are charged for imported manufactured
goods condemn them to poverty, illiteracy, malnutrition, and
unemployment. In this desperate situation, women suffer infinitely
more than men. It is no accident that the movement for the liberation
of women and their equality-based integration into world development has the classic features and problems of the vicious circle that is
visible in all facets of underdevelopment. The unequal use and
distribution of resources and power that characterize the present
world order and the resultant poverty, as well as oppressive social
structures and irrational attitudes, all militate against women's greater
involvement in national and international life.

The chapters in this volume converge in the view that women have
historically been and are currently integrated in economic development worldwide. However, although women are active participants
in economic development, they are excluded from the mainstream of
economic and political decision making and development planning
and implementation. Just as the unequal involvement of other dominated sectors (peasants in comparison with townspeople, poor nations
in comparison with rich nations) means that they can be controlled
more effectively because of their inability to compete, so in the case
of women there is a loss of decision-making authority and self-
determination.

These studies posit that although appropriate technologies are important for developing countries, they need also to have high-level
technology or they will be condemned indefinitely to a colonial and

subservient role. In the provision of high-level technology for developing countries and its maintenance in industrially developed countries, women must play an equal role. There is a danger in industrially developed countries that attention might become concentrated only on the situation of women in developing countries and that inequities in their own societies are either downplayed, ignored, or denied. Avenues for the advancement of women in industrially developed countries are opened but not filled, or filled only by token appointees. Quotas are secretly introduced and are enforced unofficially. Even when women recruitment officers or women high officials are introduced to correct the obvious injustice of certain situations, they are either coopted into accepting the status quo with minor token modifications or intimidated by the sheer weight of the male-dominated bureaucracy. They may be flattered into believing that as individuals they are exceptional and that the majority of other women are unsuited for equally high administrative posts or decision-making positions in science and technology.

The chapters in this volume show that in introducing technology in the form of agricultural modernization into rural areas in developing countries, women lose control of their cash-earning positions, their hours of labour are increased, and their role in the family and in society diminishes. It has also been found that as automation increases, the employment of women is the first to decrease. As urbanized work is introduced, young and physically attractive women become employed and middle-aged women, even when efficient, are ignored.

Those who bring science and technology into developing societies also tend to be predominantly male. There should be encouragement to increase the use of efficient women specialists in the process. Apart from the technical skill that these women specialists possess, they will in addition encourage and inspire local women and contribute to a reeducation of both women and men in society and to a more well-adjusted and balanced attitude toward the nonsexist nature of society in the future.

Women who introduce science and technology into new surroundings may be locally born or may come from abroad. They will usually have greater access to the family life and social structure of the recipient society and may also be better able to soften or deflect any harmful impacts science and technology may produce. Long-range stability and profitability, in every sense, is more likely to occur when science and technology are accepted into a society with proper adjustments and less disruption of community life. A greatly increased role for women in science and technology for development is most certainly an essential and logical ingredient in any plans that aim at a successful future for humankind.

At UNITAR, our team of research workers, both men and women of varied nationalities, agrees from its professional work on women that in the current process of restructuring the international economic and social orders and the institutional arrangements thereof, the opportunity should be taken to end the narrow confinement of "women's issues" to the social and humanitarian. As women's issues are economic and political, women should be encouraged and trained to involve themselves in issues presently not considered "women's issues." Men should be encouraged and trained to involve themselves in what are usually labeled as "women's issues," as these are in fact economic and political issues.

To this end, women must take part in international debate in such areas as the North-South Dialogue and in discussion of the establishment of the new international economic order, of the Brandt Commission Report, and of the International Development Strategy for the Third United Nations Development Decade. Attention must be directed toward the impact on women and the active involvement of women in the following: matters related to control over and benefits deriving from natural resources; energy production and distribution; monetary and trade reforms; industrial and agricultural development; expenditure on armaments; and the quality of life as it is affected by economic functions, sociocultural and religious institutions, population, health, nutrition, environment, and science and technology.

It is hoped that this volume will further demonstrate the undeniable fact that there is no sector, policy question, or operational problem in which women throughout the world are not intrinsically involved, including specifically the issue of the role of science and technology in development.

1

Technology, Economic Development, and the Division of Labour by Sex

Pamela M. D'Onofrio-Flores

Contents

1. Introduction

The contemporary Western technology that has proliferated, sometimes in modified form, throughout most of the world has evolved through three hundred years of tradition. The disposition of Western technology has been dictated by the economic, social, and political forces that historically gave rise to its development and that continue to define its parameters, condition its use, and provide Western technology with a highly political dimension. For example, Ashis Nandy cited the ideology of the Enlightenment, the Industrial Revolution, nineteenth century colonialism and twentieth century neocolonialism as forces critical to the ascent of Western technology over other forms worldwide.[1] Technology in this context "is not merely a mode of production and therefore neutral: it carries with it a code of structures—economic, social, cultural and also cognitive."[2] Any meaningful analysis of current patterns of science and technology must therefore not only probe the character of the contemporary Western form, but must also examine the role of science and technology within the structures and ideology of its generative and operative environments.

Western science and technology have historically been factors in the creation and establishment of new socioeconomic classes. Western science and technology have also been largely shaped and developed by the dominant social classes in developed Western countries, not just for their benefit, but more importantly to reinforce the structures of their dominance, at home and abroad. Techniques that could create alternative structures are either rejected or are marginalized as the preserve of small peripheral groups isolated from the power configurations in the decision-making nuclei.[3] Thus technology becomes a critical component in the structures of inequality between social classes, between regions, and between developed and underdeveloped countries. As such, Western technology can be viewed as reinforcing and perpetuating a dependent form of development in the Third World.

Although it is tangential to this paper to provide a substantive review and appraisal of the complex theoretical aspects of dependent development, it is necessary to provide a working definition of this condition. That adopted here was formulated by Theotônio Dos Santos as:

> A situation in which the economy of certain countries is conditioned by the development and expansion of another economy to which the former is subjected. The relation of interdependence between two or more economies and between these and world trade, assumes the form of dependence when some countries (the dominant ones) can expand and can be self-sustaining while other countries (the dependent ones) can do this only as a reflection of that expansion, which can have either a positive or a negative effect on their immediate development.[4]

This theory views development and underdevelopment as two related aspects of the expansion of Western capitalism in the nineteenth century. The expansion included the creation and dissemination of modern Western technology and the establishment of an international division of labour wherein the few advanced countries produced manufactured goods and the dependent countries provided raw materials and primary commodities. After the Second World War the increasing investments made by multinational corporations in Third World countries characterized a new form of dependence. Such investments are increasingly concentrated in the modern sectors, where high profits are secured for multinationals as a result of their competitive advantage and pricing policies. The type of industrialization generated by these investments is restricted to consumer goods production, directed towards the consumption patterns particularly of the upper classes in the developing countries and the upper and middle classes of the industrially developed countries; the production of capital goods remains almost nonexistent in dependent economies.

The concern of this chapter is to determine whether contemporary technology, as part of the culture and institutions of a class-bound society, promoting a dependent type of development internationally, is likely to add to the liberation of women or to their continued oppression. Accumulating evidence concerning the relation between dependent development and the division of labour by sex suggests the latter. This point will be explored in later pages.

If the priorities of the industrially developed (dominant) countries and the upper classes of the developing (dependent) countries continue to take precedence over the domestic socioeconomic needs of the developing countries, an increase in women's participation and an improvement in female status are unlikely to happen. As Saffioti observed, economic expansion is insufficient to create conditions for increased female labour absorption in regions such as Latin America. Increased female participation, both qualitative and quantitative, demands a "redivision of the world in areas and subareas of influence."[5] This does not mean to suggest that the replacement of one class by another in the leadership of the state machinery at the national level and the redistribution of resources from the industrially developed to the developing countries at the international level are conditions sufficient to produce increased female participation in political, economic, and social life and greater female status. It suggests that these are necessary conditions for such changes.

2. Contemporary Science and Technology and Social Inequality

Contemporary science reinforces class inequalities in its definition, organization, and transmission. Western society labels "scientific" those skills, crafts, and knowledge that are well integrated into the capitalist relations of production and are transmitted through a formal process of education. Those that are of no value to capitalist production and therefore are not formally taught within the institutionally recognized professions often have little market value. This is attributed to the inability of self-acquired knowledge, despite its effectiveness, to fit into the pattern of the dominant culture, which is the hierarchical division of labour that is characteristic of capitalism.[6]

The transmission of scientific knowledge and the technological expertise derived from it are conditioned by a method of teaching and an entire educational and training system that is designed to make scientific-technological training accessible to a privileged minority and hence discriminates against the great majority of people worldwide. Selective access to scientific knowledge and technological expertise is not a result of any inherent difficulty of scientific thinking or technological training but is a direct outgrowth of the gap between scientific-technological theory and practice and the lives, needs, and occupations of the majority of the people.[7]

The organization of Western science and technology is also classbound. The production of scientific knowledge and technology has been submitted to the same hierarchical division and fragmentation of tasks as the production of any other commodity. The fragmented organization of science and technology produces divisions between people and provides an organizational environment that is conducive to the increasing military uses of science and technology. This in turn has led to further hierarchization and specialization.[8]

The results of the fragmented orientation and organization of scientific knowledge and technological expertise are of great significance to socioeconomic and political development. This fragmentation has created a scientific-technological subculture that can be used only in combination with other subcultures in large industrial complexes. Western technology can be effectively operative only where there is the concentration of capital, research, and organization. In addition, priority is being given to the development of technologies that require a huge volume of production to attain economies of scale, the concentration of production, and expansion in the size of the production units. These characteristics of Western technology require its concentration in a small number of locations, usually urban centers, which increases existing urban-rural and international inequalities and creates new ones.[9]

Moreover, the technologies generated have increasingly resulted in the creation of a resource-rich, power-wielding social class internationally. The industrialists, through the development and utilization of modern, increasingly profitable technologies, have been able to determine, to a large extent, the profile and direction of social change. Investment dictated by this group in accordance with the profit motive and at the expense of wider social welfare has resulted in the growing inability of technological development to address social crises, which are in many cases created as a result of such technological advance.[10]

3. Western Technology and Dependent Development

Western technology, as used by an international elite class, which is best represented by transnational corporations in their formation of research and development oligopolies in almost every branch of economic activity, particularly in those of high technological intensity, can be viewed as a vehicle for a dependent form of socioeconomic and political development.[11]

Ward Morehouse observed the resulting concentration of knowledge as being central to the raging international equity crisis:

> Science and technology have emerged as primary instruments of power and social control, with the major industrialized countries, especially the superpowers, relying more and more on science and technology as a means of maintaining their dominance in that system. Notwithstanding beachheads of technological competence and scientific excellence in the Third World the technological gap between the North and the South has widened during this period because of the near monopoly that a few industrialized countries have acquired on the generation and productive use of the technology based on modern science. Development strategies relying on importation of capital-intensive, socially inappropriate, environmentally destructive western technology cannot but lead to a massive global equity crisis in the 1980's.[12]

The economic, social, and ideological bases of Western technology are premised on the existence of inequalities, as are its definition, organization, and transmission. As noted by Galtung, dominant countries have reached a high standard of living at the expense of the dependent countries and have attained relative levels of internal equality as a result of the exportation of their own peripheries to the Third World, specifically the exportation of jobs, "thereby cutting labor costs by something like 90%."[13] The structures of inequality no longer tolerated within the borders of the industrially developed countries and exported to the Third World are internalized by Third World countries such that regional and class structures of dependent economies reflect these inequalities.[14]

The implantation of Western technology creates its own demand for spare parts, knowledge, skills, and new technologies. The dominant countries retain their command positions by virtue of the wealth that they derive from the accumulation of profits that accrue from the sale of science and technology as commodities and through the maintenance of a monopoly on the means of intellectual production, which secures the dominant countries the role of innovators in the international scientific and technological division of labour.

The transfer of intellectual technology reinforces the uneven relations of international capitalism by providing the intellectual rationalizations it requires. As such it is a perfect example of the transfers of Western technology as a structural and cultural aggression. The transmission of information, knowledge, scholarly research, and scientific propositions are integrated into the network of contemporary international relations involving international monetary arrangements, aid programmes, the investment activities of multinational corporations, and international diplomacy. Western scientific theories are disseminated to dependent countries through the activities of prominent research foundations, through the training of Third World students, and through the creation of research and teaching "subsidiaries" in the Third World. These activities, in most cases, sustain in the dependent countries scientific interpretations of a socioeconomic reality that are amenable to the uneven contemporary patterns of political and economic exchange between countries.[15]

4. Some Internal Socioeconomic Consequences of Dependent Development for Developing Countries

The dependent positions of the developing nations have had critical consequences in determining their pattern of industrial development by defining their structure of production to include those products that can be produced with the technologies available to them and that conform to the consumption patterns that have been exported to them from the industrially developed countries.

The structure of the labour force in Third World countries is similarly affected. The lack of labour absorption in the manufacturing sectors of the developing countries is a reflection of the fact that their development has occurred through the use of imported technologies that decrease the demand for unskilled labour and that increasingly require a labour force possessing specific skills, while creating a disproportionate increase in the service sectors. The concentration of the female labour force in the service sectors is the joint product of the advantage that men have in receiving training for relatively scarce industrial jobs[16] and of sex-typed occupational definitions.[17]

Moreover, female participation is related to the stage of industrialization in which the country finds itself and its impact on the growth or decline of the primary, secondary, or tertiary sector. Madeira and Singer demonstrated the impact of the different stages of development and the rate of absorption of female labour in Brazil:

> It is generally expected in a developing country that the level of female participation in the work force will go through three phases. In the first one, during the beginning of industrialization, when the number of people employed in agriculture is still high and the number of commercial and manufacturing industries limited to the domestic circle still significant, the integration level of women in the work force is still large. During the second phase, economic development causes a large number of people to leave localized commerce and home production and at the same time there is a migration from rural to urban areas, which tends to cause the number of women participating in productive activities to decrease. Generally, together with the above described mechanisms, there is a continuous growth of female employment in the tertiary sector. Until this sector reaches a point where it is large enough to cover the departure of women from other sectors, the amount of female participation in the work force will continue to decline. The rate of female employment out of the domestic sphere will start to go up in a more advanced stage of development, as a result of the employment growth in the tertiary activity.[18]

The third phase, marked by the expansion of urbanization, capital-intensive industrialization, and state bureaucracy operating in an environment of monopoly capitalism results in an increase in the service sectors of the economy and in white-collar jobs for women in clerical work, trade, public administration, social services, and so on. Safa observed that although in all three stages a small proportion of highly educated women are employed as professionals, in the third phase this sector is significantly expanded as are intermediary occupations for women as secretaries, sales people, and other low-level white-collar jobs. In the third phase, middle- and upper-class women become economically active in large numbers.[19]

This typology is reflected in several contemporary studies demonstrating that development that is dependent on foreign capital and a relatively small modern sector does not promote the incorporation of women into the labour force and that any increases in female employment as a result of this type of development benefit women from the upper and middle strata more than women of rural or urban working-class status. Chinchilla, in her study of female occupational structures in Guatemala, showed that women of the lower classes are confined to the tertiary sector as domestic servants and that women from the middle and upper classes are engaged in the same white-collar jobs (clerks, office workers, and professionals) that have expanded female employment in the United States and elsewhere. Given that the percentage of women in these jobs is still much smaller in Third World countries than in the United States, a small minority of working women have benefited from dependent development.[20]

In Mexico, although most women are confined to the informal sector in menial and low-paying jobs as vendors and domestic servants, middle- and upper-class women can choose not to work in the absence of acceptable employment, whereas women of the lower classes work in the informal labour market to survive.[21] In the agricultural sector, Stoler observed that the stratification of the village economy in Java, which occurred as a result of demographic pressures and technological changes, had differential impacts on women of landless or small subsistence peasant families and on those of large landowning families, the greatest negative impact being on the former.[22]

In conclusion, one of the major impacts of a dependent form of socioeconomic development has been to limit the growth of the modern sector within each Third World country and to restrict the incorporation of labour into this sector to a very select educated group, largely dependent on the state and foreign capital as sources of employment. Some women, in the tradition of the industrially developed capitalist countries, have been integrated into the modern sector, primarily as white-collar workers and professionals in an expanding state bureaucracy and to a lesser extent in private foreign enterprise. Men have found some jobs in the growing capital-intensive industries of the modern sector, but women are increasingly excluded from blue-collar occupations and are restricted to more peripheral employment in traditional sector jobs such as domestic service and petty vending. In cyclical pattern the labour surplus, intensified by rural-urban migration, places further strains on the restricted capacity of the modern sector to absorb labour.[23]

5. Western Technology, Dependent Development, and Sexual Inequality

The increase in the tertiary sector in Western employment structures is largely the product of Western technology's direction toward economic, political, and social elites and toward the diminution of the industrial work force.[24] In countries experiencing a dependent type of development, where population increase is combined with a reduced capacity of the agricultural and manufacturing sectors to absorb labour, the tertiary sector emerges as that with the greatest potential for absorbing labour, particularly female labour. In this regard, Schmink observed that "many occupations in the heterogeneous service sector are favoured for female employment in Latin America as they are in the United States and Europe."[25] She noted that more than one-half of the female labour force in Latin America is employed either in the primary or tertiary sectors, with the manufacturing sector rarely absorbing one-quarter of it.[26] For example, in Venezuela, despite women's increasing participation in the labour force in recent years, female employment is increasingly concentrated in specific jobs in the tertiary sector that remain the preserve of women.[27]

Glaura Vasques de Miranda in her study of Brazil found that women's employment in the tertiary sector increased with the expansion of productive and collective services in urban centers. She noted that to a large extent the expansion of female employment is occurring in those occupations that are extensions of women's domestic activities conducted within the institution of the family. "The growth of occupations such as domestic service confirms once again that capitalist development does not always improve women's position in the wage labor market, especially that of lower class women."[28] Norma Chinchilla observed that currently in Guatemala the tertiary sector employs 22.4 percent of all workers, as compared to 16.9 percent in 1959 and 19.9 percent in 1964. The increases are not as dramatic for women, who have been concentrated in this sector as domestic servants or teachers since 1921. Although two out of every three women worked in the tertiary sector in 1973, the majority were not employed in commerce, transportation, or communication (as were 44 percent of the male workers), but in domestic service, with 64 percent of all females employed as maids in the tertiary service sector. She concluded, "while industrial growth has created new employment areas for men and women – clerical, sales and professional – the proportion of all women who are domestics has not dropped below 40 percent and the absolute number of women in this category has actually increased by 28.9 percent since 1964."[29] A similar trend of female concentration in the service sector of the economy has been noted in other regions as well.

In countries experiencing a dependent form of development, it is not industrialization or technology alone that prevents development and contributes to the marginalization of women from the labour force, but industrial finance capital and advanced capital-intensive technology, which impede modifications in the economic structure of developing economies in conformity with their internal socioeconomic needs. For women this has meant a pattern of decline or tapering off of female participation in the labour markets of countries engaged in dependent development. In Mexico, the tremendous industrial growth of the postwar period contributed to the rise of women's activity rates from 4.6 percent in 1930 to 18.0 percent in 1960; in the subsequent decade it was increased by merely 1.0 percent. Of these, 10.8 percent were in agriculture and related activity, 19.4 percent were in industry, 60.1 percent were in services, and 9.7 percent were in nonspecified occupations. As a result of male dominance in upper-level occupations, the entry of women into the professions and technical occupations is restricted. The only exception is in the textile industry, where women's participation is higher than that of men but where much of the female-performed work is done in the home[30] or in the most labour-intensive aspects of the production process least permeated with technology.

A similar trend of declining female participation in the labour force with dependent development is visible in Brazil. The highest involvement of women in the labour force was 45.5 percent of the labour force in 1875. It declined to 15.3 percent by 1920, with the greatest reduction in the agricultural sector. In industry female participation in the labour force constituted 91.3 percent in 1900 and dropped to 27.9 percent in 1920. The year 1970 marked a slight increase in total female participation in the labour force to 21 percent. However, in light of the miraculous industrial growth of Brazil in the fifty-year span this represents a proportionate decline in the economic position of women as compared with men.[31]

To some extent during the nationalist period of industrial growth in Guatemala, the expansion of the market created a demand for labour, including female labour, that was not unlike the experiences of the United States during competitive capitalist conditions, or of Mexico, Argentina, and elsewhere at the inception of national dependent development, when women workers were absorbed into the initial factories. As Guatemala's industrial growth was increasingly conditioned by the needs of monopoly capitalism, the period of a large industrial workforce composed substantially of women was circumscribed as dramatic increases in industrial production were accompanied by modest increases in employment that were inadequate to replace the traditional occupations that were eliminated or to absorb population increases. As a result most workers were frozen into the backward sectors of the economy (subsistence agriculture and domestic services).[32] In Guatemala the period between 1946 and 1965 witnessed a decline in female participation in the labour force from 22 percent to 18 percent, with the largest reductions occurring in the tobacco, textiles, chemicals, rubber, foods, and paper industries. Male employment, in contrast, is increasing dramatically in the chemicals, paper, rubber, metal products, electrical appliances, transportation, and furniture industries. New industries have created a disproportionate demand for male labour. Some industries are replacing women with male workers. In absolute terms overall male employment has risen much more sharply than overall female employment.[33]

6. The Implications for Women of the Sexual Division of Labour

In the short run it has been noted that women earn less money than do men for the same time periods of work, that they are restricted in terms of the employment accessible to them, and that in some instances, their traditional economic authority and status are usurped as a result of the destruction of independent artisan industries unaccompanied by a comparable demand for female labour in the factories or as a result of technological displacement.

The implications of dependent development and the concomitant sexual division of labour are even more far-reaching. Inadequate employment opportunities and insufficient family income for the masses of men and women in dependent economies mean that women's role in production and reproduction is increasingly critical to family survival. Deere captured the essence of this when she stated:

> Intra-familial labor deployment is responsive to the need to attain subsistence in the face of rural poverty. And what is rural poverty but a reflection of the overall pattern of peripheral-capitalist development — the concentration of the means of production which forces proletarianization yet the inability of capitalist development to absorb the available supply of labour (largely as a result of the capital intensive technologies it employs).[34]

Women's agricultural participation cross-culturally, whether they are fully proletarianized or act as a temporary labour reserve responsive to agriculture's seasonal demand for labour or as subsistence producers on plantations, haciendas, or independent land parcels, has served as a force for the maintenance of low wages. Boserup concluded that in the Asian and African cases, the plantation circumvents the payment of a wage sufficient for family subsistence to the male by relying on women's agricultural participation as a rural producer or as a rural wage-earner.[35] Caufield pointed out that this is also true of West Indian plantations, where the recruitment of entire families by plantation owners enables them to utilize the wage labour of women and children only during peak agricultural periods. Plantation owners can then rely on women's subsistence production of food to feed their families from the small plots provided them. This use of the labour performed by women and children maintains the male wage at an absolute minimum.[36] The Zambian copper mines provide yet another example.[37] Van Allen asserted that the high profits extracted from Africa's export industries "would not be possible except for the unpaid labour of the wives of their African workers who feed, clothe, and care for themselves and their children at no cost whatsoever to the companies. Far from being a drag on the modern sector then, as it is sometimes claimed, the modern sector is dependent for its profits on the free labour done by women."[38]

Moreover, while the exclusion of women from advanced sectors of commercial production depresses the wage of workers in the marginally productive industries and services, the wages of workers in advanced sectors of industry are augmented by the narrowing of the labour force channeled into these jobs. The differential wage, artificially heightened in these sectors, stimulates greater investment in the capital-intensive advanced sectors and adds to the distortion of the economy, the overinvestment in import substitution, and the intensified neglect of local level and subsistence sectors.[39]

The failure to place a market value on women's work means that their contribution to production is undervalued. This aggravates the unevenness of capital investment in development. The savings on women's unpaid labour in domestic production accelerates the accumulation of capital for the investment sector, thus reinforcing the existing inequalities that are currently and have historically been responsible for women's oppression.

In addition the sexual division of labour within which women occupy a subordinate role, can be translated into minimal participation for women in the labour movement. Because women move in and out of the productive process according to the need for the household to cover different points of production (e.g. seasonal agricultural labour, crisis situations such as war or periods of economic expansion followed by cyclical patterns of inflation and depression), women as a group do not formalize a permanent relation to production that is concentrated over time. This is aggravated by the supplementary and peripheral nature of the economic spheres in which women are concentrated in relation to the centers of investment and productive activity. The above-mentioned position of women in the labour force is reinforced by social conditioning in accordance with an ideology that defines women's work as secondary to the unpaid household-related functions they perform and projects women as inferior members of the labour force.

This restricted nature of women's relation to the productive processes, which is largely determined by a labour-demand structure created by dependent development, means that women remain "the masses" relative to other workers. As such they are denied comparable equitable education and training.[40]

This point was made concrete by Glaura Vasques de Miranda in her case study of Brazil. She concluded:

> Dependent capitalist economic development therefore does not necessarily increase employment in the primary and secondary sectors of the labour market, where lower class women have the educational requirements to work as wage labourers. And these same women did not benefit from the expansion of the educational system. In all probability expansion of educational opportunities to women of all classes in a later stage of economic development will lead to an increase in job requirements. Thus these women will continue to have relatively poor opportunities in the wage labour market, unless changes in the very process of economic development begin to facilitate the incorporation of women into the labour force.[41]

Just as the unequal involvement of other sectors (peasants in comparison with townspeople, rich nations in comparison with poor nations) means that they can be controlled more effectively because of their inability to compete, so in the case of women there is a loss of decision-making and self-determination. Moreover, as a consequence of women's peripheral and limited position in the labour force, women as a group are increasingly isolated, lacking identification with the interests of other workers. Their isolation becomes the vehicle for their further and future oppression by circumscribing their effective political participation.

Modernization and economic growth are critical to development and it is difficult to envision modernization in the absence of "advanced" western technology, but it has become painfully apparent that the development of technology is not tantamount to development in a social sense. Advanced technology cannot be seen in a vacuum, but carries with it fundamental aspects of the society out of which it has grown. Much of it has been designed to save labour and to utilize capital inputs and has been constructed in accordance with a framework of a highly centralized and regimented organization of production and dissemination.[42] Just as technology cannot be viewed in a vacuum, neither can it be seen per se as purely technical, as its definition, choice, development, and deployment are highly politicized. Science and technology have been utilized by an international male elite class to perserve and reinforce the political economic and social bases of its dominance. Moreover, this technology, which is derived from a class-bound and patriarchal tradition, reinforces the division of labour between nations, classes, and the sexes. As such, it is doubtful that this form of organization of technology – unaltered – can bring about a process of development that the majority of people can be involved in and that is responsive to their needs.

Notes

1. See Ashis Nandy, "The Traditions of Technology," *Alternatives*, Vol. IV, No. 3, January 1979, pp. 371–386. Nandy also attributed the patriarchal nature of Western science to the fusion of the seventeenth century western European identification of science and technology with power, activism and aggression with the masculinity principle in the Judeo-Christian cosmology.

2. See Johan Galtung, "Towards a New International Technological Order," *Alternatives*, Vol. IV, No. 3, January 1979, p. 227. Galtung described these codes of structures inherent in Western technology:

> The economic code that inheres in western technology demands that industries be capital-intensive, research intensive, organization intensive and labor-extensive. On the social plane, the code creates a 'center' and a 'periphery' thus perpetuating a structure of inequality. In the cultural arena, it sees the west as entrusted by destiny with the mission of casting the rest of the world in its mould. In the cognitive field it sees man as the master of nature, the vertical relationships between human beings as the normal and natural, and history as a linear movement of progress.

3. Ibid., p. 286.

4. See Theotônio Dos Santos, *El nuevo carácter de la dependencia* (Santiago: Cuadernos de Estudios Socio-Económicos (10), Centro de Estudios Socio-Económicos (CESO), Universidad de Chile, 1968).

5. See Helieith Saffoti, "Women's Mode of Production and Social Forma-

tions," *Latin American Perspectives,* Issue 12-13, Vol. IV, No. 1-2, Winter-Spring 1977, pp. 27-37.

6. See Hilary Rose and Steven Rose, *The Political Economy of Science* (New York: Holmes and Meier, 1976), p. 62.

7. Ibid., 62.

8. Ibid., 62.

9. See Johan Galtung, "Towards a New International Technological Order," *Alternatives,* Vol. IV, No. 3, January 1979, pp. 277-300; 284.

10. See A. Rahman, "Science and Technology for a New Social Order," *Alternatives,* Vol. IV, No. 3, January 1979, pp. 317-333.

11. See Vinod Vyasulu, "Science and Technology for Underdevelopment," *New Scientist,* 18 January 1979, pp. 183-185. This notion was also discussed in a national seminar on "Technology Choice in the Indian Environment" held in October 1977 in Bangalore.

12. See Ward Morehouse, "Science, Technology, Autonomy and Dependence: A Framework for International Debate," *Alternatives,* Vol. IV, No. 3, January 1979, pp. 387-412; 387.

13. Johan Galtung, "Towards a New International Technological Order," *Alternatives,* Vol. IV, No. 3, January 1979, pp. 290-291.

14. Ibid., 291.

15. See Michael Chossodovsky, "Dependence and Transfer of Intellectual Technology. The Case of the Social Sciences," *Economic and Political Weekly,* Vol. XII, No. 36, September 3, 1977, pp. 1579-1583.

16. See Marianne Schmink, "Dependent Development and the Division of Labor by Sex: Venezuela," *Latin American Perspectives,* Issue 12-13, Vol. IV, No. 1-2, Winter-Spring 1977, pp. 153-180. See also Elsa Chaney and Marianne Schmink, "Women and Development: Access to Tools," in June Nash and Helen Safa (eds.), *Sex and Class in Latin America* (New York: Praeger Publishers, 1976).

17. Valerie Oppenheimer, *The Female Labor Force in the United States: Demographic and Economic Factors Governing its Growth and Changing Composition* (Berkeley: Institute of International Studies–University of California Population Monograph Series No. 5, 1970.) See also her chapter entitled "Rising Educational Attainment, Declining Fertility and the Inadequacies of the Female Labor Market," in Charles F. Westoff and Robert Parke, Jr., (eds.) *Demographic and Social Aspects of Population Growth,* Commission on Population Growth and the American Future Research Reports, Vol. 1, pp. 305-328.

18. See Felicia R. Madiera and Paul I. Singer, *Estructurado Empregoe Trabalho Feminino no Brasil, 1920-1970* (São Paulo: CEBRAP Cuaderno 13, 1975).

19. See Helen Icken Safa, "The Changing Composition of the Female Labor Force in Latin America," *Latin American Perspectives* Issue 15, Vol. IV, No. 4, Fall 1977, p. 126.

20. See Norma Chinchilla, "Industrialization, Monopoly Capitalism and Women's Work in Guatemala," in Wellesley Editorial Committee (eds.) *Women*

and National Development: The Complexities of Change (Chicago: University of Chicago Press, 1979), pp. 38–57. Also see a variation on this article reproduced in *Signs*, Vol. 3, No. 1, Autumn 1977, pp. 57–73.

21. See Lourdes Arizpe, "Women in the Informal Labor Sector: The Case of Mexico City," *Signs*, Vol. 3, No. 1, Autumn 1977, pp. 25–37.

22. See Ann Stoler, "Class Structures and Female Autonomy in Rural Java," *Signs*, Vol. 3, No. 1, Autumn 1977, pp. 74–87. These points are summarized by Helen Safa in the "Introduction" to Wellesley Editorial Committee (eds.) *Women, and National Development: The Complexities of Change*, where all their articles are reproduced in revised form.

23. See Helen Icken Safa, "The Changing Composition of the Female Labor Force in Latin America," *Latin American Perspectives*, Issue 15, Vol. IV, No. 4, Fall 1977, p. 126.

24. Galtung, op. cit., p. 284.

25. See Schmink, op. cit., pp. 153–180.

26. Ibid.

27. Ibid.

28. See Glaura Vasques de Miranda, "Women's Labor Force Participation in a Developing Society: The Case of Brazil," in Wellesley Editorial Committee (eds.) *Women and National Development: The Complexities of Change*, pp. 261–275.

29. See Chinchilla, op. cit.

30. See June Nash, "Women in Development: Dependency and Exploitation," *Development and Change*, Vol. 8, No. 2, 1977, p. 169.

31. Ibid.

32. See Chinchilla, op. cit.

33. Ibid.

34. See Carmen Diana Deere, "Rural Women's Subsistence Production in the Capitalist Periphery," *Review of Radical Political Economics* Vol. 8, 1976, pp. 9–17.

35. See Ester Boserup, *Women's Role in Economic Development* (London: George Allen and Unwin, 1980), pp. 77–78.

36. See Mina Davis Caufield, "Imperialism, the Family and Cultures of Resistance," *Socialist Revolutions*, No. 20, October 1974, pp. 67–85.

37. See Deere, op. cit.

38. See Judith Van Allen, "Women in Africa: Modernization Means More Dependency," *The Center Magazine*, Vol. XII, No. 3, May-June 1974, pp. 60–67.

39. Nash, op. cit., p. 161.

40. See Batya Weinbaum, "Women in Transition to Socialism. Perspectives on the Chinese Case," *Review of Radical Political Economics*, Vol. 8, 1976, pp. 34–58.

41. See Vasques de Miranda, op. cit.

42. *New Scientist*, Vol. 82, No. 1151, 7 June 1979, p. 831, "UNCSTD: A Matter of Involvement."

2
Women and Technology in the Industrialized Countries

Maria Bergom-Larsson

For thousands of years people have dreamed of being able to fly. Today, when the craft has become reality, they have to crawl under the ground like rats to protect themselves from their dream.

—Elin Wagner, 1935

Contents

1. Introduction

The recommendations of the UNCSTD Programme of Action observe, "Not much is yet known about the impact of technology on the work of women or about the implication for society of technology-induced changes in women's work. Existing data are inadequate and,

29

often, inappropriate for the identification of needs at the community level." It is important to establish that research has charted the effect of technology upon women's life and work only to a very limited extent. It should be emphasized that it is of crucial significance to investigate this before we can formulate a concrete action program for the solution of women's problems.

Technology's revolutionary influence on patterns of culture and life in underdeveloped countries is posed in the United Nations as a historical problem. In 1951 and 1952 the following resolutions were included in UNESCO's program:

> (3.231) To study possible methods of relieving tensions caused by the introduction of modern techniques in non-industrialized countries and those in the process of industrialization; [and]
> (3.24) To bring together and to diffuse existing knowledge and to encourage studies of the methods of harmonizing the introduction of modern technology in countries in the process of industrialization, with respect for their cultural values so as to ensure the social progress of the peoples.

In the study *Cultural Patterns and Technical Change* (1953), edited by Margaret Mead, technology's unforeseen consequences and potential damage are emphasized.[1]

> Technical change is also as old as civilization and since time immemorial the ways of life of whole peoples have been transformed by the introduction of new tools and new technical procedures, as inventions like the plough, the domestication of animals, writing, the use of steam, the factory assembly line, and the internal combustion engine, have been diffused from one country to another. Relationships of relative dominance between two peoples, population balances, dynasties, and whole religious systems have been upset by some change in technology, just as the inventions which underlie technological change have themselves arisen from changing conceptions of nature and of man.

To this it can be added that, since this report was written in 1953, technological development has accelerated and the perspective of the future presented, for example, by the new weapons technology, the neutron bomb, computer technology, and so on, appears to be more and more alarming.

Cultural Patterns and Technical Change views technology as part of a cultural context. I concur emphatically with this comprehensive kind of view. Each new technology introduced is accompanied by profound political, ethical, social, and human consequences. Ultimately, our choice of technology reflects the society we live in. No new technology is neutral in its values. It has built-in political valuations. This is part of the society's culture. For culture

> covers not only the arts and sciences, religions and philosophies to which the world culture has historically applied, but also the system of technology, the political practices, the small intimate habits of daily life, such as the way of preparing or eating food, or of hushing a child to sleep, as well as the method of electing a prime minister or changing the constitution. This survey is based on the assumption, itself drawn from field work among many kinds of societies, that a change in any one part of the culture will be accompanied by changes in other parts, and that only by relating any planned detail of change to the central values of the culture is it possible to provide for the repercussions which will occur in other aspects of life.

This view is particularly important to maintain in studying women's relationship to technology. Women's relation to technology is a cultural question.

In this chapter I am going to base my study of women and technology in industrialized countries upon conditions in Sweden inasmuch as these lie within my area of experience and knowledge. But I am convinced that conditions in Sweden, on most points, can be generalized to other highly industrialized societies in the Western world.

This study shuttles between two levels, the first being a metalevel on which I have tried to take up women's criticism of male technology—a critique that has evolved from the female consciousness formed by women's position in the production process as unsalaried producers in the home. A second level documents quite concretely the way in which women suffer from technological development. These two levels are intimately related. Out of specific experiences in work outside and inside the home with downgrading of labor, social control, stress, and isolation, women's protest grows against a technology that does not inquire after their fundamental needs. Against a technology that, increasingly, is threatening the life on earth and in our wombs, women today, increasingly, are saying no in order to safeguard their physiological integrity. The risk of congenital and genetic damage and cancer in the future for unborn children constitutes a direct threat to our lives and our children's lives. The drastic drop in the birth rate in all highly industrialized countries (in Sweden the number of births is about 11 per thousand) demonstrates the extent to which technology becomes manifest in women's consciousness in the form of a birth strike.

2. Women in Sweden

Swedish women got the vote in 1921. They obtained civil
rights – the right to schooling and education and the right to work – according to the law. But formal equality has not led to actual equality.

A higher proportion of women are gainfully employed in Sweden
than in most other Western countries. In 1978 the average gainful employment was 43.9 percent among women. Almost 70 percent of mar-
ried women work outside the home – but over half of them work part-
time. Nearly half of all women (48 percent in 1977) work part-time.
Yet this extensive female labor has not meant that women get the
same jobs or the same conditions as men. The labor market is
characterized by strict segregation into one male- and one female-
dominated sector.

- 70 percent of the women work in low-salaried female-
  dominated occupations requiring little education and involving
  assembly-line and part-time work during inconvenient hours.
- 80 percent of the employees in offices and shops are women.
- 92 percent of the employees in social work and health care are
  women.
- 97 percent of nurses' aides are women.
- 90 percent of part-time employees are women.
- Only 25 percent of women employed part-time could support
  themselves on their wages (in 1974).[2]

The women's occupations – that is, those occupations that are 90
percent dominated by women – are very much focused on the personal element; the men's occupations are oriented toward machines. As people are valued less than machines in capitalist society,
women are consistently low-paid. Often women's occupations represent an extension of the old housework. Where a male vocational
tradition did not exist and there was no technical equipment, women
entered in. They came to be dominant in areas such as textiles,
needlework, the manufacture of food, tobacco, shoes, and leather,
and in unqualified labor on the fringe of production, such as packaging and warehousing. During the last decade, when they have also
entered such traditionally male areas as the electronics industry, they
have wound up mainly in assembly-line work not requiring any vocational training.

By employers as well as the trade union movement, women have been regarded as "irrational" labor because their biology – giving birth, nursing, and caring for children – disturbed their work rhythm. As deviant labor power, they have had to pay for their responsibility for society's reproduction with low wages, poor education, difficulty in getting promoted, monotonous jobs, and part-time work. (Gunhild Kyhle, *Gästarbeterska i manssamhället* [Woman guest worker in the male society], 1978.)

The situation in the labor market is replicated in the decision-making bodies that influence social development. The proportion of women in parliament in 1977 was 23 percent; in the country's municipal governments, 23 percent; and in county councils, 24 percent. Whenever women happen to land in ministerial posts, it is in traditionally female areas such as welfare, education, housing, and aid programs (associated with women's ancient philanthropic work for the world's poor and starving children). The heavy ministerial posts – treasury, defense, energy, and the labor market – have consistently been reserved for men.

In the private sector it can be shown that women are underrepresented on the boards of companies and banks: only 11 board members out of a total of 2,000. The agencies that make decisions on technological research and social planning are almost completely male-dominated. The Research Institute of the Swedish National Defense (FOA), the National Swedish Board for Technical Development (STU), the Swedish Medical Research Council, the Swedish Natural Science Research Council, the Federal Power Commission, the Delegation for Energy Research, the Commission on Energy Production Research, and the Parliament's Traffic Commission all have exclusively male directorates. On the Data Inspection Board there are two women out of eleven members.

In other words, women have not participated in the crucial decisions made concerning technological development, arms technology, energy and traffic planning, and computerization of work. Under these circumstances it is not difficult to understand that women's needs for technology did not win a hearing until men took over their jobs. This applies to every area from window washing to health care.

At the same time, it is important to emphasize that it is overall economic development – including centralization, large-scale production, capital concentration, and structural rationalization – that has undone women in particular, because economic profitability and efficiency do not make allowances for the requirements of reproduction.

Karin Andersson, Chairperson of the Swedish government's Equality

Commission, believes equality and an ideology of economic growth are impossible to combine:

> We have a work economy with the sort of efficiency requirements that women with the responsibilities for reproduction cannot enter in without doing violence unto themselves. The capacity of the holy machine must be utilized day and night. In the processing industry today, for example, the fixed costs of the technical plant constitute 70 to 80 percent of manufacturing costs. With further technical development, even more capital is committed to fixed costs, and interruptions in the operational – for human beings' natural circadian rhythm, for example – become increasingly expensive and impossible. And it's the people who have to pay the price through shift work and stress, through a lack of camaraderie on-the-job, through a sense of powerlessness, through layoffs and unemployment. And through diminished prospects for equality.
>
> The physical social development – the development that has meant concentration and segmentation – has also deteriorated prospects for equality. The policy of concentration has led to major portions of our country being deprived of jobs and service. The fact that this has largely been leveled at women is demonstrated in large differences existing in women's rate of gainful employment among various regions of the country.
>
> In the areas of concentration, this build-up in sectors has produced great distances to be traveled and sterile environments to be endured. We now have large areas that are purely residential and without functioning services; we now spend much more time every day commuting to workplaces. And for this commuting we have a poorly functioning public transportation system. Moreover, it is mainly the women who have to use it since, according to all the surveys, the men are the ones who use the family car to go to work.
>
> No, indeed, the prospects for equality in today's society are not promising. They're going to be even worse tomorrow if development toward a highly technologized concentration society is allowed to continue unchecked. (*Dagens Nyheter*, 5 June 1979)

3. Women in the Male System

The men were the first to become wage earners in the infancy of industrialism. It can be said that it is male values and male organizational models that have determined the design of the work economy, defense, and politics. The labor movement has also given priority consistently to the opposition between labor and capital and devoted only an abstracted interest to the conflict that is also central but that primarily afflicts women: namely, that between production and reproduction, or paid work and family.

What these three systems have in common is the fact that they are hierarchically structured, with a small leadership stratum—an elite—requiring obedience from the large mass at the bottom. They are based on mathematical rationality, efficiency, impersonalness, competition, and economic profit. Objective criteria, such as profitability and consideration for the interests of production, also dominate over subjective criteria, such as human consideration, feelings, intimacy, and experience.

While the men's value system prevails in the working economy and society at large, the women's value system has been dominant in private life and the family. Thus, we have acquired a divided world in which men's suppressed needs for subjectivity, feelings, intimacy, and humanity are projected onto the private life and women, who at the same time have this private life as their workplace insofar as the responsibility of caring for home and children is theirs. Two cultures faced off against each other, the one designed by the demands of the production apparatus and the machine, the other grown out of reproduction. This explains why women, despite their formal equality, have had such a hard time holding their own in the world of work and politics. This also explains why women organize differently from men. The women's movement has always preferred a decentralized, nonhierarchical organizational model to the male society's hierarchical one because women know from their own experience that the weaker are oppressed in an elitist system.

What happens when the caretaking organized in female fashion is socialized? Sociologist Rita Liljeström gave two illuminating examples of how an industrial thinking apparatus governs the organization of two public institutions—the hospital and the school. The hospital is described as a "controlled production system" having two "main products," open and closed care, and offering for sale an assortment of products consisting of various types of treatment. Liljeström maintained, "The controlling of a nurses' aide or a patient involves approximately the same problems as the control of a somewhat complicated robot. . . . These theorists of organization describe the hospital as a completely industrialized production system devoid of all human relations, a system in which what counts is to get the patients in as fast as possible, to 'process engineer,' to treat them and put them on the assembly line heading out."[3]

In a similar manner the school is compared to an oil refinery that refines crude oil into various expensive finished products. The organization theorists recommend economic models to measure schools' productivity so that the "human capital" invested is looked after as efficiently as possible. It may be pointed out that when men and technology take over reproduction, the division of labor, hierarchies, efficiency, and the profit motive of industrial production do the organizing of the caretaking sectors. We get a little elite of (mostly male) hospital bureaucrats and professors at the top and a large group of women at the bottom with the most impoverished jobs and without any influence over their working situation or the form of the care. Women's experiences of the work of caretaking have no place in this system. Liljeström wrote:

> If industrial capitalism's first historical offense was to sever hand and brain, theory and practice, intellectual and manual, its second is no less serious: here reason dispels feeling, brain and heart are disengaged, two knowledge processes are kept from fertilizing each other. And at accelerated speed we are heading for a separation of hand and heart, a disintegration of qualification. We organize and divide labor so that systematically it destructs and squanders the most valuable combinations of human life resources. (*Kultur och arbete* [Culture and work], p. 144)

4. Women's Culture and Women's Consciousness

Men and women live in different cultures on account of their different placement in the production process. The gap between these two cultures tends to enlarge. The UN talks about three discrepancies that have grown worse during the recent decades: the one between rich and poor countries, the one between rich and poor within each country, and the one between men and women in all countries. While women are in unsalaried production in the home, men work as salaried employees outside in the labor market. Even when women take the step into the work world, they take their reproductive role with them into the occupational areas available; moreover, they still bear the major responsibility for reproduction in the home. In other words, they have two jobs. Studies from all over the world unequivocally show that the time women spend in unsalaried production has not decreased during the past fifty years.

Out of women's work with children, the sick, and the old, with childbirth and its preparation, with clothing and upkeep of the home – that is, in the daily maintenance and restoration of our lives and our labor force as well as in the recreating of the human species – generation after generation, through birthing and caring for small children grow values at variance with the male society. One U.S. study shows that women prize aesthetic, social, and religious criteria; men favor political, economic, and technological criteria.[4]

Women have learned greater prudence with living things – learned not to waste nature's resources, learned to use leftovers – and have, together with children, developed greater psychological sensitivity. All this knowledge is today invisible. If it were to become visible, it would become a challenge to our entire social system.

Out of women's and men's different positions in social production, with person-oriented versus machine-oriented labor, emerge totally different relations to causal relations and to time. Women who work with and among human beings see a network of causal connections, visible and invisible, reaching out over a long period. The seeds being sown here and now in reproductive labor will not bear fruit for some decades to come. "The moment is the history of the future" sums up this style of understanding. Men's sense of the causal, on the contrary, is decided by machine production and imbued with linearity (if X, then Y): It is set on measurable tangible results.

Like the Norwegian women's studies scholar Bjørg Aase Sørensen, one can speak of women's rationality of responsibility. Women inquire as to the long-range consequences of social decisions rather than short-range technical and economic gains. Men as a group, on the other hand, are bearers of the Western industrial society's *techno-economic* rationality in which economic goals are permitted to legalize exploitation or disregard other human beings. (*Forskning för jämndställdhet, människan och arbetslivet* [Research for equality, people, and work], RG 1979: 3, Stockholm, 1979.)

Women's time and men's time also differ from each other. Women's concept of time can be called organic, the time that it takes to get something done; men's time is one-dimensional. Liljeström has drawn the differences in this way in her study *Culture and Work* (1979):

Women's Time	*Men's Time*
• is time that is used to make and maintain social ties, to secure access to mutual help if anything should happen.	• is time used to further objective economic interests, in exchange for an acknowledged interest of one's own.
• is unsold time. There is no quantitative yardstick that ascertains the activity's value.	• is sold time. The wages spell out clearly what the work is worth.

- is coordinated time. Women alternate various activities and often do several things at the same time.
- is marked by an indistinct scheduling of time. Unpaid labor, symbolic interplay, and relaxation relieve each other and interfuse in a continuing current.
- has less visible results: How are support to other people's growth and actions fostering others' independence to be accounted for? The results must be valued in qualitative terms.

- is segregated time. Attention can be concentrated on one task.
- is marked by strict scheduling of terminate, exact time units, clearly drawn boundaries between work and leisure time.
- has more visible results, a striving to maximize in quantitative terms.

To sum up, the qualities that have been detected in women's culture are:

1. horizontal organizational model without a leadership stratum or elite;
2. valuations based on aesthetic, social, and religious criteria;
3. an organic conceptualization of time;
4. a multidimensional, complex conception of causality (rationality of responsibility);
5. an orientation in terms of persons instead of machines.

All these qualities have consequences for women's way of relating to technological development.

5. The Patriarchal Natural Sciences

Research in the natural sciences often has the reputation of being "objective," of standing outside any context of social interest. It purports to seek knowledge for its own sake. This freedom of values has been strongly challenged by female scholars and philosophers. Elisabet Hermodsson has summarized the views she expressed in her book *Synvända*:[5]

It's not so many years ago that the progress of science and technology was viewed as something exclusively beneficial. The measure of progress was defined technologically (increased speed, increased technical efficiency, bigger machines). Today the situation is different. More and more people are talking today about the menace to nature and the danger for humans' life environment. People have begun to realize that, all the while, the development in the natural sciences and technology has been matched by an ongoing devastation of nature. It is not only a matter of depleting irreplaceable natural resources. It is also a question of modern science and technology setting in motion processes, and creating combinations of substances, that are unknown in nature – substances and processes against which nature has no defense and which therefore jeopardize the ecological balance.

States and governments are still acting largely in the optimistic spirit of nineteenth century development, and groups of critical scholars and laypersons who demand a new direction (alternative research, alternative technology), are labeled romantics or innocent troublemakers.

However, today we must ask ourselves not only how the findings of research are used by political powers, how economic resources are distributed by agencies in charge, which type of research is given priority, how major industries can buy research resources to such an extent that they can affect the whole research approach, and how commercial interests can steer research in a destructive direction. We must also wonder whether there isn't anything destructive in modern science's very manner of seeing the world.

One of the principles of natural science is the freedom of evaluation. Research is conducted "for the sake of knowledge itself." The models and images of reality, nature, matter such as it "actually" is. Research declares itself free of responsibility in relation to its object, nature. In modern science, nature has been reduced to "only matter." The attitude of research to nature, on these principles, is destructive.

Let us transpose this relationship to pertain to a relationship between people. Thus, if one person studies another person and subjects this other person to experimental investigations but at the same time is totally irresponsible as to the object of these investigations, coldly observing "objectively," then this relationship becomes the same as a destructive relationship. In other words, it is not an objective relationship in the sense of being value-free, but it is a question of a relationship that is controlled by negative valuations – that is, by *not taking responsibility*. Not sharing existence is the same thing as being nonethical. A nonethical way of relating is *destructive*. When it comes to the relation between people, there is an awareness that the methods with which a person is studied, affect the person and affect the investigator in turn. But in the relationship of natural science to nature, an equivalent relationship is not thought to exist.

Natural science is "in principle materialistic." Matter is "only matter." What does "only" mean in this connection? It means the same thing as reduction, a simplification, a slanting so that the process in nature, when subjected to methodical investigation, is to respond to this reduction, this slanting. The investigation becomes not only a survey, but also a steering in a certain direction.

We might inquire as to what the Western culture would have looked like if the women had not been subjected to an oppression of many thousands of years. If the women had had a different effect on our culture's search for knowledge than fixing meals and typing manuscripts for their world-finding and world-winning husbands, would we have had the image of the world we have today? And would we have had the technology we have today?

We can ascertain that sex roles in patriarchal society are distributed according to a conceptual realm in which the man is seen as the brain (reason, technology, abstraction) and the woman as the senses (the emotions, the heart, nature, the immanent, etc.).

With the patriarchal social order comes private property, the class society, the subjugation of woman. The growth of capitalism and of natural science – technology – are interrelated and both are a product of patriarchy.

The hypertechnocratic civilization can be seen as the ultimate consequence of patriarchy's desire to master what is nature, woman, and life. Humanity defined as man, as aggressive conqueror, as the right of the stronger to rule the world, has clarified, researched and tamed nature's forces, demystifying nature but at the same time committing rape upon nature, on Mother Earth, performing ruthless exploitation of the natural resources and creating the technical possibility for human exterminating humanity. Women who have been excluded from codetermination in political and cultural development have not been involved in creating this hypertechnocratic culture. The women who are now fighting for the liberation of women's strength to intervene in social development want the action pattern – the modes of development, value, competition, and class that patriarchy has imprinted upon society – to be changed. Progress must not be defined as it has to the present, as something solely technical. The prestigious word "development" is used when one internal machine is replaced by another internal machine or when one fast airplane is replaced by another even faster. But development must be based on social values and consideration for nature and it must imply an appreciation of the basic values of equality between people and equality between nature and people.

6. Women's Criticism of Male Technology

Women's culture has served as the grounds for a growing women's consciousness of supertechnology's threat to the most basic preconditions for life. As a collective body women have been outside the development of modern supertechnology. Berit Ås, a Norwegian social scientist and politician, has pointed out the irrationality in what she calls male technology:

> Why is its first solution to the transportation problem the use of the private automobile, a form that ruthlessly kills and cripples humans, distributes the chances of mobility inequitably among the population, and pollutes air and earth and lays waste to precious farmland? The UN has documented the fact that the automobile in many instances is the worst source of air pollution.
>
> Why doesn't it instead create clean and expanded public transportation that will be of use to everybody?
>
> Why does the male security-police mentality take the form of more bombs and rockets, of an accumulation of arms that today can blow up the earth 48 times over? Here too there is an abundance of documentation on the threat of the arms race to world peace. In 1977 the UN issued a report showing, with clear-cut examples, how economic and social development is impeded by the arms race, how inflation and a deficit in the balance of payments in almost all countries have arisen in its wake, and how extremely dangerous it is to world peace and to security.[6]

What is the sense of 200 million Americans using up as much energy on air conditioners as 800 million Chinese use in all? Or of medical research spending millions on incredibly sophisticated "luxury medicine" such as heart transplants while schistosomiasis, for example, has not yet been wiped out? Why have we got superjets and micro-processors but not solar-heated housing or good elevators in geriatric chronic-care wards? Lars Ingelstram from the Bureau of Future Studies maintains that if technology once liberated the human being from the tyrannization of nature, it is increasingly clear today that to a larger degree it is technology that is enslaving humans. "The nuclear race is the most important example, spacecraft the most grotesque, and a harshly mechanized work environment is a striking illustration and reality for many."[7]

Ås pointed out that it is the women who have sounded the alarm on super technology's devastation of the air, the water, and the soil. Rachel Carson was the first, in *Silent Spring* (1963), to discuss mercury poisoning of animal life. In Scandinavia a great number of women have protested against the destruction of the environment. In 1941 Elin Wägner and Elisabeth Tamm began with *Fred med jorden* (Peace with the earth).[8] Monika Nilsson, after having had a miscarriage, singlehandedly led the fight against a chemical-technical company in Teckomatorp (in the Swedish province of Scania), which caused an environmental disaster with the highly poisonous substances they discharged.[9] Merit Paulsen has mobilized the women of an entire district against spraying the forests with *hormoslyr* (two types of phenoxyacetic acid) in Yttermalung, in the province of Dalarna.[10] Birgitta Hambraeus was the first in parliament (in 1972) to question the gruesome risks to human beings and nature that are involved in nuclear waste from atomic power. The author Sara Lidman has protested against the devastation of the forest in the rational, industrialized timber industry. She wrote:

> But the cleared area looks as if a war had been raging over the ground. There is a sadness that comes out of this kind of ground that makes all that lives despair. . . . Something inside us withers in the presence of the burned-black birch stumps. We grow gloomy, ashamed, and unable to look each other in the eye. On the edge of a cleared area people's living standard drops so drastically that no matter what whopping profits the lumber industry makes on this area, it cannot compensate us for the loss—not even if these profits are made available to the public. (*Dagens Nyheter,* 18 August 1977)

In Norway and Denmark, too, it is the women who have protested against the defilement of nature. In Southern Zealand Bodil Mertz has led the interdisciplinary women's protest movement against aerial spraying of fields of blooming crops. The Norwegian author Sidsel Mörck has written about highly dangerous transport.[11] Women have protested against the 1,000 lakes now dead as a result of the great radioactive fallout from Western Europe; against the poisoning of Mjösa (Norway's largest lake) as a result of silo discharge and an insane farm policy; against the lead in the air of big cities that now threatens the nervous systems of children. In Sweden the politicians are saying openly that the choice is now between children and cars and at the same time—by their passivity—are demonstrating that they have already chosen cars.

What is characteristic of these female protests is that responsibility is being taken for coming generations. There is a strong conviction that what we do here and now is going to affect people in the future down to the third and fourth generations. While men live their own lives in the present, the women's capacity to reproduce suffers. The contamination threatens their physiological integrity with deformed fetuses, abortions, and cancer in children and grandchildren. Moreover, the women's protest has been buttressed by the fact that it has always been women who have tended technology's victims. It is women who most often are nurses, psychologists, welfare workers, and therapists. They look the victims in the face and for this reason also have a more difficult time rejoicing over the territorial gains of technology.

One last example of the difference between female and male attitudes to the risks of supertechnology concerns nuclear energy. In both Sweden and Norway women's skepticism toward atomic power has been extensive. In Sweden one study from January 1979 conducted by the Swedish Institute of Public Opinion Research (SIFO) showed that 55 percent of the women in a referendum would vote against nuclear power as compared with only 28 percent of the men. After the accident in Harrisburg women's resistance rose to 75 percent.

In Norway the woman centrist Tove Bye has managed to organize an extensive critique of a planned Norwegian nuclear energy program. One of Norway's best known political TV reporters, Herbjørn Sørebo, wrote after Harrisburg: "One might wonder, reading the statistics, how people who object to nuclear energy ever dare to sit down in a car. The statistics give those of you working in nuclear energy plants a greater chance of survival than any given passenger in the back seat of an auto" (*Dag og Tid* [Day and time]).

Sørebo's comment demonstrated a conceptual gap between male and female thinking. He does not look beyond his own immediate existence here and now, but Bye, in her argument, is particularly concerned with the long-range consequences of a nuclear energy gospel and the complex of causes that in the future can damage all human life. Like all the other women active in the environmental struggle, she has been extremely sensitive to what happens to the earth. Whether this is the result of social tradition passed down through women or is quite simply an expression of daily habit in the preparation of nature's products and the fixing of food, it is difficult to say. But Bye's whole line of reasoning is based on the responsibility for children, for future generations, and for nourishment. It's up to us in the present to see to it that children don't get poisoned by food. In order to show Bye's reasoning, I shall quote from one of her lectures:

Radioactivity cannot be reduced through human intervention if the global level becomes too high. The radioactive material that is released in the use of nuclear energy has a halflife that indicates the length of time it takes for the number of radioactive nuclei to be reduced to half. The halflife is a characteristic trait of radioactive nuclei and cannot be altered.

From nuclear energy plants and related operations there will be a constant discharge of radioactive material that may be harmful to human beings and to the environment. The power plants may be built and operated so that the amount of radioactivity released is minimized. It is the local area in which the radiation level of radioactive materials emitted from a plant is the highest. The size of the area depends on geographic and meteorological conditions: a radius of about 50 kilometers is usually given. (In the U.S. it is estimated at 80 kilometers.) If foodstuffs are produced in the local area that are consumed by specific groups outside the area, these groups can also get corresponding levels of radiation. The group of people who get the highest level of radiation from the discharge of a nuclear technology plant are referred to as the exposed group for the particular plant in question. An exposed group may be the people who live next to the plant, and who get a radiation level from the dischage of radioactive material in the air, but it may also be people who get an increased amount of radioactive material in their bodies from eating food produced near the nuclear technology plant.

Radioactive isotopes of iodine, strontium, and cesium have long since been known to be those materials capable of causing the highest radiation levels to humans in the contamination of farm products. Children may often be exposed to a higher radiation level than adults themselves if the amount ingested is the same. Milk production and geographical distribution of grazing land should be specified in detail for the area situated within 10 kilometers from a nuclear power plant. Also, relevant information should be gathered from areas located within a distance of up to 50-70 kilometers from the possible building sites. In the application for a license to operate a nuclear power plant, the contracter must account for possible radiological consequences anticipated for the environment of the plant operation. This assumes that a radiological analysis has been made of the configuration of the nuclear power plant and the environment. Because of the major role that milk can play in transmitting radioactivity to people, milk production must be charted in greater detail than production of other agricultural products. If milk production is not especially large in an area in which radioactive fallout can be expected, vegetables will probably be the products that contribute most to the population's radiation level. (This information is taken from: *Innledende radioökologiske studier for Kjernekraftverk ved Oslofjorden* [Introductory radioecological studies for power plant works at Oslofjord] [NVE June 1974].) One critical group will be children (aged one) on those farms which produce milk and where estimates indicate a high bacteria contamination.[12]

As I read the radio-ecological studies mentioned above, it occurred to me that it may be high time to demand an investigation of imported agricultural products to check to see if they are contaminated by radioactive materials. One cannot disregard the fact that some of the farm products we bring in may be raised in the neighborhood of nuclear power plants abroad and that unacceptably high levels of radioactivity may have developed in them.

One of the arguments in Bye's article regards the irrevocability of the nuclear technology process. Modern supertechnology sets in motion processes that cannot be stopped if they prove to threaten human survival in a more long-range perspective. This approach conflicts with the established notion that technological research provides control – quite the contrary. Ås maintains that it does not give control but instead commits to processes that are impossible to surveil or stop.[13] With all its built-in control systems the automobile has one simple flaw: it cannot be braked immediately. As a result, it annually kills thousands of people. The bombs that are released can never be called back. The pollution of the seas cannot be undone.

Television may be said to function as a different sort of device for violence. It forces us to sit still three or four hours each day in an attentive state without the chance to channel feelings that are brought to life – something that has never before happened in the history of the world. Kerstin Stjärne, a Swedish scholar of children's culture, has described television in its function as a corrective device in child rearing:

> TV came as a gift from above to bewildered parents who, after having oppressed children since at least time immemorial had had it made clear to them that neither beating nor frightening children was any longer allowed. Why, here was the perfect electronic childcare that miraculously made noisy youngsters quiet, complaisant, and still – and to top everything off it made them love their own pacification.
>
> Too late it was discovered what a terrorist had been let into the house – who undermined eating habits, sabotaged group activities, bedtime routines, holiday traditions, small talk, fights, and discussions. In short: human intercourse in the family.[14]

Moreover, the enormous resources put into technological research cannot be restructured or used for anything meaningful. The $500 billion or so squandered annually on the arms race cannot be recouped. This money is stolen from the poor and sick people of the developed countries. We cannot get any use out of the enormous sums wasted on the world's 400,000 arms technology experts (who use half of the world's research funds) because their technical expertise is specialized in weapons of destruction.[15] The time that they have spent is lost, the educational material made for them is forfeited, and so are the efforts of the teachers. In addition to the actual destruction these weapons inflicted in Dresden, Hiroshima, and Vietnam, there is also the ghastly waste of resources implied in the laying out of $500 billion on something *not* intended to be used.

Disarmament expert and Undersecretary of State Inga Thorsson has pointed out what invisible violence is contained in this waste of the world's meager resources. With only 5 percent of the world's annual military budget

- all the children in the underdeveloped countries could be vac-cinated against the most common diseases;
- 700 million people could get instruction in writing and reading;
- great portions of the Third World could get preventative health care;
- 500 million people could get enough land to support themselves;
- 300 million living in the slums today could get new housing;
- 200 million undernourished and malnourished children could get extra food rations;
- 60 million pregnant women suffering from undernourishment could be helped;
- 100 million more children could be sent to school;
- everybody could have pure water by 1990.[16]

All this for only 5 percent of the world's annual military appropria-tion. In order to make the problem even more concrete, Thorsson demonstrated that one nuclear submarine costs as much as it costs to keep alive 16 million children under one year of age. Why is it mainly women and not the men making the crucial political decisions who point out these types of facts and arguments? There are two possible explanations for this: (1) There are different value systems, different patterns of solidarity, and different notions of causal conditions underlying men's and women's thinking; and (2) Understanding based on research is largely meaningless. It is power and not knowledge that forms the basis for political decisions.

7. Women and the Peace Movement

Through its title, "Equality, Peace, and Development," the 1975 In-ternational Women's Year Conference in Mexico not only served as a reminder that women are oppressed, their conditions deteriorating in almost all of the countries of the world. It also related to women's traditional connection to peace work. It is tempting to turn in rage against individuals who now – at the last minute – blame women for international crises, war, and injustice in general, particularly as we know that women are not represented in the major peace negotiations, have no influential organizations, and no resources of their own for independent peace research on their own terms. But it is also conceivable that this is not mainly a search for scapegoats but that the title actually indicates that the male society of the UN feels it has lost control over the arms race and weapons technology and is looking to women for possible guidelines for something qualitatively different. (After all, none of the preceding conferences – in Stockholm, Rome, and Bucharest – had the peace question affixed to their title.)

As early as 1854, in *The Times*, the Swedish author Fredrika Bremer published a proposal for a peace federation:

> We propose the establishment of an alliance in the name of the Prince of Peace, extending his healing regenerative activity over the entire earth. . . . We propose in this respect to recognize a common native land, to consider ourselves as one family, to reach out our hands to each other as sisters and to recognize as our children and relations all those whom misfortune deprived of their support or means to a livelihood and who our caring attention can possibly reach, whatever their race or creed. . . . Individually, each of us is weak and able to do but little, but if we reach out our hands around the whole world in the name of Christ's love, we shall take the earth into our arms like a child.[17]

Significantly more concrete in her criticism of militarism was the Austrian baroness Bertha von Suttner who in 1889 wrote a flaming protest novel against war, *Die Waffen Nieder* [Down with weapons]. Like Fredrika Bremer, she invested all her energies in the struggle for peace. With foresight, she warned of the development of arms technology and the brutality of war: "With our age's formidably developed arms technology . . . and the unspeakable size of the armies, the next war will be not only a dreadful business but also a gigantic catastrophe. The next war, which people speak of so easily and freely, will not mean the gain of one or the loss of the other but the *defeat of all*." Bertha von Suttner never knew what a prophet she was. She died a couple of days before the outbreak of World War I. In 1905 she became one of the first to receive the Nobel Peace Prize.

Her fight was carried on by a great number of women. In protest against the nationalism and militarism then raging, the American Jane Addams, at the height of the war in 1915, assembled a peace conference in The Hague, where the Women's International League for Peace and Freedom was formed. It still has branches today in most countries.

The Swedish author Elin Wägner participated in The Hague conference and worked untiringly for peace until her death in 1949. In 1924 she formulated the slogan "Humanity ought to exterminate war before war exterminates humanity." And in 1935 she proclaimed "The Women's Unarmed Revolt Against War," which won a wide hearing among Sweden's women. Here it was said, among other things:

> During recent years the threat of war has constantly made new forays, on each occasion advancing nearer. We were promised disarmament and have gotten involved in armament. The language of war has grown increasingly provocative, and its resisters more and more compliant.
>
> This fateful development has thus far taken place largely without either assistance or resistance on the part of the women. But it has now reached the point that they must make up their mind one way or the other. The war machinery has been developed into a technically perfected mass killer that aims right at the population, crossing frontiers, fleets, and fortresses. It therefore by necessity forces the population to put on protective cover turning the earth into a fortress, closed off against the sky.
>
> Women, unite and demand that men consider where they are taking humanity. The best and wisest of them see this and try to turn the tide.
>
> But when you demand that they lay down their arms, let them then understand at the same time that you intend to lay down yours: that you refuse to enter the war machine, refuse the discipline of cellar and gas mask!
>
> Women, tell them you don't believe in gasmasks, cellars, and other defense weapons. Tell them you turn your back to the idea that some people will be picked out to be saved and others left to perish. Tell them you don't want to be left with your children to the poison and fire outside an overcrowded shelter, but neither do you want to be rescued at the expense of others, and then to step out into a world laid waste. (Clayhill, *Den antimilitaristiska kamptraditionen i den svenska kvinnorörelsen* [The antimilitarist tradition of struggle in the Swedish women's movement], 1979, p. 23)

But war came despite the women's vain protests. In 1941 Wägner wrote her thought-provoking pacifist work, *Väckarklocka* [Alarm clock], instilled with great pessimism about the West's male-controlled culture of violence. But she still has hopes for women.

In 1945 the work for peace was resumed. Then the Women's International Democratic Federation was formed with representatives from thirty-nine countries. The first demand was that the UN have control over the A-bomb. In Sweden there was a tough fight against the Swedish atom bomb. The author Moa Martinson urged women to "become just as ruthless in the struggle for peace as the men in the fight for war." The Social Democratic Women's League, under the leadership of Inga Thorsson and with the support of Ulla Lindström in the government, managed to stop the introduction of a Swedish atom bomb.[18]

Since the 1950s, Sweden has seen a great number of women working for peace and disarmament nationally and internationally, ranging from Alva Myrdal, Inga Thorsson, Maj Britt Theorin, and Maj Wechselmann to all the women who participated in the march against the neutron bomb on Whitsuntide in 1978. Like Myrdal, they have all placed the arms race in a cultural context as part of a destructive culture of violence:

> The very fact that war is sanctioned as a natural exercise of power for nations, I think, plays a decisive role in the preservation of what I call the culture of arms and violence and which I believe to a great extent characterizes our age.
>
> This militarization proceeds not only through acts of war and purchase of arms. It is also fostered through military education, defense instructions, etc., in which exercises and exhortations wear down the basic ethical values of "Thou shalt not kill," which religious proclamations as well as international law on human rights and humanitarian warfare otherwise attempt to reinforce. (Alva Myrdal, *The Game of Disarmament*)

Why are women, as a collective body, more involved in the cause of peace than men? Women have other historical prerequisites for the understanding of war than men.[19] Women and men have different relationships to property and territories:

> It is the men in the world who have been property owners. Women have had to follow their husbands to new countries and cities. The right of inheritance has not existed for girls either: it has been only half of what the boys got or the women have themselves been property that has been bought or traded off.
>
> During specific acts of war they have *become helpless victims*. Nobody has ever tried to make them believe that if only the generals were good enough, the strategies superior, and the desire for revenge were there, their efforts would be crowned with victory.
>
> "In war, rape is a natural thing," say the generals, and this was certainly the experience of the women of Bangladesh. In terror bombing, the women, children, and old people of the civilian population are "reified." The reason villages are bombed to dust is so that those men at the front watching "their people" getting wiped out will be demoralized. The rela-

tionship to *men in the army* is for women, to a greater extent than for
men, a relationship to sons. For men, the members of the army are
fellow soldiers and comrades whose actions may decide whether or not
they themselves live or die.

The different relationships to territories, to the active or passive role
during war, and to the army, make women view the problem of war
and peace differently from men. Therefore women work to avoid
war – but not at any price. Peace cannot be bought with other people's
starvation, death, and torture. Nor have women been socialized since
childhood to be aggressive, competitive, and belligerent. They have
not been indoctrinated by the "hero ideologies" in the major mass
market novels. They have not been forced to obedience, subordination, and an aggressive masculinity cult in military service. Consciousness, thinking, and reasoning evolve out of human praxis. The
more men develop, buy, and use technology, the harder it will be for
women to live and survive. "The technological supremacy of the West
achieves its shining perfection in the arms technology," said one West
German industrialist and arms expert on a television program. Here I
shall give a couple examples of military reasoning. Maj Wechselmann,
scholar and debater on questions of defense, did three programs for
Swedish television during the spring of 1979 on the nuclear strategy in
Europe. She tells here of her conversations with a German military
man on the neutron bomb:

> The weapon is tested in the Nevada desert – the medical effects of this
> weapon are known. It is emphasized very strongly by those military
> men with whom I talked in Germany that this is now considered to be
> the only sensible weapon that can be used in limited nuclear war. The
> one I talked to is the rank under general, a lieutenant colonel, and a
> teacher at the Academy of Military Science in Hamburg. He believes
> that the neutron bomb can be used to provide a rapid atomic display and
> then conventional war would be restored to its former state. It should be
> remembered that the neutron weapon has the form of radioactive radia-
> tion that provides the greatest biological effect. Very low levels kill, very
> low levels do damage. Neutron radiation damage sources are insensitive
> to other forms of radioactive radiation and X-ray radiation. Actually two
> instances are known in which people were exposed to this form of radia-
> tion contained in neutron weapons. Their death was unspeakably pain-
> ful and appalling. The slow death awaiting people who are exposed to
> neutron radiation is probably what makes the neutron weapon the worst
> antipersonnel weapon invented so far. From German quarters this
> weapon is very much in demand. In Sweden last fall there was also a
> conference at the Research Institute of the Swedish National Defense

(FOA) in which many West German military men and experts participated and after, the neutron weapon was described in exactly the same terms as the German military personnel use today; as the only "clean" weapon, that does not cause radioactive fallout and that lets things remain standing undamaged. The fact that—in its effect—the bomb has the same radius as a large atom bomb (when it comes to killing people) is not mentioned. Instead it is stressed that the bomb only destroys material objects within a very small circumference and that its halflife for radiation is very short, which of course does not have any effect on those who have already been exposed for they die in any case.

The military personnel that Wechselmann interviewed assured her

that it was very enthusiastic, spirited technicians who were permitted to provide aeronautics research, "vanguard technology" which they never would have a chance to develop otherwise. I think it is in this area that we find much of armaments' own dynamic—that is in the technician's desire to break the Olympic record when it comes to accuracy of aim for bombs, etc.[20]

In contrast to the military's view of the neutron bomb as the only "clean" weapon, Wenche Haland, a member of the Norwegian Disarmament Commission, emphasized in her statements the devastation that the neutron bomb inflicts on human beings. Here data is taken from Dr. R.J.H. Kruisinga, the Dutch physician and defected defense minister. The effects of the bomb include the following:

- 10,000 units of radioactivity will produce brain damage followed by death one to forty-eight hours later.
- 1,000–10,000 units produce stomach pains leading to death two to six days later, with enormous suffering for which no medical help is possible.
- 250–1,000 units produce leukemia followed by death in the course of two to six weeks.
- 50–250 units produce leukemia or other forms of cancer in the course of five to twenty-five years. All dosages at this level may have genetic consequences and produce damage in unborn children.
- Within a radius of 200 meters material things will also be destroyed, but beyond this radius, material will not be laid waste.[21]

Why don't these facts reach the mass media? Wechselmann gave an illuminating example from her work in West Germany:

> I interviewed one TV producer who deals with these questions, and he said: "In this country I can't make a movie showing the effect of these weapons – the damage they actually do. My photographers just love weapons because they're movement, action, speed, explosions. These weapons are always photographed in direct light. If you check in the German film archives, you'll see that on each weapon there is a bunch of index cards. In other words, you can get undreamed-of quantities of films on every weapon produced in Germany today and they are incredibly beautiful. However, they say nothing about the effects.

Moreover, she had never met a single woman journalist, technician, planner, or arms expert.

It need not be emphasized that the gap between the increasingly advanced arms technology, with its studied precision in snuffing out life, and women's daily existence, which aims at just the opposite, the recreation and sustenance of life, is enormous and growing. The technicians' attempts to conceal what they are actually doing behind seemingly objective, "unhysterical," and matter-of-fact concepts such as "clean" weapons and "megabody" deaths (one million dead, according to Herman Kahn in *The Thermonuclear War*) attest to a frightening lack of moral and human responsibility. Reflected in these concepts is a total alienation in the face of inhuman suffering and despair: a natural consequence of the development of nuclear weapons.

In a lecture on United Nations Day Thorsson asserted that "today's arms situation in the world is a declaration of bankruptcy by the present world order." Bergfrid Fjose, formerly a member of the Norwegian parliament and Minister for Social Affairs, concluded an address "Smi sverd om til hakker!" (Turn swords into ploughshares!) "It is our mission to hold fast to the basic principle of the right to live and to reject war as an unacceptable means of conflict resolution."[22]

8. Women and the Computerization of Work

Klaus Traube, formerly Planning Chief for the German nuclear energy establishment, who was dismissed for his critical attitude, said in one interview: "Supertechnology determines the lives of millions of people today in the industrialized countries. Nonetheless, it is totally lacking in political control. . . . The most important thing is to stop microelectronics, which is more dangerous than nuclear energy viewed in sociocultural terms."[23]

The microelectronic revolution, it is thought, will bring with it profound changes throughout the industrialized world. At this point they are already making factories in Japan, for example, completely without workers, with nothing but robots. But workers in manufacturing industry aren't the only ones who are going to be hit: so are the people who work in offices. In November 1976 the Siemens Group did a study showing that 25 to 30 percent of all office work is going to be automated during the next few years (Michel Bosquet, "The Golden Age of Unemployment," *Le Nouvel Observateur* 4, 10/12/1978). Of the two million typists in Germany, 40 percent are going to become superfluous. "The consequences for the employees may be equivalent to catastrophe," summarizes one English report.

Unemployment is one side of this catastrophe; the impoverishment of work the other. Philippe Lemoine, advisor to the French Ministry of Industry, said: "No one can continue to claim that the data processing is going to liberate humanity from repetitive, dull jobs. At the various levels in the chain of information processing, the job is simplified, sliced up, taylorized, abstract, and devoid of content. The office jobs, even the technicians' jobs, are going to be broken down" (*Revue de l'Entreprise*, September 1978).

How will this development hurt women? The Central Bureau of Statistics (SCB) in Sweden estimates that, by 1975, between sixty and ninety thousand jobs had disappeared or not materialized because of computer technology. The areas of commerce, banking, and insurance as well as public administration are responsible for about sixty thousand of these jobs.[24] "Those occupational groups that have been cut back most in the industrial sector are the category of office staff, clerks, typists, purchasing agents, etc.—mainly female employees."[25] Commerce, office work, and health care are some of the areas being computerized more and more rapidly. They are expressly female-dominated sectors. Since women were already stuck in the most unskilled, low-paid assembly-line jobs, it is obvious that they may be the first to be replaced by computers. In other ways, too, computerization affects "the development that occurs in the direction of equality between the sexes in the area of the labor market and the working environment," said Gunilla Bradley, a researcher of the social consequences of computer technology, in her report, "Computer Technology, the Work Economy and Communication," (pp. 19–20).

"At least 90 percent of those employed in executive posts in Automatic Data Processing as well as systems programming and application programming are men. Also the area of the Automatic Data Processing operation that encompasses planning, managerial, and public relations work with regard to the Automatic Data Processing operation plus preparations for data processing and the running of computers is for the most part (80%) a 'male' occupational area. Only data entry is dominated by women." Thus, in the new hierarchy that has arisen in computer jobs, women have also wound up at the bottom.

Bradley made one further comment on the computerization of work that is relevant for women: "Many of the simpler routine-type chores may, as mentioned earlier, disappear, which in several respects is a desirable development. But at the same time this will probably result in jobs being regarded as retirement posts for older employees or employees with reduced working capacity as well as "training posts" for young people made redundant by rationalization. Hence, computer technology would lead indirectly to a general increase of requirements for competence in the workplace. Clearly, this means that, as a result of computerization, the mechanisms for eliminating people in the work economy are going to be made even more effective, that the division of the labor force into one A team and one B team is going to become more and more evident. The women today who (on account of their responsibility for reproduction) already belong to the B team—doing a lot of part-time work among other things—are going to have an increasingly difficult time holding their own on the labor market, as are other not very powerful groups."

The threat to the employment level is one of the consequences of computerization. The impoverishment of the content of work is the other. The Swedish Confederation of Trade Unions' computer expert Birgitta Frejhagen emphasized that both office and banking work have been impoverished by computer technology:

> Previously the bank was extremely dependent on its bank tellers and it was on their occupational skill and carefulness that the reputation of the bank depended. Today many of the sensitive steps have been put into the computer system, and the bank tellers just have to listen to what the customer says and punch it in. They don't need to know how things are supposed to be handled or which things are supposed to be checked. That's the computer program. This means that requirements in experience and education can be reduced by the employer. The value of the work is less, and so are the wages, of course.

At the same time the elimination process increases, as those demands that the computers make are extremely special:

> You should be able to stay alert the whole time, you should be able to

work at a monotonous job without breaks, which is completely against human nature. It is an extremely harsh type of demand that is made and as a result, it is difficult for those employees who get a little older to find a job. Between the ages of twenty and thirty-five only – not before nor after – can a person manage to handle this terrible pressure."[26]

Women in sales jobs and health care suffer from the same problem. In stores the clerks are about to be deprived of their familiarity with the merchandise and are getting turned into transport workers, and about 10 percent of their working hours have disappeared. At hospitals the nurses' aides, without training, have had to cope with the monotonous computer jobs.

9. The Example of the Textile Industry

Textiles are a typical women's industry. For a long time the industry has required a great deal of labor. Women's wages were lower than men's, and so the capital owners preferred female labor, which was more profitable. As before the breakthrough of industrialism it was the women who, in unsalaried production in the home, wove cloth and sewed clothes, it was also natural that they were the ones to enter the new textile and garment industry. Even though wages were low, the companies' aim all through the twentieth century has been to cut down wage costs by means of rationalization and automation. With the new technology that came in the 1930s, in the weaving mills for example, the distribution of labor increased. The tendency has been that, the more expensive the technology to be introduced, the greater the division of labor and the lower the wages for employees.[27]

The main effect of the division of labor has been to increase management's control over work. Detail workers are simpler to manage than diversified workers who know the entire production. Wage differentials also created divisions among the workers, which helped to strengthen the power of capital. The wave of rationalization in the 1930s with automatic looms was followed up in the 1960s with shuttleless looms and eventually computerized machines. At Rydbyholm's Weaving Mill, now moved to Taiwan, 330 looms were replaced by 64; and where there previously were seventeen weavers, four are now enough. The wage expenditure per meter produced could be brought down from 2.5 to under 25 Swedish *öre*. By moving the supermodern weaving mill to Taiwan where the worker's wages are 2 crowns an hour instead of 32 crowns an hour, they could cut costs further.[28]

By means of rationalization, 20,000 workers could be put out of work during the period 1968–1974 while keeping production at the same level. In the 1950s the textile branch was Sweden's second largest industry, with about 115,000 employees. Today about 38,000 are left. Unemployment has hit women hardest. Eighty-five percent of those unemployed are women even though only 70 percent of the people employed in textiles are women. Probably this is because men are foremen and work in the office while women are on the shop floor and thus far have been more vulnerable to rationalization.

What is happening to the Swedish textile industry today? In today's modern Swedish garment firms – for example, Lapidus in Borås – pattern grading and cutting are done by means of computers. To gradate a jacket, for example, with thirty pattern parts in twenty to forty sizes can take ten days for one grader. The computer does the same work in ten minutes. A numerically controlled machine is responsible for the actual cutting. With the same precision it can cut up to one hundred layers of cloth. The capacity is twenty-five thousand garments in one forty-hour week. The work goes more than ten times faster than in manual cutting. And soon we will have the computerized sewing machine, which sews six thousand stitches a minute and can store up to fifty of the most complicated steps. The old occupational skills are programmed into the computer, and the remaining work is downgraded, becomes monotonous, psychically taxing, unskilled, and low paid.

Other areas, such as the woollen mills, have been completely eliminated, which is particularly absurd. In an age when energy for heating homes is growing more and more expensive, we have gotten rid of an entire manufacturing industry that would be able to help us keep warm in other ways and thus enable us to drop the temperature indoors.

Other areas of industry are anxious to preserve national independence, but the textile business has made itself completely reliant on foreign manufacture. Today three-quarters of Sweden's ready-to-wear clothing is imported. The Garment Workers Federation has demanded that Sweden become 30 percent self-supporting, but the government has not taken any steps to stop rationalization of this basic industry.

But technological development afflicts women not only as producers – as workers whose jobs are lost or downgraded in the computerized spinning mills or sewing machines – but also as consumers. The internationalization of the textile industry has also brought lower quality, a briefer lifespan for the clothing, and a stronger orientation toward fashion in order to shorten the product's period of use. Good basic merchandise to meet consumer's needs has almost completely vanished from the business. The deteriorated quality is a result of the new technology, rotor spinning, which yields an enormous increase in productivity. The cotton used to be carded to separate the stronger fibers from the weaker ones. Today there are for the most part only three qualities. With the new technology the threads are not sorted out: The fiber lies there unadjusted, which makes the thread weaker. Fine yarn can no longer be spun. It becomes coarser than the yarn in sheeting, for example. The new technology not only downgrades the jobs but also makes products worse qualitatively.

For the new rotor-spinning technology a special short-fiber cotton has been developed. But the short-fiber cotton produces lower quality than the long-fiber. The short-fiber type has the advantage that it can be harvested mechanically and ripens simultaneously over the entire field. And for the rotor machine, the length of the fibers does not make any difference. It might be noted that the picking machine, the seed, the quality of the cotton, and the spinning technology are controlled by the same international capital. Only short-fiber cottonseed is sold today all over the world, which means that the old spinning technology is also eliminated even though the new one produces more rapid and larger concentrations of capital. At the same time the new technology brings immense concentration of power. Today 90 percent of the cotton trade is controlled by U.S. and Japanese firms. They dictate the conditions for the 125 million people in the Third World working on cotton plantations.

Kristina Torsson, a textile artist, journalist, and researcher at the Swedish Center for Working Life, has worked closely together with the seamstresses at Algots Nord in the province of Västerbotten, who organized a political movement around the demands for alternative production rather than a plant shutdown and unemployment. In several articles[29] Torsson has related the introduction of the new technology in the industrialized countries to the situation in the underdeveloped countries. Her perspective is grounded in solidarity, not only with the Swedish seamstresses – who today are losing their jobs as a result of rationalization and competition with low-priced imports from free zones of the underdeveloped countries – but also with women workers being forced to submit to inhuman conditions in multinational industries in the underdeveloped countries. Her criticism also evolves from a political consumer consciousness of the insane waste of global resources entailed in deterioration of quality and increasingly rapid fashion shifts. Torsson wrote in the anniversary publication of the Amalgamated Clothing Workers in 1978:

> The struggle for the Swedish textile industry is in principle an important fight for both workers and consumers in Sweden. In the near future probably more branches of industry will encounter the same course of development as the textile industry as more and more underdeveloped countries are industrialized and begin competing with the same advanced technology but lower wages.

Today we have to decide whether we are still going to have a textile industry, and if so, how it ought to be organized. Torsson continued:

> Another important question is the development of product and quality. How are we supposed to make demands and develop quality when we no longer have any control over the manufacture? Demands for minimum quality and specification of merchandise can be countered by arguments that such demands amount to restraint of trade. It is partly a result of cheap import, also, that the general standard of quality has deteriorated on Swedish products. The pressure and pace of work increase, and the faster and faster machines spit out cloth of increasingly poor quality. The marketing of clothes becomes more and more sophisticated: It is a matter of creating needs to find a market for the products, not of producing what people really want. The idea of marketing is for people to be satisfied by consuming one lifestyle after another.
>
> In order to determine how this form of commercialism is to be dealt with, it is also important to view questions of consumer politics in a global perspective. In principle, it takes just as much raw material to manufacture a garment of poor quality as one of high quality. The difference is that the consumers have to buy a new one more often if the garment is of poor quality. With fashion constantly changing, we, in any event, tire of the garment quickly and the consumption of textiles fibers increases in the industrialized countries.
>
> In the West we annually consume 20–25 kilograms of textile fibers per person. The U.S., Canada, Japan, and Sweden top the list. In the underdeveloped countries the equivalent figures are 2–5 kilograms per person. At the same time the major portion of the world's population lives under such conditions that they cannot satisfy their most elementary needs of food, clothing, and a roof over their head.

The underdeveloped countries get paid less and less for their products in relation to what they have to pay for goods they import from the industrialized countries, as a result of which the gap is growing wider and wider. In 1955, for example, a jeep could be bought for 124 bags of coffee. In 1975 the discrepancy in the exchange value had increased so that one jeep now cost 344 bags of coffee. This means that more and more land had to be used for export crops.

In the mid-1970s, during the worst drought and famine in Africa, agricultural products were exported to the consumers of the West for millions and millions of dollars. Mali was one of the countries that was hit hardest by the drought. During the most critical period the cultivation of corn and millet for the population's needs declined; however, production of cotton for export increased.

When their own production of food crops falls off, the underdeveloped countries become even more dependent on importing grain themselves, going even further into debt and assuming an even weaker position and greater political dependence. But the worst consequence of this development, which it may never be possible to do anything about in the future, is that the soil's yield successively declines when cultivation is one-sided, which means that the cotton acreage must be constantly expanded at the expense of food crops.

Cotton is exported to the Third World from the United States, which makes it vulnerable to pressure, claims Torsson:

> The U.S. generally calls the plays when it comes to marketing the cotton. The fashion in blue jeans comes from the U.S. It is now estimated that the market for jeans in the West is for the most part saturated. The markets of the future are in the underdeveloped countries, primarily the Far East and Latin America. In Sweden we consume at least 10 million pair of jeans annually. In Japan the consumption is 47 million pair, but the blue jean companies plan to double the figure within a few years. So the question is where will the cotton be grown? It takes about eight square meters of productive cotton land to "grow" one pair of jeans. Doubling the sales of jeans on the Japanese market alone means that in principle an additional 376 million square meters of the arable surface of the earth is going to be used for fashion production when the land is actually needed for food crops.
>
> As long as cotton is a cheap raw material, the international textile capial will keep this merry-go-round going. But one of the demands of a new economic world order is that underdeveloped countries be better paid for their raw materials. A cotton worker, for example, earns not even one crown out of the 150 crowns that a pair of jeans costs over the counter in Sweden. When the cotton workers get better pay for their work, the prices of raw materials will go up. It will then be necessary to manufacture clothes that last longer. Another positive aspect of this is that once again it probably will become more profitable to refine Swedish raw materials – flax, wool, and rayon fiber – which myopically have now been rationalized away almost completely.
>
> If we go along with this and let the Swedish textile industry be sold out

to multinational capital, we are going to be caught up completely in the merry-go-round of international fashion. This means accepting the spread of commercialism, more waste of the earth's resources, and a widening of the gaps between industrialized and underdeveloped countries. In a few years it will be possible to do away with generations of textile workers' occupational skill while it takes decades to build that knowledge up again.

If we have any textile industry left in Sweden at all in the future, it will be concentrated to a few large units with production very much geared to fashion. The work in these factories is going to leave people extremely downgraded and isolated: a few persons will be sitting there staring at computer screens controlling the major processes.

Multinational capital is going to strengthen its hold on the Swedish economy. This is because in the future capital investments are going to be very large when the new technology is implemented. The fashion merry-go-round is going to be built into the manufacturing process. Both from the point of view of private economy and a global perspective, it remains all the more untenable for us to be forced to consume more and more meaningless things so that people can keep their jobs.

Therefore we must now have an open discussion on the consequences of the development of industrial production in Sweden – from the perspective of consumer politics as well.

The introduction of computer technology in production in several respects is comparable with the introduction of nuclear power. We will be building our way into computer-controlled social and environmental production with consequences that will be impossible for us to control in the future.

An internationally competitive Swedish industry must invest in computers and nuclear energy. The nuclear energy is needed to maintain an export industry in which, more and more, people are going to be replaced by machines.

During the years to come we are going to have to go through a structural change in the textile industry, commerce, and officework because computers are being introduced in these areas. Many women are going to be its victims.

Half of all the women who lost their jobs in industry during the seventies worked in the textile industry. By the beginning of 1979 there will be about 33,000 employees left. At that point 44,000 jobs will have disappeared during the seventies, an average of 5,500 jobs a year. If the trend continues the way it has been going up to now through the seventies, the textile industry will be eliminated by 1985.

What we have been through so far has been only the beginning of a global structural change on the conditions of multinational capital. We must be prepared to fight this development!

Torsson has worked together with the seamstresses at Algots Nord for alternative production and alternative technology. In their publication *We Have An Alternative* (1978), they described what they mean by alternative technology:

> Alternative technology, we think, is something that is based on people's needs. It is meaningful jobs, variety in work, opportunities to develop in the job, to get a better sense of self, etc. This means that one must consistently move against the division of labor, the undermining of occupational skill and content of work, the fragmentation of the working community that capital's technology and work organization stand for. In short, a technology that does not exploit people and wear them out.

10. Technology in the Household

In the industrialized countries women's everyday existence in the home has been influenced by the new technology. Women may be adversely affected by new technical developments not only as producers but also to a great extent as consumers. The new technology barges right in on their daily life but has only to a limited degree taken place on their own terms.

Before industrialism the home was the center for both production and reproduction. When production was separated from reproduction the man was in practice separated from the woman and children. At the outset it was not a question of any great physical distance, but in time the distance has increased, both physically and psychically. This basic division of labor has seen its most evident spatial expression in the modern city—reproduction is assumed to take place in the so-called bedroom communities, and production occurs far away—or when guest workers are forced to leave their families in Turkey or Greece in order to work in Sweden, for example.

But the distance between production and reproduction is not only physical but also psychic. In the home, where the major share of reproduction work still occurs, rules other than those of the labor market are at work. Housework is indistinct in its nature and dimension. Important and trivial tasks are mixed up together. Nobody checks the work, it is usually performed in solitude, and it is never finished.[30] It is done almost exclusively by women.

Because certain qualities and ways of relating have more or less been reserved to the outside world of work and others to family life, both environments have become needlessly monotonous and arduous. Moreover, housework has for a long time been invisible in the sense that it has been social work not recognized as work by virtue of its being unpaid; also, it is motivated more by ideological incentives, such as love, than by economic ones, such as financial support. Housework has been invisible in the sense that it has never been included in the GNP and has never been quantified or actually defined.[31] Some studies of women's work in the household in developing countries exist that can form a data basis for such quantifications, and similar studies must be made in industrialized countries.

Kerstin Anér emphasized the irrational, blind neglect of women's everyday drudgery with an example from Africa, but one that is of general value for our purpose here:

> In the labor market statistics in the African countries a worker is called "employed" if he lays a water main to a house in the town. If a woman carries water jugs of forty kilos for one or two hours every day, she is called "just a housewife" and is not included in the country's labor force. But this daily hour or two could be used toward more productive ends. In a village like this 500 women spent an average of 5 hours a day fetching water from a little river during the dry season. That is, 2,500 working hours every day, and an enormous investment of energy. However, there were known water supplies in the area not far below the surface of the ground. One might think that those 2,500 working hours could also have been used to dig a great number of shallow wells. Then the women could use their time learning to read, devoting more time to their children's education and upbringing, or even resting.[32]

When new technology has been introduced into the workplace, it has been done in order to rationalize the operation and increase productivity per employee. By their nature, nursing and caretaking jobs are the sort of work that cannot be rationalized by being done faster. Productivity cannot be increased by caring faster for a child, a sick person, or an old person, and the supposed rationality we have become accustomed to in production might just very well become irrational when it is transposed into areas that obey completely different laws. However, other portions of housework can be rationalized by new technology – or at least apparently be rationalized as it seems that the time housewives save as a result of this new technology is minimal. However, from capital goods such as freezers, washing machines, etc., the producers have received a return on their products. And this was probably the main purpose of rationalization. According to a blueprint Swedish commission on the energy situation, in a high-energy society, women are going to be liberated in this way:

"Increased electrification in the household work, cleaning robots, electronic ovens, dryers in each apartment, etc., make an essential contribution to women's liberation from earlier conventional 'housewives' chores such as cleaning, preparing food, and taking care of clothes." That is, housework is going to stay in the home but be made easier by mechanical equipment. Also left at home in this bourgeois dream is obviously the woman who, since the servant girl has disappeared, will now have to settle for supervising her electronic oven and her cleaning robot.

Society's attitude on housework, as reflected in official studies, has been ambiguous. On the one hand there have been attempts to make the housewives' work easier through better equipment, but on the other, there has been an effort to avoid "unemploying" her by moving the chores outside the home. Sometimes the people doing the studies admit that the only sensible and rational thing to do would be to deal with a certain task in a collective fashion, but the next minute they stop and say you mustn't forget the sense of contentment created by having a number of chores still in the home and that it's important not to leave the housewife unoccupied *since she's kept at home anyway* by caretaking chores and (though it is not clearly stated) by the shortage of jobs outside the home. This attitude is particularly prevalent in studies that came out in the 1940s.[33] Since then the household has become smaller and smaller, more and more women have gone out into the labor market, and consequently fewer and fewer households have an adult working at home. Yet despite this enormous change that has taken place—especially during the past fifteen years—meaning that today's labor market is populated by masses of people (men as well women) who also have caretaking responsibilities, neither the organization of the workplace nor that of the household actually has changed. Planning is done as if households still consisted of mother, father, and a couple of children, although actually 65 percent of all households today consist of one or two persons.

The work economy is still keyed to men who have their home service arranged for them and to women without children, and in practice even housing and residential areas have been designed as if there was a housewife in each living unit. The savings of time that might have been achieved by mechanical equipment in the home have been eaten up by increased commuting time. For while the experts of those surveys of living habits were busy measuring the distance between the stove and sink to make the housewife's work easier, the housewife was in the process of leaving both the stove and the sink to venture out into the labor market, and there she was frustrated much more by the distance to her workplace, the day care center (if there was one), and the grocery store than by the distance to the kitchen sink. And when she came back home after her day at work, the housework was still there—for naturally it didn't suddenly disappear just because women left home. The "solution" to the problem, in far too many cases, has been that women have taken upon themselves a double workload.

Statistical reports from various sources and from countries with completely different social systems and different official ideologies all agree that, when it comes to equality between men and women, the prime responsibility for the housework still rests with women, and men's contributions are not increasing in households in which both spouses are gainfully employed.[34] All the same, in Sweden, for example, which has an official myth of equality, the latest figures from the Central Bureau of Statistics (SCB) on men's participation in the family housework say that

- 71 percent of all men never clean
- 52 percent of all men never shop
- 73 percent of all men never prepare food
- 89 percent of all men never do the washing
- 64 percent of all men never do the dishes.[35]

Predictably, the leisure time for men in families with children and in which both spouses are gainfully employed is 2.3 hours longer a day than for the women. Thirty-six percent of the women in the Stockholm region suffer from "general fatigue." Considering the circumstances, this is a surprisingly low figure.

In reviewing technical development in the household one finds in fact that this development has not taken place in the household at all but in industry. The job of the home has been to buy and use the products that industry has turned out, and although new technology has been introduced to households through the consumption of merchandise, the organization of the household has gone practically unchanged despite technological development. Indeed, perhaps because of technical development! Perhaps the relief that the washing machine, the refrigerator, and the dishwasher have brought have made women put up needlessly with the grotesquely impractical and extravagant manner of organizing society that all these little households actually represent: Each and every person every day is supposed to organize a complicated business of purchasing, transport, and extremely small-scale production of miscellaneous merchandise and services.

One tends to take it for granted that technical innovations have led to savings of labor and time. Such is not the case, as is demonstrated by one study from the Bureau for Future Studies and the National Swedish Board for Technical Development (STU) (Sangregorio and Cronberg, *Innanför den egna tröskeln* [Inside your own threshold], 1978). The study surveys three areas: laundry, television, and shopping and storage (refrigeration/freezer units).[36]

Laundry

At the start of the century all laundry was done by hand. It was the heaviest portion of the housework and monopolized women full-time. Often it was done outdoors, summer and winter. Often working-class women washed for wealthy families. In the 1920s and 1930s the majority of apartment buildings had a laundry room equipped with hot-water heater and rinse tub. In the winter the women had to manage the drying in the attic, which meant they had to lug the wet wash up the stairs. A big wash by hand often took two or three days.

In the 1930s people began to get laundries equipped with machines. Often there was also a wringer and drying room adjacent to the laundry. This reduced the time it took to do a big wash to half a day. But the breakthrough of washing machines was not particularly rapid. Even in the beginning of the 1950s 70 percent of laundry was washed by hand.[37] Not until the 1960s did washing machines become popular. It is estimated that in 1974 nearly 90 percent of the population had access to a washing machine and that every other household had its own machine.[38]

Laundry has been studied by a number of government commissions. Consistently, they point to the advantages of collective laundries. During the 1940s and 1950s it was predicted that washing would be discontinued as housework. Nevertheless, home washing machines became popular, even though this is the most costly alternative (per kilo of wash) and the one that demands the most energy.[39] The amount of time it takes to wash has been reduced only modestly since the 1930s. The privatization of laundry has gone on despite society's ambitions toward collective solutions. To summarize:

1. The technical performance of the equipment has been improved enormously.
2. It has been very difficult to manage without a certain type of appliance: the textile material is largely adapted to the washing

machine, the washing machine is included in the standard equipment of the apartment, and other alternatives are disappearing.

3. We have more clothes and wash more often.
4. Further development of the equipment does not save time: on the contrary.
5. Needs and desires are influenced strongly by the producers.
6. Equipment for private use is displacing alternatives based on communal use. Natural opportunities for personal contact are disappearing. Instead there arise artificial, often commercialized opportunities to meet people such as Bingo, pensioners' meetings, etc.[40]

Television

But before there was TV it was fantastic how lively it was here. People went back and forth to each other's place, and there were folks out on the streets all the time. But the year TV came things became dead-like – not a person out – as if it was completely depopulated. Everybody got themselves a TV, and when you went to visit somebody, you just sat down and were quiet, and then said "so long" when it was over. Folks used to come to my place, and I went to visit the neighbors and chat awhile. Now nobody comes at all, and it's not worth going anyplace 'cause you interrupt the program.[41]

Television became popular immediately when it was introduced in Sweden in 1956. After four years 75 percent of the population had television at home. Today 95 percent have a television. In a 1951 commission report on television great hopes are attached to television's possibilities for increasing contact between people:

Some of the important things television can do are to break down feelings of isolation, to create common experiences and possibilities for active participation in the exchange of ideas between people as well as to bring together individuals from different environments and occupational groups.[42]

Despite these high hopes for television's social functions, nothing was done to make television a communal meeting place. Instead the model became one private television receiver for each household. The way in which television's entry into the home has broken down a deep-rooted local culture has been described vividly by social anthropologist Åke Daun:

The pure social life generally played a much smaller role than it did before 1961. That year it became possible to watch TV in Batskärsnäs, in both Swedish and Finnish. The Workers' Educational Association's lecture operation stopped short, and only one study circle attracted participants that year. Since TV came it was mostly young people that went to the movie theater at the People's House, which adults had visited just as much previously. Nor did the ice hockey team, so popular earlier draw a big crowd anymore. People stopped "bumming around the place" or "cruising around town," as it is called. People came and went much more than before. Often they came to borrow something, salt and matches, and then they got a cup of coffee, and then they came again the next day to return it, one worker recalled. . . . One woman complained that nowadays it was very rare that anybody came to visit. When you have to invite them to get them to come, it's not worth it, she added. (*Upp till kamp i Batskärsnäs* [To the struggle in Batskärsnäs], 1969)

On the average a Swede watches television eleven hours a week. Almost half of our leisure time is devoted to television-watching. This time has been taken partially from radio listening, partly from sleep, but certainly also – as Åke Daun's example shows – from social life in clubs, contact with neighbors, and other social intercourse.

It may also be of interest to ask ourselves not only how much time goes to television, but also whose time it is. It appears that men watch more than women, retired people and children watch most, and young people least; those with less education watch more than people who are highly educated.[43]

TV is a good example of how a technical innovation that has been introduced for a certain purpose (to provide information and entertainment) has had consequences in completely different areas, including family life and spontaneous contacts with people beyond one's own family. TV helped to reinforce a tendency that already had had an effect in other areas: the reasons for leaving one's own home were decreased. The sort of thing one previously had to leave home to participate in – movies, theater, political discussions, sports contests – suddenly existed in one's own living room.

Shopping and Storage

Shopping and storage have undergone a radical change since the 1960s. On account of structural rationalization, the local shops have been rapidly eliminated. In Stockholm county one-fourth of the grocery stores disappeared between 1968 and 1972 alone. In practice it has meant that more and more households have had farther and farther to go to shop for merchandise needed every day. More and more households became dependent on a car for their shopping. A refrigeration/freezer unit has come to be included in normal standard housing, which has facilitated large purchases and longer storage in the home.

In other words, the ideal consumer, according to the producers' calculations, has access to a car and has a good deal of storage space and a planning capacity for one week. The reality, it turns out, looks different. Out of three million households only 1.8 million have a car.[44] In only 27 percent of those households that have a car (as of 1971) do the housewives – usually the ones responsible for shoping – have access to the car. In 73 percent of the households, that is, it is the men who have the car at their disposal.[45]

Only 25 percent of all households (in 1971) had room to store the fresh goods needed for one week. Forty-four percent had a storage capacity suitable for less than half a week's supply of fresh goods. Nor did the planning capacity prove equal to one shopping trip a week. In addition, there is the fact that two persons are needed to carry the grocery supply for a whole week. Studies on buying habits show that households go shopping on an average of six times a week. At least an hour a day is spent on shopping in families with children. The number of mothers who spent time shopping on the day the count was taken was 60 percent; the equivalent figure for men was 5 percent.[46]

Less powerful groups in society have suffered a great deal from the change in the structure of shopping – for example, retired people and mothers with small children and no car. Expenses for shopping and storage have also increased as the costs for transportation and storage have been turned over to individual households. Technical development has been used to make things cheaper and easier for the producers and distributors rather than for the consumers. Thus, the fact that individual households have refrigerators and freezers, for example, is more a matter of businesses' need for returns on their products than a case of consideration for women. They have had to pay for improved storage space in the home with increased driving or walking time to the stores and worse service. *The saving of time and rationalization in the work economy has occurred at the expense of women's time budget. Savings in paid time have been passed on to women in the form of increased utilization of unpaid time.*

Development in this area, as in others, has meant that possibilities for human contact have disappeared from the immediate environment (in the form of food cellars and neighborhood shops, for example). The raised standard in each apartment has led to fewer and fewer excuses to visit the residential area outside the house. Little by little, technical improvements such as water mains, central heating, vacuum cleaners, refrigerators and freezers, washing machines, and so on, have made it unnecessary to leave home to fetch water, chop wood, beat carpets, visit the food cellar, do the wash, etc. Moreover, television has also moved politics and entertainment into the homes.[47]

To sum up, it is doubtful to what extent the technology of everyday life really helps women on their own terms. The time saved in one place is consumed in another—for example, in long hours spent commuting or repairing and maintaining machines. But one thing seems completely clear: The immense technical and social changes of the most recent decades have had little effect on the organization of housework. Although households have grown smaller and smaller, housework has been kept within the framework of the small household.

Sangregorio and Cronberg have pointed out that the technology a society produces is not neutral. The new technology that has reorganized the sphere of reproduction has at the same time entailed a far-ranging privatization of society. More and more activities have been moved inside the home; local neighborhood environments have been impoverished. As Evelyne Sullerot points out in *Demain des femmes*, women as a group are always treated unfairly by individualism, with its economic consequences—private ownership and individual enterprise—"while they are favored by all collectivistic systems, or systems and societies in which the economy is not based on private ownership."

Although women's material needs have been satisfied, this has happened in such an individual way that the preconditions for satisfying the nonmaterial needs of community and self-realization have been reduced. Studies also indicate that technological development is being directed away from total dominance by the forces of the marketplace to more socially oriented technology. "A robust and adaptive technology that tolerates collective use—unlike technology produced today—should also manage to become accessible to the majority of humanity that does not belong to the world's overclass."

11. Conclusion

In the foreword to Margaret Mead's study, *Cultural Patterns and Technical Change*, it is established that:

Rapid changes in the industrial or social structure in any country are apt to lead to unforeseen disturbances even when such changes are initiated or supervised by nationals of that country. When men and women with technical skills set out to help in shaping new developments in a country or a culture other than their own, there are clearly many more possibilities of producing unfortunate consequences. Sometimes great harm can be done to the people of that country, especially through the creation of social psychological stress and the disorganization of family and community life.

This is true of the conditions in the underdeveloped world as well as in the industrialized countries.

The gap between men and women is widening. Women's situation in all countries has grown worse. Women have been left out of the crucial decision making on society's economic and social planning. They have also been without influence in technological research and the application of new technology. Women and men live in different cultures. It is out of these facts that women have developed their criticism of a major portion of Western technology, which, according to one German weapons expert, "achieves its perfection in arms technology."

The World Federation for Mental Health, in a plan presented to UNESCO, pointed out that

> No programme of technological development can hope to succeed in the long run if it leaves people unhappy and maladjusted. In the long run also, such unhappy and maladjusted people are the ones who are more likely to turn to violence and even war, because of their dissatisfaction with the conditions under which they live. This is not a necessary consequence of technological development, but it is a possible one. It can be rendered much less probable if adequate attention is paid to the effect of technological development on people. The most important single fact to be kept in mind is that new techniques must be introduced with proper regard for the existing culture and with as little violence as possible to the folkways of the groups concerned. (Quoted in Margaret Mead, *Cultural Patterns and Technical Change*)

It is remarkable how little inquiry has been made into women's needs from technology or the consequences to women and women's culture when new technology is introduced.

The microelectronic revolution has hit women harder than men both in the form of unemployment and in the downgrading of the content of work. The pollution of earth, air, and water affect both women and men, but women seem more vulnerable emotionally than men as a result of their daily responsibility for child care and feeding. The technologization of everyday life has been harmful to women in terms of increased isolation and privatization.

New technology today is not subjected to political decisions. It is passed off on us as an intrinsic law of evolution in the guise of "the technological imperative": what can possibly be researched and given concrete form as new technology must also be put into practice — everything possible is also necessary. The social and human consequences are not given any consideration at all in this view of things in which technology is attributed an intrinsic dynamic of its own. Against this expressly male manner of observation, women raise demands for human consideration. Anér writes in her book *Framtidens insida* [Inside the future]: "The question of how technology is used and what purposes it serves will become just as important as the question as to the effectiveness of technology. Or more precisely: a technology is *not* effective if it places great social burdens upon the people around it, even if these burdens are not taken into account in the business's cost estimates."[48]

Undersecretary of State Thorsson has suggested that "technology evaluations" be used to bring about a discussion of technology's social and political implications, and a discussion of a society's scale of values. Before it is put to use, a new technology should be "analyzed impartially, with consideration for long-range consequences insofar as is possible and with the results of various alternative solutions clearly accounted for."[49]

Some guidelines for such a technology evaluation could be:

- No technology should be superimposed upon any culture if it appears to jeopardize the values of that culture, in either industrialized or underdeveloped countries.
- The dangerous consequences of a one-sided development of technology must be pointed out.
- The connections between the innovators' ideology and goal and their social and cultural ties must be indicated.
- Criteria for the evaluation of deterioration and improvement resulting from new technology should be developed.

Society's evaluation of centralization, capital concentration, large scale, increased efficiency, and more technology may be the primary obstacle to women's equality. Today's highly industrialized society takes no consideration whatever of the demands and needs of reproduction. Therefore new technology favoring women would be based on collective solutions; it would be partly small-scale and surveyable; and it would consider the ecological balance. Obviously, women do not want this to happen for their own sakes alone – such a development will also serve men's need for a more fully human life. However, because women are closer to the reproductive and caring functions, they also acquire experience in handling many different activities and problems of daily life simultaneously. I have already summarized some of the characteristics of what is perceived as women's culture. Women are in many ways generalists where men are specialists, and they are thereby often in a better position to judge and predict the multiple consequences for people's daily lives of different technological innovations.

We therefore need to understand more about the relationship between women and technology, or more specifically

- how women in particular are affected by technological developments;
- how women perceive technology and its consequences for society at various levels; and
- how, on this basis, women can constructively contribute to selecting the types of technology that would generate better life conditions for all women and men and their dependents.

To this end, women themselves must start to collect data and formulate a plan of action based on their own felt needs and their specific skills and experiences. A possible framework for this would be:

1. Women's deteriorated conditions as a result of technology must be analyzed carefully before any measures are taken. Women shall not be subjected to measures developed on the basis of male experiences and priorities. Every action program must emerge out of women's own experiences and priorities and be formulated *by* women and *for* women.
2. Technology's lack of success for women must be analyzed and evaluated in industrialized as well as in underdeveloped countries. Women themselves must be able to decide which research areas and questions are relevant.
3. A special investigation must be made of the correlation between increased profit and increased wages in male society and the expansion of women's working hours in unpaid production.
4. There is a need to investigate ways in which women can protect their traditional workplaces when men's unemployment is increasing and the pressure upon these workplaces is growing

increasingly heavy. How are both paid and unpaid work to be distributed equitably between the sexes in a situation with widespread male unemployment?

5. All social development – in industrialized as well as under-developed countries, in labor as well as capital, of women and of men – must undergo a technology evaluation.

Notes

This chapter was written under the pressure of a heavy schedule and may be regarded as an early draft. Many of the points made here will require further development. Those individuals who have contributed material and views are Berit Ås, Maj Wehselman, Inger Lisa Sangregorio, Elisabet Intermodsson, and Kristina Torsson. I would especially like to thank Berit Ås, without whose enormous knowledge and enthusiasm this chapter would not have been written. It was translated from the Swedish by Verne Moberg.

1. M. Mead, *Cultural Patterns and Technical Change*, Tensions and Technology Series, UNESCO, 1953.

2. The information in this section is based on the following publications: G. Kyhle, *Gästarbeterska i manssamhället. Studier om industriarbetande kvinnors villkor i Sverige* [Woman guest worker in male society: studies on conditions of women working in industry in Sweden] (Stockholm, 1979); E. Höglund, *Deltid. Bakgrund och fakta om deltidsarbetet* [Part-time: background and facts on part-time work], (ILO, 1979), and "Kvinnor i arbetslivet" [Women in working life], *Arbetaren* [The worker] 10, 1979; Fredrika Bremer Förbundet, statistics on female representation in the society's decision-making bodies.

3. R. Liljeström, *Kultur och arbete* [Culture and work], (Stockholm: Sekretariatet för framtidsstudier [Bureau for Future Studies], 1979), p. 137.

4. G. W. Allport and P. E. Vernon, *A Study of Values* (Boston: Houghton, Mifflin and Co., 1931). On women's culture see especially B. Ås, "On Female Culture: An Attempt to Formulate a Theory of Women's Solidarity and Action." *Acta Sociologica* 2, 1975, p. 4.

5. The following is Elisabet Hermodsson's own summary of the criticism in *Synvända* [Vantagepoint] (Stockholm, 1975).

6. B. Ås, "Den manliga teknologin" [Male technology, in *Rusta för fredrädda livet* [Arm for peace: save life], ed. by M. Bergom-Larsson (Stockholm, 1979).

7. L. Ingelstram, *Teknikpolitik. En bok om tekniken, människan och socialismen.* [Technopolitics: a book on technology, human beings, and socialism] (Stockholm, 1978).

8. E. Wägner and E. Tamm, *Fred med jorden* [Peace with the earth] (Stockholm, 1941)

9. M. Nilsson, *Min seger över BT-Kemi* [My victory over BT-Kemi] (Malmö, 1978).

10. M. Paulsen, *Malungskullorna* [The girls of Malung]. Play at Stockholm's city theater, 1978.

11. S. Mörch, *Stumtjenere* [Dumbwaiter] (Oslo, 1978).

12. T. Bye, *Tjernekraften—en kostbar blindvei?* [Nuclear energy: an expensive dead end?], lecture in Oslo, 1979.

13. Ås, "Den manliga teknologin."

14. K. Stjärne, *Fler passningar. Om barn, vald och framtiden i världen,* [On children, violence, and the future of the world] (Stockholm, 1979).

15. Information from A. Myrdal, *The Game of Disarmament* (New York: Pantheon, 1976).

16. Reprinted from a talk given in Oslo on United Nations Day, 1978. Quoted by B. Ås in "Den manliga teknologin."

17. Reprinted from H. Clayhill, "Den antimilitaristiska kamptraditionen i den svenska kvinnorörelsen," in *Rusta för fredrädda livet,* ed. by M. Bergom-Larsson.

18. U. Lindström, *I regeringen* [In the government] (Stockholm, 1969).

19. B. Ås, "Kvinner i forsvaret—eller: kvinnerne og krigen" [Women in defense—or the women and the wars] in the political pamphlet *Ett alliancefritt* [An alliance-free Norway] (Oslo: *Norge,* Socialistisk opplysningsforbund [Socialist Education League St. Olavsg. 27, Oslo 1]).

20. Interview conducted 3 March 1979.

21. Address by Wenche Haland, "Nei till nytronbomben—Ja til nedrustning" [No to the neutron bomb, yes to disarmament] at a meeting of the Nobel Institute, 6 June 1978.

22. B. Fjose, "Smi sverd om til hakker!" [Turn swords into ploughshares!]. Address at a Christian People's Party conference on arms control and disarmament (May 1978).

23. Interview in *Arbetaren* 16, 1979.

24. TCO arbetsgrupp för datafragor (Swedish Central Organization of Salaried Employees, Committee on Computer Questions), *Datorerna och arbetslivet* [Computers and the work experience in the economy] (Stockholm: TCO, 1978).

25. G. Bradley, *Datateknik, arbetsliv och kommunikation* [Computer technology, the work economy, and communication] (Stockholm: Delegationen för langtidsmotiverad forskning [Delegation for Research with Long-Range Justification], 1977), p. 18.

26. Interview conducted 12 April 1979.

27. G. Bradley, *Maskin Makt, Teknikens utveckling och arbetets förändring under industrialismen* [Machine power: the development of technology and the transformation of work under industrialism] (Stockholm, 1977).

28. Factual material in this section is based largely on an interview with Kristina Torsson, 11 April 1979.

29. *Dagens Nyheter* [Daily news], 11 March 1977, 4 April 1977, 17 June 1977, and 13 September 1977; the Amalgamated Clothing Workers, ninetieth anniversary publication in 1978; Algots Nord seamstresses' publication *Vi har ett alternativ* [We have an alternative], 1978.

30. Cf. A. Oakley, *The Sociology of Housework* (London, 1974).

31. According to the Norwegian Study on Living Conditions, NOU, 1976, p.

' 28., women's "caretaking services" in Norway amount to nearly half a million jobs annually or more than the total annual working hours in Norwegian industry. Attempts to quantify this can be found, for example, in S. Lingsom, "Arbeidstid hjemme og ute" [Working hours at home and outside the home] in *Hvis husmor ikke fantes* [If there were no housewives], ed. by Grennes, (Olson, 1978), and in Oakley, ibid.

32. K. Anér, *Framtidens insida* [Inside the future], (Stockholm, 1978).

33. K. Anér, *Familjeliv och hemarbete* [Family life and housework], Statens offentliga utredningar (Public Government Reports), SOU, 1947, p. 46.

34. Lingsom, "Arbeitstid hjemme og ute," quotes figures from nine countries.

35. National Central Bureau of Statistics (SCB), Living Conditions. Report No. 20. Sex and Equality (Stockholm, 1980).

36. Based on the study by T. Cronberg and I. L. Sangregorio, *Innanför den egna tröskeln. Ny teknik och dess konsekvenser för livsstilen—Boendet som exempel.* [Inside your own threshold: new technology and its consequences for life style—housing as an example] (Stockholm: Bureau for Future Studies and the research group on consumer technology of the National Swedish Board for Technical Development, 1978).

37. Deliberations of the Committee on Collective Housing, SOU, 1955, p. 3.

38. *Boendeförhallanden 1974* [Housing Arrangements, 1974], Levnadsförhallanden [Living conditions] Report No. 3 (Stockholm: Liber, SCB, 1974).

39. Gothenburg City Housing Corporation, "Kostnader och service vid olika tvättälternativ" [Costs and service in various laundry alternatives], mimeo, 1968.

40. Summary from L. Ingelstram, *Teknikpolitik.*

41. Å. Daun, *Upp till kamp i Batskärsnäs* [To the struggle in Bastskärsnäs] (Stockholm, 1969).

42. Å. Daun, *Televisionen i Sverige* [Television in Sweden], deliberations of the 1951 Commission on Television, SOU, 1954, p. 32.

43. R. Sjödén, *Etermediernas public* [The audience of the broadcasting media] (Stockholm: Sveriges Radios Förlag, 1967).

44. R. Sjödén, *Samhället och distributionen* [Society and distribution], deliberations of the Commission on Distribution (Stockholm: SOU, Liber, 1975), p. 69.

45. *Samhället och distributionen, Bilagor och företag, oanställda och hushall* [Society and distribution, supplements and businesses, unemployed and households], deliberations from the Commission on Distribution (Stockholm: SOU, Liber Förlag, 1975), p. 70.

46. *Hemarbete och servicekontakter* [Housework and service contacts], deliberations from the Commission on Distribution (Stockholm: SOU, 1965), p. 65.

47. Cronberg and Sangregorio, *Innanför den egna tröskeln*, p. 47.

48. Anér, *Framtidens insida.*

49. Thorsson, "Teknik och humanism" [Technology and humanism], *Tiden* [Time] 9, 1977.

3

Women and Technology in Peripheral Countries: An Overview

Zenebeworke Tadesse

Contents

1. Introduction

The centrality of women in the development process or lack thereof has finally become a theme worthy of serious intellectual and political inquiry. The last decade has witnessed an avalanche of literature on women and development.[1] Scattered through the literature one finds the impact of technology on women in peripheral countries. This chapter is an attempt at an overview of the issues raised in the literature on women supplemented by the relevant issues in the literature focusing on technology transfer. The selection of studies, the organization of the text, and the emphasis on certain trends is dictated by my understanding of technology as the social relations of production in the different phases of the global capital accumulation process; it is not limited to innovations, know-how and/or machinery.

Generalizing about the impact of technology on women in peripheral countries is an ambitious and risky endeavour. The impact varies in accordance with the economic, social, and political differences among these countries and the different regions of each country. The specificity of each situation depends on the role that a country plays in the international division of labour, the type of development pursued by a particular state, the extent to which it mobilizes political support from one or another of the classes engaged in the productive process, and the sexual division of labour. Despite these differences, the existing literature indicates substantial common features for generalization. The most common — and one that has had a profound impact on every other aspect of their development — is the integration of these countries into the world market as subsidiary and complementary to the metropolitan system, thereby distorting their autonomous development. Consequently, peripheral countries are characterized by heterogeneous economic structures and relations of production, low productivity in agriculture, limited industrialization, a relative degree of extensive poverty, and extreme inequalities of income. Within this framework the issue of technological dependence and technology transfer has been amply documented elsewhere. The main argument here is that the majority of women in these countries are much more negatively affected by all the asymmetrical relationships: first, as members of peripheral societies and second, because of the sexual division of labour that assigns to women a disproportionate role, both in production and reproductive activities, without a concomitant remuneration.

A cursory examination of most studies of women in development indicates a failure to document these variations, serious weakness in theoretical development, lack of conceptual clarity, and a lack of operational definitions of key concepts such as "development," "integration," etc. One glaring shortcoming that has led to faulty conclusions is the choice of a unit of analysis in studying issues concerning women. Most studies limit their scope to "women," a superficial rural-urban dichotomy, or at best a given country. Thus accepting the dualism of conventional theory that divides peripheral countries into modern export enclaves and rural subsistence hinterlands and a "neglect theory" that argues that policymakers and development experts have neglected women, these studies advocate the "integration of women in development." There seems to be a consensus that the most common result of "development" is to relegate women to the subsistence sector in agriculture and low-paying jobs in manufacturing and industry. Technology, credit, and know-how are concentrated in the hands of men, and women are assigned the nonmodernized subsistence sector, i.e., food production for domestic consumption.

These deleterious effects of "modernization" and "development" have been supported by massive data across countries, but the conclusion reached, the need for the "Integration of women in development," is dubious. Does it mean that there is a process of "development" that includes all males? What are the relationships between the subsistence sector and cash crop production sector and women's role in each of these sectors?

Recent studies have argued that the proper conceptualization of problems that women face requires a broader understanding of a particular social formation, the mechanisms of its insertion into the world market, and the resultant changes in the sexual division of labour.[2] In the words of one such writer, "The fate of women, the way they carry out their daily tasks, and the view of the world they derive from these experiences depends, in the final analysis, not so much on the policies of their government or the 'enlightenment' of the men around them as on the function that the economy of which they are a part serves in the world system."[3] Contrary to assumptions that women have been left out of development due to "lack of proper planning," these studies point out that women have in fact been integrated as reproducers of labour power, producers of subsistence foodstuffs for family consumption, and very often as unremunerated familial labour in cash crop production or as cheap seasonal labour in large plantations. Women are important constituents of the labour reserve for capital on the one hand and the use of female wage labour is closely related to the maintenance of low wages on the other.

In the rural areas, as it is men who tend to be hired in permanent wage labour, "the burden of the reproduction of the family falls overwhelmingly on women assuring that the division of labour by sex enhances capital accumulation through the lowering of the value of the wage to capitalists."[4] In industrial production, the factors that determine when and where women are employed, the general occupational structure, and changes in the allocation of work by sex can only be fully appreciated if viewed within the framework of an international context of investment, production, and control.[5] In any case, here, too, women's employment and low wages enhance capital accumulation.

Furthermore, these studies emphasize that a comprehensive grasp of issues affecting women has to give analytical priority to questions of class relations, "as the relationship of both men and women to the production process is not indicated by gender alone, but, more importantly, by access to strategic resources which crosscut sexual distinctions."[6] Likewise, capital accumulation governs the dissemination of technology. Technology has had varied socioeconomic outcomes in the many countries in which it has been introduced. It is therefore clear that the consequences of the introduction of technology into a given economy vary depending on its social utilization.

In spite of differences in emphasis and conceptual clarity, there is growing cross-cultural empirical evidence that indicates a sharp sexual division of labour attributing certain tasks and differential power to men and women. Penetration of capital invariably accentuates these patterns in the direction of enhancing male dominance and the subordination of women. Nor have societies that have undergone serious societal transformation solved this problem of inequality. Consequently, technological innovation and interventions have differential impacts on males and females, and these differences are significant for the household's productive capacity and welfare as well as a country's ability to fully utilize its human resources. However, the nature and consequences of technological change in various areas are uneven and different. A comprehensive examination of the impact of technological change on women therefore requires conceptual clarity about the sexual division of labour. One of the most comprehensive conceptualizations has been presented by Deere:[7]

> The division of labour by sex is conceptualized as an aspect of the labour process; although an economic category, its specific form and content is determined by the mutual effectivity of the ideological, political and economic aspects that characterize the social formation. [Hence] the division of labour by sex is rarely static, but changes over time, it is more than a socio-cultural convention and is responsive to material conditions of production. [Furthermore] as an economic variable, the rationality of the sexual division of labour is class specific and varies according to social relations of production and reproduction.

She also cautioned that the sexual division of labour is neither mechanical nor voluntaristic, that it is imbedded in the dominant value system that interacts in a complex manner with changes in economic parameters.

Although the specificity of what is considered as "women's work" varies across countries[8] and classes, women seem to be charged invariably with the myriad of duties required for the daily maintenance and care of children and the family. In order to carry out these tasks they perform a large number of functions related to food processing, water carrying, handicrafts, marketing, and other types of household work that in industrialized countries are performed outside the household and allocated through the market. In addition, women participate in agricultural production, where they are often given the responsibility of cultivation, weeding, harvesting, processing of food, and storage as well as helping out with animal husbandry. The absence of labour-saving devices renders women's production and reproductive activities drudgerous, physically demanding, and time-consuming. It has been estimated that their actual number of daily working hours is as high as fifteen to sixteen, with a high proportion of the time spent on tasks that could greatly be simplified by the introduction of simple technology.[9]

In spite of this sharp sexual division of labour defining the tasks performed by women and distinguishing them from those done by men, women's work is central to production and integrated with that of men in terms of functions and space.

> The primary contradiction that women face under these conditions is related to subsistence itself, drudgery of work, dominance of nature, and in a class society, the inequalities in the control of the means of production and the appropriation of output. The most basic problems faced by women in the rural areas of the Third World include the satisfaction of the most basic needs for themselves and their families. Malnutrition, high infant mortality rates, unsafe water, lack of the most basic health services, and abject poverty are among the problems in rural women's daily lives.[10]

These problems of survival affect both men and women, although they have differential impacts on the sexes. Given the reality of the periphery, these problems of survival are not limited to rural women but characterize the lives of the urban poor as well.

In an important contribution to conceptual clarity, a recent study has argued that, *"subsistence production is not defined by the nature of the work involved but by the performer's relationship to the means of subsistence. Both women and men from the households of the rural poor* engage in subsistence activity in this social sense." Consequently, "the greater the pressure on the means of subsistence of the rural poor, the more arduous and difficult the activity tends to increase along with the precariousness of survival."[11] The following sections will attempt to synthesize the impact of technology on women. To discuss the condition of women's lives under the umbrella of the impact of technology is an attempt at pointing out simultaneously the current distortions and the immense potential that technology has for changing women's lives for the better. Both these distortions and the potential for change are reflections of the sociopolitical reality and, as such, their solution is necessarily tied up with struggles, adjustments, and consolidation of different class forces.

2. Women and Agriculture

The heterogenous nature of Third World countries has earlier been noted. Although one finds the coexistence of different agrarian structures, general characteristics of differing rural areas include shifting agriculture and low population density in Africa, plough cultivation tied with individual property rights and high population density in Asia, and the hacienda system in most parts of Latin America. One finds marked variations even in a given country, however. As has been pointed out:

> The changing form of incorporation of the national economy into the world market has influenced the pattern of regional integration. Regions have been integrated in different historical periods as areas of commodity production or as sources of labour power for other regions of the social formation. Integration into the national or international economy has brought periods of growth as well as of stagnation of regional economies, and in turn, affected the relations of production, and corresponding economic and social institutions. Thus we find in rural areas, diverse forms of land tenure, as well as varying processes of production, which link rural households to the national economy.[12]

Overall, the incorporation of the periphery into the world market at different historical stages has shaped the current relations of production in agriculture and the sexual division of labour within the household unit according to the requirements of the world market. This international division of labour has affected women, who play a key role in subsistence production and in the reproduction of the labour force. The ongoing transformation of agrarian structures and the introduction of new technology are principally geared towards commercial crops for export.

In all three continents, these changes have resulted in a new sexual division of labour within and outside the household unit of production. In Africa, the subsistence sector was left to women, as men turned toward export crops or migrated to the cities or the mines, thereby increasing women's work load.[13] In Latin America, the increasing integration of latifundia into commercial agriculture and the increase in population have led to the parceling of land and to the semiproletarianization of men, because the minifundia were no longer capable of providing enough for family subsistence. Thus, the minifundio is integrated into the economy not only through the production market but also through the labour market. These changes necessitated the active participation of women in agriculture, because men migrated seasonally to the plantations, mines, or cities in search of additional income.[14]

In Asia, irrigated agriculture requires a large labour force. Hence, the patterns of labour recruitment utilized the entire family labour force, rather than fragmenting the household production unit. In addition, small plots are allocated to women to grow food for household consumption. In all these cases where women grow food for household consumption, wages paid to male workers are reduced to the minimum, as they are premised on the partial and daily reproductive needs of the single male worker. In other words, the rest of the family and the long-term reproductive needs of the male worker would have to be taken care of by the women's subsistence activities. Available data indicates that the extent to which women participate in agricultural production alongside men, or on their own, varies across regions and class background.

In spite of these variations, women represent a high proportion of the labour force in predominantly agricultural areas.[15] In subsistence agriculture, the predominance of women in the cultivation of foodstuffs is estimated as high as 60 percent in most African countries and even 80 percent in some.[16] In most Asian countries, 75 to 85 percent of women live in rural areas and spend half of their working time in agricultural activities.[17] Although existing data indicate a lower participation rate for Latin American women, recent studies have challenged this assumption and pointed to issues of underevaluation and underremuneration of rural women's agricultural participation.[18] Overall data indicate that there are wide interregional and interdistrict differences in women's labour force participation rates in agriculture. Furthermore, it can be argued that there is a clear correlation between the extent of women's participation and the four determinants of the choice of technology, i.e., the objective of production, the size of the production unit, the type of ownership, and the internal class and power relations of the unit.[19]

Women's participation in the agricultural sector is inversely related to regional development. In areas where no new technology has been introduced one finds a high percentage of women. On the other hand, in areas dominated by commercial agriculture, such as coffee plantations, women have fewer opportunities to work as permanent labourers. They, however, make up a large portion of the seasonal labour supply and continue farming in the subsistence sectors if plots are available.[20] In the case of the introduction of the high-yielding varieties with the resultant extra yields and intensive cultivation, there is an initial short-term increase in demand for labour, including that of women. Later on, the introduction of the so-called seed-fertilizer revolution with its components of labour-saving mechanical innovation leads to a substantial displacement of labour, the larger proportion of whom are undoubtedly women.

A case in point is that of wheat production in the Punjab, in India.

> Rather suddenly a market for rapid mechanical reaping has come into existence with the change in varieties, and, some machines have already come in the market . . . in the latter part of the decade reapers will become commonly available and make profound impact on demand for labour. It is estimated that by 1983–84, this device will reduce human labour by 33 percent in the month of April, most of which will be casual and women workers. The reaper thresher system will reduce demand for human labour to about one-fifth of that required by the traditional method. Combines, which are making their appearance, will reduce it to no more than three percent of the traditional level. These machines will greatly affect female labour in Harayna.[21]

These data are predicting future trends, but other studies have shown the current rate of displacement of women from agriculture in India, where commercial production has generated a considerable decrease in small subsistence holdings. The percentage of women cultivators of small holdings decreased from almost 56 percent in 1961 to less than 30 percent in 1971.[22] Similar trends of displacement have been noted in Brazil,[23] Chile,[24] and other peripheral countries.

3. Cash Crop Production

Certain trends become visible when technological innovation takes place in agriculture. There are clear-cut differences in access to essential resources, such as land, labour, cash, education and know-how, between men and women, with men being relatively much more privileged. Consequently, because of lack of access to resources, coupled with the existing division of labour, women are the first to be displaced from tasks that can be mechanized or remunerated. Depending on the type of change, there is a tendency to increase the burden of women's work by increasing the demand for unpaid family labour in tasks that are labour intensive (e.g., weeding, transplanting), and for which there is no remuneration. As one study has pointed out, "In proportion to the amount of labour extracted from the subsistence economy, there was not only increased demand for female labour in agriculture, but an increased demand for child labour as well. The entire household labour force was mobilized to intensify subsistence production."[25]

4. Access to Resources

Existing studies indicate that in most cases women have no access to various inputs, physical, capital, skills, and materials. In other words, they are denied access to land, farm produce, farm inputs, credits, cooperative membership, and other technological innovations. In the case of Africa, the disappearance of communal land tenure rights has tended to dispossess women of land and decrease their control over productive resources by recognizing men as the new owners of land. African women have little opportunity to learn about agriculture, cooperatives, and animal husbandry. Credit and loans are less readily available to women, as they are made against land titles and the land is held in the men's names, or else they are made through cooperative societies of which mainly men are members.[26]

The determinant of women's access to resources, however, is not primarily and always their sex. An understanding of women's access to resources can only be achieved if viewed vis-à-vis the process of differentiation that determines a household's access to strategic resources, particularly that of land. For instance, contrary to the trend noted above of women's access to resources, some women in Ghana own and manage cocoa farms.[27] In Southern Nigeria, women who are active in agriculture and trade participate in cooperatives, have access to credit, and organize work parties to alleviate their work and saving societies to provide them with extra capital when it is required.[28] In these as in other cases, the class composition of the household always plays a determinant role.

A global and sex-specific bias in women's access to resources appears to be a persistent unequal channeling of agricultural extension services to men and women, although here, too, the degree of differentiation determines the approach. It is noted, for instance, that in Botswana, "the results show first how little direct agricultural extension is reaching rural people. Where it does make contact (through an agricultural demonstrator) both men and women are reached but the process appears to function mainly through men and favours households with a male head."[29] And yet the proportion of female-headed households is very high in countries like Botswana, Lesotho, Swaziland, and Malawi, where other studies have noted a male preference in extension services.[30]

The discriminatory ways in which finance and technical knowledge are disseminated are not *always* sex-specific, although they do affect women more. In cases where extension services and qualifications for loans, training, and follow-up is based on the "progressive farmers" approach, a large number of farmers are excluded for not qualifying as "progressive" or not being members of "Improved Farmers' Schemes."[31] As one study points out,

> "The reinforcement of success" approach was of immense disadvantage to women. Legally, there was no barrier against women applying for loans, however, their chances of getting loans were diminished by the fact that none of them become "progressive" farmers. In colonial days, only the man, as head of the family and therefore breadwinner, was conceived of as a farmer. Women could not join the "Peasant" and "Improved Farmers' Schemes" which were the backbone of "progressive" farming. Such attitudes persisted after Independence. In addition to difficulties in securing loans, the first few years of the inception of training programmes did not include women producers. When training was extended to women towards the end of the period, they received instructions in homecraft and, later, poultry.[32]

Lack of agricultural extension services for women, even in areas where they assume full responsibility for agriculture, has been noted in many cases, as in the cultivation and adoption of innovative cash crops in Kenya,[33] rice transplantation in Senegal,[34] or wet rice cultivation in Liberia.[35] This unequal channeling of resources has resulted in the increase of men's labour productivity and a deterioration of that of women, as changes in production processes usually mean additional tasks for them to attend to. Nor is this process limited to Africa. Observing the same trend in Latin America, one author has ventured to point out that "modern technology imported by foreigners brings with it a preference for male employees."[36]

Women's access to training in productive skills is reinforced by existing courses that are primarily focused on cooking and sewing. Moreover, "stereotypes that women cannot manage technology are reinforced by the fact that illiteracy is more wide-spread among women, who therefore cannot read instructions."[37] This situation of unequal access to new techniques and institutions is reproduced through the nature of existing educational institutions. As one study has observed,

> New techniques based primarily on know-how such as application of fertilizer or the use of improved seed varieties, obviously do not carry an inherent sex designation for utilization. But to a certain degree, the acceptance and use of improved agricultural methods depend on education. And unequal education for the sexes with primarily boys sent to school or boys remaining in school longer than girls, creates an ever widening gap between the sexes.[38]

This process of unequal channeling of resources between men and women continues to lower productivity of food crops and is particularly damaging in areas where men migrate and women are the only full-time agriculturalists.

Uneven regional development on a world scale and the development of commercialization in agriculture has witnessed a simultaneous creation of a nonagricultural labour market, to which men are often the first ones to migrate. The resultant effects have been a marked change in the sexual division of labour as tasks traditionally regarded as those of males are by necessity taken over by women. For instance, in Kenya, male migration implied that women had to add full responsibility for the care of livestock and the cultivation of cash crops, such as coffee, to their previous and continued responsibility for food crop production. Yet extension services are not available to them. Explaining this predicament, one study noted that "over 98 percent of the agricultural staff in this district are men. The society is characterized by communication between men on governmental matters and by symbolic male authority over households, despite extensive male absence in rural areas."[39]

In the case of Southern Africa as well, male migration has led to definite changes in the sexual division of labour in the household. For example, in Lesotho, "Women both herd and tend livestock, contrary to the strong Bantu prohibition that exists against any contact between women and cattle."[40] Similar changes are noted for the whole region, where a constant flux of male out-migration has led to women being the sole agriculturalists for the most part. Yet subsistence agriculture in this region "is not perceived . . . as a locus for change and innovation."[41] Women's increased responsibility for family maintenance and subsistence agriculture, however, implies that reproduction of the labour force takes place in the subsistence sector and wages for migrant males need not cover a portion of family maintenance and of reproduction of the labour force.[42]

In Latin America, temporary male migration has led to the breakdown of sex roles as it necessitated a greater female involvement in agricultural work. In almost all cases, the introduction of cash crops has meant concentration of land in the hands of few households, concentration of infrastructural inputs to that sector, and hence, a marked decline in the importance of agriculture in generating familial subsistence. Concurrently, increased demand for female labour affects the time available for food growing, food preparation, and general child care. In many parts of Africa, time constraints on women have led to women's rejecting food crops that require a higher labour input. According to one case study,

> When a woman becomes responsible for food crop production, her available resources were not so that she could take over yam production. . . . She needed a crop into which she can put her labour in small portions and . . . which gives the highest possible output per labour hour, since time is her scarcest resource. Women therefore replaced yam with cassava (traditionally regarded as a low value hunger crop) since cassava gives a much higher output of starch per labour hour than yam.[43]

Cassava growing, however, means an inferior nutritional value and lack of both the vitamins and minerals that yam used to provide. Thus malnutrition, particularly

> kwashioker—a serious malnutrition disease that affects children—has appeared in districts where it was unknown before, coinciding with a shift from growing yams, bananas and so on to cash crops like tea or sugar, usually with official encouragement. The drive for foreign exchange is officially justified by the need to import fertilizer and machinery to produce more food. But the peasant seems to be the loser.[44]

One clear trend that can be observed is that technological changes have led to the concentration of women in domestic roles (food production, household maintenance, and child care), nonmarket productive work (both agricultural and nonagricultural), and labor-intensive activities in general.

5. Women and Plantations

Depending on the nature of commercial farming, women, as indicated earlier, get seasonal employment opportunities. In fact, some large-scale plantations "prefer" a female labour force, e.g., cotton, coffee, and tea. Women workers seem to be preferred for certain jobs like harvesting tea, as in Taiwan, or plucking the ripe coffee berries during the coffee harvest season, as in Tanzania and Kenya. In the major tea and rubber plantations in Sri Lanka, Malaya, and India, the labour force is almost 50 percent female, whereas in East, Central, and West Africa, many fewer women are employed. The reason behind this preference for females is that women have a "better skill and nimble touch and are more careful in handling the harvest."[45] The growth of large commercial agriculture, particularly the above indicated types of plantations, implies that the seasonal and nonpermanent character of female employment is on the increase.

In some African countries, women represent the great majority of seasonal workers. For example, in Malawi, more women than men are found in the cultivation of tobacco and cotton. Women are employed not only in the harvesting and grading work, but also in tobacco nurseries and in planting and spraying of cotton.[46] In Latin America, women and children are employed as temporary workers, particularly in the harvesting of coffee and cotton. As payment is often in terms of piecework, it has encouraged the participation of children alongside women, thereby maintaining low wages.[47]

Wage rates for women in plantations are lower than men's across countries. In Sri Lanka, the minimum female daily wage rates in tea, rubber, and coconut plantations in 1969 were on the average about 70 percent of the minimum rate for male labour. A similar pattern, or worse, can be found in other countries. In some cases, women's wages are close to half of men's—as observed in sugar plantations in Colombia and other Latin American countries.[48] Moreover, there are cases in which women and children do not even receive a direct payment, as the plantation pays the male worker for the work done by his wife and children.[49]

6. Crop and Food Processing and Storage

Given the lack of infrastructure in the rural areas, food and crop processing is one of the many laborious and time-consuming tasks that rural women have to perform. Theoretically, technological development in the processing of a given crop or food item can save women both energy and time. However, the impact of technological change on rural women is class-specific. Whereas women in the middle peasant and landlord classes can benefit from the time saved, technological change in the processing of food and crops can eliminate supplementary sources of employment on which poor women have to depend. A case in point is the introduction of rice hullers in Indonesia, which in Java alone resulted in the loss of the major regular source of income for women in poor households. It is estimated that in Java the loss amounted to 12 million women's days of work, which is equivalent to $50 million in earnings. As they received 10 percent of their earnings in food, they lost an amount that would have served four months of food consumption for the household.[50] "For larger landowners, the hullers save cost, and, more importantly, preserve rice better than pounded rice and facilitate sale."[51] Again, in Java, larger farmers sell their rice before harvesting to middlemen who bring in outside harvesters using better tools, thereby reducing labour by as much as 60 percent. Whereas women from large landholding households are freed from the job of harvest management to invest time in lucrative trade, poor women lose another source of employment.[52]

Likewise in Tanzania, introduction of a diesel pump, which stored water in a tank, replaced hired women water carriers, resulting in a loss of 2,531 women-days of work and income equal to 7,972 Tanzanian shillings.[53] In other circumstances, the introduction of labour-saving devices are highly appreciated by women. In the Sudan, the introduction of *dura*-grinding mills has led to the elimination of long queues of women who waste time waiting to get *dura* ground for their families.[54] Similarly, the introduction of corn grinders saves women many hours of manual work, although it implies carrying approximately a 24 kilogram (53-pound) load for four miles and then taking a bus for a further five miles to have the maize ground. Unfortunately, the cost of grinding and busing amounts to about two-thirds of the value of the maize itself.[55] The construction of wells in one area of Ethiopia could save rural women ten hours of walking to fetch water.[56]

Food processing in the rural areas takes a considerable amount of time and energy as it implies traditional manual tools, collection of fuel, and fetching water from long distances. For example, in Zaire, fetching water entails long walks with loads as large as 10 to 15 litres (11 to 16 quarts) at a time.[57] In a rural Indian household, gathering firewood takes approximately six hours a day.[58] In a Javanese village, women aged thirty spend five and one-half hours per day on domestic tasks and child care, 20 percent of which is spent on housework, 56 percent on food preparation, 1 percent on collecting firewood with the help of children, and 22 percent on child care.[59]

A related problem is that of storage and waste. Studies indicate that 75 percent of the grain grown in Ghana is stored in traditional storage structures. Estimated weight loss in maize due to insect infestation is 35 percent in six months of storage. In Nigeria, losses of 30–70 percent have been recorded for between six and eight months of storage. In Ivory Coast, the loss is estimated at between 20 and 90 percent of maize stored; in Benin it is estimated at between 30 and 50 percent in five months of storage.[60] Reduction of food losses cannot be achieved without training the women who store the food. New technologies require the provision of improved technical knowledge. Yet rural women are either illiterate (83.7 percent in Africa) and/or are not given access to concepts of scientific principles, e.g., mixing of insecticides or principles of solar drying. "Thus attempts should be made to undertake a more effective dissemination of scientific knowledge to women."[61]

Most of these studies have documented in great statistical detail the nature, duration, and intensity of housework. Recommendations include access to new water technologies to ease the water-carrying burden, re-afforestation programmes, solar energy as an easily controllable source of heat, teaching women themselves how to handle these "appropriate technologies," and finally, training women in income-generating activities to utilize the time saved. Often, these recommendations, although they are useful in themselves, remain simply well-documented recommendations with a few cases implemented in one or two areas of a given country. Lack of infrastructure in the rural areas is a major reflection of the intensity of rural poverty and underdevelopment. No doubt some of these recommendations can be and are gradually being implemented, albeit in selected areas. It would seem, though, that the real solution requires a transformation of priorities in rural development and the political participation in all aspects of decision making of those involved in production.

7. Trade and Commerce

Large numbers of women engage in trade and commerce as a supplementary income-generating activity (in the rural areas) or as a full-time occupation, particularly in towns. The majority are found in petty trading, where they retail agricultural surplus, cooked food, fruits and vegetables, handicrafts, and small imported items. In many parts of Africa, particularly West Africa, women dominate what has come to be known as the internal market. Studies estimate that 40 percent of West African trade is undertaken by women. They dominate markets in Dakar, Zaire, Zimbabwe, Zambia, and Malawi.[62] In Peru, Paraguay, and Bolivia, rural women play significant roles in the market.[63] Likewise, in Mexico City (as in other Latin American, Asian, and African cities), women make up a large sector of the informal labour market.[64]

Similar trends concerning the impact of commercialization of agriculture on women have been noted for women's role in trade and commerce. Thus, increasing penetration of capital reduces their relative importance. At times, however, stimulation from commercial agriculture can actually increase the absolute volume of their trade while their relative share in the economy is declining.[65] These recommendations have so far been based on implicit assumptions that visualize technology outside of the international and local social and political structure and a failure to confront the crucial question "appropriate" for whom? African data support this assertion; it is noted that the percentage of women in commerce decreased in Dahomey from 95 percent to 89 percent between 1961 and 1967 and that of petty traders in Nigeria from 84 percent to 70 percent between 1950 and 1963.[66]

One of the most comprehensive and analytical studies of women's role in trade has shown this global phenomenon to be to the benefit of male traders, facilitating women's exclusion from trade in export commodities. Mintz noted:

> The Haitian economy provides such women with scanty space for innovative maneuver, and with little or no opportunity to reinvest in new forms of production. It is the men who control coffee, sisal, and livestock production and sale, for the most part, men and foreign firms who control the licensed purchasing and bulking of export commodities. . . . Thus it is not surprising that market women often give over much of their earnings to the education of their children, as the major means of "reinvestment."[67]

Here, as in the other cases, one ought to add the qualification that not all men benefit. These male traders are members of the class that is directly tied up with and benefits from export sectors of the national economy. In fact, numerically they are a very small number of men.

Incorporation of the periphery into the world economy has resulted in structural and organizational changes in marketing. Thus, the functions of wholesalers, retailers, and hawkers are taken over by chain stores; corporations and joint partnerships replace family-run enterprise.[68] These changes displace most small traders but very often affect poor women disproportionately, as they have no access to capital and are denied membership in marketing cooperatives.

Finally, women's income-generating activity is undercut when handicrafts are replaced with factory-made commodities. Likewise the introduction of large-scale breweries in Africa has undercut women's income from home-brewed traditional beer.[69] Similarly in Java, the importation of Coca Cola and ice cream displaced local soft drinks manufacture, thereby undercutting women's resources.[70] Bakeries and milk cooperatives have also displaced women as governments sponsored milk cooperatives for men and encouraged bread production in bakeries through loans and partial ownership of flour milling facilities.[71]

8. Women in the Formal Labour Market

Women's participation in the formal labour market is characterized by three interrelated phenomena: occupational segregation by sex, pay differentials, and displacement of women at times of considerable oversupply of labour or introduction of capital-intensive technology. Across countries, both industrialized and peripheral, with the exception of East European countries, the majority of women are found in relatively unskilled, less prestigious, and low-paid sectors of the economy. A complex set of institutions, economic, legal, familial, and cultural, have both created and presently reinforce occupational segregation by sex. The nature of occupational segregation as it presently stands mirrors the division of labour between the sexes in the reproduction of labour power. As indicated earlier, a comprehensive understanding of women's participation in the formal labour market, or lack thereof, has to be located within the context of the production process of the world capitalist economy.

Simultaneous with the introduction of capitalism in agriculture, incorporation of the periphery into the world economy meant the establishment of industry, a modern bureaucratic state structure, and an ever-growing service sector. This process, which is to be understood as the progressive extension of the market exchange of commodities, led to the breaking up of precapitalist social relationships, i.e., displacement of people from agriculture, forcing them into the labour market. Thus, although the first to be hired in the new institutions were men, women, too, entered the labour market *initially* on a relatively large scale. Reinforcing the preexisting sexual division of labour, and based on women's lack of the necessary skills, women were hired in those sectors that required no previous skills and thus received low pay.

In the history of industrial growth, the dynamics of surplus value accumulation has often led to substituting capital for labour, thereby displacing workers. To begin with, industrialization makes up a small sector of peripheral economies, which concentrate on primary sectors of the labour market. Moreover, capital-intensive industrial growth further limits labour absorption in industrial employment, which has not been expanding at an adequate rate in proportion to the increase of available labour, leaving large numbers of workers with no possibility of finding formal employment. Thus, "industrial growth has meant increasing inequality of wealth and opportunity overall and greater inequality of employment by sex."[72] As in agricultural production and commerce, here, too, women have been the first ones to be displaced and/or never promoted to skilled posts.

9. Sectoral Distribution

Women's participation in the formal labour force varies according to the type of industry, sector of the economy, and stage of industrialization. However, across countries, the majority of women seem to cluster in the most servile, lowest-paid sectors of the economy. Women professionals, for instance, are to be found in nonsupervisory "feminine" occupations such as nursing and elementary school teaching. It has often been observed that the sectors that largely employ women are extensions of their reproductive roles in the household.

The hypothesis that expansion in industry exerts a preferred demand for male labour while female employment continues to be concentrated in tertiary employment is supported by cross-country data.[73] Women across countries are overwhelmingly concentrated in the tertiary sector. In Mexico, for example, women are concentrated in the dress manufacturing, food, electrical equipment, and textile industries in manufacturing, and 40 percent are engaged in jobs of extremely "low productivity" and income. Women rarely hold high administrative or professional posts.[74] Likewise, in Guatemala's earlier phase of industrialization, women were employed in the sectors of the economy with the largest numbers of workers, making up 35 percent of those in food, 20 percent of public employees (including teachers and nurses), 10 percent of those in electricity, and 9 percent of those in "specialized arts and industries" – musicians, office workers, typesetters, fireworks makers.[75] Similar trends have been noted for Africa and Asia.[76]

Large proportions of those who are employed are professionals, operatives, clerical, and service workers. Women employed as operatives constitute those employed in textiles, weaving, and footwear manufacturing, i.e., light industries. Another concentration of females is professionals – elementary school teachers, nurses, social workers, clerical personnel, and service workers. Males, on the other hand, are clearly far more evenly distributed both by industry and occupation.[77]

10. Wage Differentials

A number of studies have documented a wide gap in wage differentials between men and women in the labour force. Many reasons are given for this discrepancy. The most conventional is that women are generally less skilled than men and hence do not qualify for equal pay. Recent studies have argued that wage differentials between men and women are the result of women's primary concentration at the domestic level.

> Wages are not related to marginal productivity, as orthodox economics have it, suffice it to recall the extreme cases in which women's wages are lower than men's even when women are preferred workers and perform similar jobs to men. On the other hand, if wages are viewed as the cost of maintaining and reproducing the labour force, and if society views the male worker as the one responsible for providing maintenance, female earnings – whether from wages or any other type of labour – do not need to cover even the female worker's own costs of maintenance. Female earnings constitute a complement to family income, not the main source which is represented by male earnings. . . . As long as society views men and women's roles in that way, women will be subject to and are likely to view exploitation and wage discrimination as the natural outcome of these roles.[78]

On another level, wage differentials between men and women are also the result of women's occupational segregation by sex.

In all cases, the gap is considerable, particularly for nonprofessional jobs. For example, in Mexico City, 72.2 percent of working women received less than the official minimum salary in 1970. In the services, which employ 42.9 percent of the total female labour force, the figure is 72.9 percent. Of the total salaried labour force between twenty-one and twenty-six years of age in Mexico City, 18.1 percent of the men are in those low-income jobs as compared to 35.6 percent of women.[79] In Ethiopia, it was found that factory women as a group earn much less than their male counterparts, as little as one-fourth of the pay men receive for the same type of work.[80] In India, women's wages are said to be uniformly lower then those of men.[81] A comparison of male and female distribution of weekly paid workers in Venezuela showed a consistent pattern of wage differentials.

> In the two lowest income categories women's proportion was nearly always greater than men's, while in the upper two categories the reverse was true. In the middle income category, the relationship hovered around unity. The only exceptions were in the utilities and transportation and communication sectors, where employment of women amounted to only 2 percent of the total female labour force in 1970. On the other hand, great discrepancies are visible in the manufacturing and services sectors, two branches that accounted for more than three-quarters of the female labour force in 1970.[82]

Finally, basing its explanations on the dual labour market analysis, a study has argued, "Thus, we may replace the familiar statement that women earn less because they are in low paying occupations with the statement that they earn less because they are in women's jobs."[83]

11. Decline in Women's Employment

A trend similar to that of technological intervention in agriculture is observable in industrial production. The early phase of industrialization creates a labour demand for both men and women. In fact, at times, depending on the type of industry, women have been employed at a faster rate than men, e.g., in textiles and food production. However, when industrial production is further mechanized, women tend to be replaced by men or both are replaced by machines.

Cross-country data from India to Bolivia support this observation. In Bolivia, for example, women entered the labour force in the early period of tin mining after 1880 in increasing numbers, up until 1940, when new methods displaced female workers, who were replaced by male workers in the sink-and-float plants. Since 1960, no women have worked in the large mines as metal concentrators, because the concentrators have been completely mechanized.[84] Similarly, the above-described sectors of the Guatemalan economy where women concentrated have shown a declining trend.

> The industrial census of 1946 and 1965 report a decline in female workers from 22 to 18 percent. The largest declines are in tobacco, textile, chemicals, rubber, foods and paper. For male workers, on the other hand, employment is rapidly increasing in the areas of chemicals, paper, rubber and metal products as well as electrical appliances, transportation and furniture which first appeared in the 1965 census. Thus, not only have new industries created a disproportionate demand for male labour but men are replacing women in some industries. In absolute terms, overall male employment climbed much higher than overall female employment in this period.[85]

Likewise, in India, though total employment in factories has been increasing steadily, women's employment in this sector has decreased since 1964, their share being reduced from 11.43 percent in 1951 to 9.1 percent in 1971, i.e., a decline of 21.7 percent. In mines, the number of women declined from 109,000 to 75,000 between 1951 and 1971, whereas total employment increased from 549,000 to 630,000. The women's share of employment declined from 21.1 percent to 11.9 percent, i.e., a decline of 47.4 percent, the heaviest decline being in coal mines, from 55,000 to 2,000.[86]

The same study points to reasons behind the decline of women's employment.

> After examining the situation in the particular industries where the decline in women's employment has been substantial, viz., the textiles, jute, and mines, we find that the most important factor contributing towards the decline is the extent and nature of modernization methods. Industries which have adopted a higher capital intensive technology resulting in displacement of labour have found it easier to displace women rather than men. They have justified this on the ground that women lack skills and are illiterate and unwilling to learn new processes. While a chance for on-the-job training is generally denied to women, there is evidence to show that wherever such training has been provided, women have proved themselves capable of acquiring new skills and a few have even proved to have greater aptitude than men (e.g. in some of the new industries). Similar trends have been noted for Mexico[87] and Brazil.[88]

Globally, this trend has been noted for industries such as metal trades, textiles, clothing, leather footwear, food and drink, and printing and allied trades. An extensive study of textile industries by the International Labour Organisation (ILO), found that when a new machine is installed, the tendency as a whole was to "substitute male workers for women workers and to keep women workers on the older and nonautomatic machinery."[89] Another observation by the ILO concerning the employment of women in postal and telecommunication services was that rationalization measures that introduce new technical equipment often result in the abolition of temporary or part-time posts. Thus, automation in telecommunication does away with operator's jobs; computers eliminate clerical or bookkeeping work. "Such posts are frequently occupied by women, it is the female staff who are the most affected by the adoption of new techniques."[90] A study on the repercussions of scientific and technological progress on the status of women has concluded that women are not employed in heavy industries "involving changes in science and technology as they are not yet physically and psychologically equipped for such . . . work . . . mainly because of the lack of facilities for scientific training and research. . . . But being deprived of such additional technological knowledge equally results in widening the skill and wage gap between men and women."[91] It is not clear what exactly is implied by "physically and psychologically equipped," as the phrase smacks of biological determinism. It is true, however, that women, for many reasons, mainly socialization, are excluded from existing scientific training and research.

As a consequence of all these factors, but particularly because of the generally rising level of unemployment in peripheral countries, a disproportionately larger number of women than men face unemployment. In India, women were found to be victims of unemployment and underemployment. The number of unemployed women in rural areas was estimated to be 4.5 million, as against 3.2 million males, in 1971. Women constitute nearly 60 percent of the rural and 56 percent of the total unemployed in the country.[92] In Mexico, women's unemployment has risen at a faster rate, 14 percent, than that of men, which is estimated at 5.7 percent. By 1980, female unemployment will overtake male unemployment, and 60 percent of the unemployed will be women. Although educational background correlates with unemployment, women with the same level of schooling as men have higher unemployment rates.[93] However, it is the poor uneducated women in particular who often face unemployment and underemployment. Nonetheless, it is true that, statistically, the distribution of women in the labour force does tend to reflect the level of development of a country. A detailed analysis of female labour participation according to the level of development of the Mexican states showed that "for every unit increase in the index of economic development there is a corresponding increase of about three percentage points in the aggregate level of women's labour force activity."[94] Consequently, women's labour force participation does not decline or taper off in all sectors of the economy.

12. Services and Professions

There is a decline in women's employment in certain sectors of the economy, but this trend is matched by a simultaneous growth of their numbers in the services and professions. Industrialization has necessitated expansion of education, health services, and production services, which comprise occupations in commerce, real estate, credit, transportation, communication, and storage. These new structures, both public and private, create a demand for professionals and technicians and globally, a growing number of the relatively few women with technical and professional training join the labour force. As has been pointed out, "Industrialization increases bureaucratic and clerical activities for women."[95] In most peripheral countries, however, it is the expansion of the public sector that has created an increased job market. In Brazil, for example, a sectoral analysis of the economy and women's participation within it points out that,

> In other categories it is possible to observe some increase in women's labour force participation, especially in collective consumption and professional activities in the developed regions. This increase is probably due to the expansion of the educational system which employs a large number of primary school teachers, and the expansion of civil service activities, especially in bureaucratic service, where women are willing to work for lower salaries and are generally more stable employees than men.[96]

Likewise, in India, there is a continuous growth in the number of women employees in the categories of professional, technical, teaching, and other related services in the public sector. There is a marked increase in the category of clerical and related workers, service, sports, and recreation. In the last category, however, the majority are working as maids, cooks, housekeepers, cleaners, and sweepers. Although there was a general slump in the employment of women in all categories in 1963, the decline was more marked among administrative, executive, and managerial workers, from 5,000 to 1,000. New industries, such as advertising, market research, hotel management, and cottage industries, are employing women in the management cadre. A review of the available data on the changes in the occupational structure reflected two trends: (1) concentration of women in the professions of teaching and medicine; and (2) recognition of certain low-prestige jobs in the clerical services as particularly suited to women.[97]

Similar trends are observable in Africa, where since independence a growing number of women have joined both the public and private sectors as teachers, nurses, bank clerks, secretaries, and service workers in general. For example, in Nigeria, women make up 23 percent of the teaching force at the elementary level, 19 percent at the secondary level, and 10 percent in the universities.[98] In Cameroun, a study points out that 12 percent of women are in banking and adds that, although two-thirds of the males in banking are engaged in clerical activities (accountant, bank teller, etc.), half of Camerounian female bank workers are employed as typists. As for differences in the educational background of clerical workers and typists, 41 percent of the men in clerical posts have a post-primary education, as opposed to 14 percent of the women; the figure among typists is reversed, with 14 percent of males and 33 percent of females having post-primary education. Hence, as typing becomes stereotyped as a "feminine" occupation, it attracts women with increasingly higher levels of formal qualification but includes men with lower educational status.[99] Similarly, in Senegal, a growing number of women are obtaining secretarial, teaching, and health worker posts, and as for university graduates, they are found in the liberal professions and the relatively new professions, such as librarians and social workers.[100]

In all these cases, women's participation in the formal labour market varies according to their level of education, age, marital status, and socioeconomic status. As a study of the Brazilian labour force has clearly pointed out:

> the rates of labor force participation increase with the level of schooling for both single and married women. Among illiterates only 6.4 percent of married women and 19.7 percent of single women work, as compared to 65.8 percent of married and 77.2 percent of single women with university education. Participation differences by marital status are larger in the lower levels of schooling; in the higher levels, differences tend to diminish, perhaps because married women have domestic help for household and child care activities. Low socio-economic status women earn low salaries which do not cover the costs for the unpaid

work they do in the home; only when the salary covers the cost can these women enter the labour market.[101]

The issue of socioeconomic status has also been indicated in the case of Senegal and India. A study by the Indian Council of Scientific and Industrial Research in 1971 revealed that out of 400,000 women degree-holders, only 150,000 were employed, representing only 4 percent of the total working women in the country.[102] Those not employed came from middle-class families that upheld values of a woman's place being in the home.

13. New Trends in Occupational Structure

Historically, the subdivision of the labour process in industrial production has meant the use of less skilled labour in one or more subportions of tasks, i.e., unskilled women. Currently, the decline in women's employment in capital-intensive industry is balanced by a new source of employment. The new international division of labour has ushered in an increasing subdivision of the manufacturing process into separate partial production tasks in different locations around the world. Traditionally these have been high concentration areas of women in manufacturing, i.e., textiles, clothing, and the electrotechnical product groups.

A case in point are West German textile and clothing subsidiaries:

> Foreign employment in West German textile and clothing subsidiaries in low wage countries as a proportion of the total foreign labor employed abroad in that industry has increased from roughly one-quarter in 1966 to about one-half in 1974. A breakdown by sex and age reveals that in low wage countries an extremely high percentage of young female workers are employed. Roughly one-half of the employees in the foreign subsidiaries of the West German clothing industry are younger than 20 years, and more than 90 percent are females.[103]

The other change in the international division of labour is the creation of free production zones, and a new type of facility, the world market factory.

> Free production zones are industrial enclaves set up for industries with a World Market orientation at sites offering abundant cheap labour. World market factories are installed on these sites (but also elsewhere) to utilize this labour. In 1975, 79 free production zones existed in 25 underdeveloped countries in Africa, Asia and Latin America. In 14 other underdeveloped countries world market factories have been

operating on sites outside the free production zones. During 1975, such zones were in the process of being established in 11 countries where they had not existed before. Our case study reveals that in 1975 there were considerably more than 700,000 workers employed in world market factories in both free production zones and other locations (although mainly in the former).[104]

The largest share of production in 1975 was held by the textile, clothing, and electro-technical product groups, and production tasks are noncomplex, involving the manufacture of parts, their assembly, or the final assembly of components only.

> The employment structure in free production zones and world market factories is extremely unbalanced. Given the virtually unlimited supply of unemployed labour, a highly specific type of worker is chosen, mostly women in the younger age groups. The selection criteria are unmistakable: Labourers are employed who require the minimum remuneration, "can be utilized the most" (a fresh labour force can be expected to provide the highest labour intensity), and are predominantly unskilled or semiskilled.[105]

14. Education and Training

As in all other issues considered, the type of economic development taking place in peripheral countries has not resulted in high levels of education for women, nor even the same level of educational opportunity as that of men. However, there has been a phenomenal increase in the enrollment of girls at every level of the educational system, although in most cases they drop out at the elementary level and tend to be concentrated in certain fields. The total number of students enrolled, enrollment by sex, availability of schools and level of education, and type of subject matter pursued vary in accordance with the economic development of different countries. Educational opportunity is primarily related to socioeconomic status. Higher levels of parent's schooling and higher family income correlates positively with girls' education careers. Regional imbalance in the location of educational institutions limits rural school attendance, particularly that of girls whose mobility is culturally limited. Finally, the societal view that girls will eventually drop out and become housewives has led to the addition of subjects "suitable for women" in the school curricula in which girl students concentrate, those same courses offered in nonformal education courses for women and, finally, denial of on-the-job training for women workers, who are always considered temporary. Thus the educational system, both formal and informal, preselects women away from scientific and technological subjects and continues to reproduce the sexual division of labour and resultant subordination of women. It is important to note, however, that in most peripheral countries, education with technological content is not given its due importance. Biases in favour of law, medicine, and recently, accounting and business management predominate to the neglect of pure science and engineering.

15. School Enrollment

Cross-country data indicate the differential participation rates for boys and girls at all levels of the educational system, with a dramatic decrease in the rate of female participation at each higher stage of the educational process.[106] In Ghana, for example, in the 1973–1974 academic year, girls accounted for 43 percent of the total population enrolled in elementary schools, 28 percent in secondary schools, and about 15 percent in all three Ghanaian universities.[107] In India, in the same academic year, girls enrolled at the primary level numbered more than 24.4 million (a ratio 62 girls per 100 boys), at the middle level more than 4.5 million (ratio 43 per 100), at the secondary level more than 2.3 million (ratio 36), and in colleges and universities about 0.9 million (ratio 31). The distribution of all girls enrolled between different stages of the educational system by 1970–1971 was 75 percent in primary schools, 14 percent in middle schools, 7.3 percent in secondary schools, 2.4 percent in universities and colleges, and 3.3 percent in professional schools.[108]

Other than economic status, the differential rate of educational participation between boys and girls can be traced to patriarchal ideology. That is, differences in expectations for boys and girls with regard to schooling make girls start dropping out of school around the age of twelve or thirteen. Particularly in the rural areas, this ideology works at two levels. Where girls are expected to stay home and look after the house and children, education is considered a waste. In addition, girls are expected to do housework from an early age and boys are not. Thus, their motivation to stay in school is greatly limited.

16. Areas of Specialization

Cross-country data again support the observation that the educational system reflects the sexual division of labour in society and channels women into "suitable" tracks. For example, in Nigeria, out of a total number of 2,113 students in trade and vocational institutions in the old Western State in 1973–1974, only 283 (13.4 percent) were girls, and of these, 63.6 percent were undertaking housekeeping/matronship courses.[109] Contrasting educational opportunities in two African countries, the following study provides information about some factors in women's choice of educational specialization:

> Educational development is also associated with an accentuated institutionalization of educational and occupational hierarchies. In turn, this institutionalization induces increased divergences in the academic trajectories of the two sexes, both through the influence of informal patterns of socialization and through the mechanisms of selection used by educational authorities.[110]

An ILO report has pointed out that, conforming to this cross-cultural pattern, few girls are enrolled in technical and vocational education, few are to be found in vocational training outside the school system, and those enrolled learn sewing, dressmaking, housecraft, childcare, and embroidery. To be sure,

> There is sometimes a failure to distinguish clearly between home economics and vocational training outside the school system . . . although measures are now being taken to bring girls into agricultural schools, colleges and into extension work and services. Some governments (e.g. Egypt, Lebanon, Chile), are making special efforts to encourage the training of girls for some modern occupations such as laboratory technicians and industrial designers and to encourage their subsequent employment.[111]

17. Non-Formal Education

As earlier noted, rural women are denied access to extension education, and the vast majority of the world population that are illiterate are women. Their substantial role in agricultural production is almost always neglected in the formulation of informal education for rural women, and informal women's education is geared to nonproductive activity in urban centers. Attesting to this a study notes that "in nearly all countries, agricultural training at low, middle and high levels is given to men only. This of course produces exclusively male instructors—instructors who, in turn, address themselves to the male farmers, overlooking and disregarding women, even in cases where the wives, daughters and hired labour are doing the work."[112]

Across countries, non-formal programmes emphasize family

welfare – nutrition, child care, health, family planning, and home economics. Very few countries have provided women with access to new knowledge, technology, and other services to improve their production. In urban areas, training concentrates on sewing, embroidery, tailoring, and handicrafts. As there is no link between the production and the marketing, the training does not result in much productive employment. "The multiplicity of schemes and wastages of resources in administrative duplication limit the scope of these programmes which make only a marginal impact on the employment needs of women. Lastly, the classification of these programmes under welfare rather than under economic development prevents their receiving adequate sources from public funds."[113]

Women's lack of scientific and technological education, particularly that of poor women, affects their own welfare and that of the household and a given country in many different ways. As has been pointed out, their lack of skills both limits and is one of the causes of their exploitation in the production process. Multinational corporations and local firms have also taken advantage of women's illiteracy to introduce improper birth control methods and baby foods that have increased malnutrition of children and health problems of many women.[114]

18. Conclusion

From their inception in human history, technology and science have had contradictory impacts on society. They have been both labour-saving and labour-displacing, lifesavers and potential killers. In all societies, the impact of technology varies according to its social utilization. For those who control it and those who have access to it, the advantages are undoubtedly immense. On the other hand, the reverse is the case for those who not only have no access to it and do not control it but whose livelihood has been deteriorating because of the way technology is presently utilized. The degree of women's access to technology is a consistent index of a country's level of socioeconomic development. In most peripheral countries today the majority of women are negatively affected by many of the technological changes. That this negative impact has now and will continue to have in the future serious repercussions should be the cornerstone of any discussion on women and technology. Yet one has to add that positive changes in the status of women and thereby the transformation of a given country depend on the use of technology within a totally different socioeconomic framework.

Many mechanical proposals isolated from the socioeconomic reality of the world and the historical period have been made concerning women and technology. Studies on technology transfer and technological dependence have clearly pointed out that the path to technological liberation is political and necessitates a radical reorientation of the existing productive base and the full utilization of internal natural and human resources. There can be no special and long-lasting solution for women outside this context. However, history has shown that no societal transformation is complete if it fails to focus on the special needs of women and redress the gap and the resultant inequality that is reproduced via the existing sexual division of labour.

Notes

1. See, for example, collection of books, articles and conference paper in Mayra Buvinic, *Women and World Development, An Annotated Bibliography,* Overseas Development Council, 1976. Also, Suzanne Smith Saulnius and Cathy A. Rakowski, *Women in the Development Process: A Select Bibliography on Women in Sub-Saharan Africa and Latin America,* 1977. More recently and in the case of Africa, see Zenebeworke Tadesse, "Survey of Principal Social Science Research on Women in Sub-Saharan Africa," unpublished manuscript, 1979.

2. Some of these include Claude Meillasoux, *Femmes, Geniers et Capitaux* (Paris: Maspero, 1975). Also, Carmen Diana Deere, "Rural Women's Subsistence Production in the Capitalist Periphery," *Review of Radical Political Economics,* Vol. 8, No. 1, Spring 1976; and Marie Angelique Savane, "Les femmes africaines dans la problematique du développement," paper presented at a seminar "Africa and the Future," African Institute for Economic Development Planning (IDEP), Dakar, 1977.

3. Norma S. Chinchilla, "Industrialization, Monopoly Capitalism, and Women's Work in Guatemala," *Signs,* Vol. 3, No. 1, 1977, p. 39.

4. Deere, op. cit

5. Chinchilla, op. cit., p. 39.

6. Ann Stoler, "Class Structure and Female Autonomy in Rural Java," *Signs,* Vol. 3, No. 1, 1977, p. 77.

7. Carmen Diana Deere, "The Development of Capitalism in Agriculture and the Division of Labor by Sex: A Study of the Northern Peruvian Sierra," Ph.D. Dissertation, University of California, Berkeley, 1978. See also Lourdes Beneria, "Production, Reproduction and the Sexual Division of Labour," ILO Working Paper, WEP 10/WP 2, 1978.

8. See, for example, Seemur Anwar Khan and Farz Bilquees, "The Environment, Attitudes and Activities of Rural Women: A Case Study of a Village in

Punjab," *Pakistan Development Review,* Vol. 15, No. 3, 1976, pp. 238–71; Ester Boserup, "Traditional Division of Work Between the Sexes, A Source of Inequality," in International Institute of Labour Studies, Research Symposium on Women and Decision-Making, Research Series No. 21, 1976; and Donald Mickelwait, Mary Ann Riegelman, and Charles F. Sweet, *Women in Rural Development* (Boulder, Colo.: Westview Press, 1976).

9. UN, Centre for Social Development and Humanitarian Affairs, "Water, Women and Development," E/Conf. 70/A 19, February 1977.

10. Lourdes Beneria, op. cit.

11. Gita Sen, "Rural Women and the Social Organization of Production: Some Conceptual Issues," unpublished manuscript, 1978.

12. Carmen Diana Deere, Jane Humphries, and Magdalena Leon de Leal, "Class and Historical Analysis For the Study of Women and Economic Change," paper prepared for the Role of Women and Demographic Change Research Program, ILO, Geneva, 1979.

13. Savane, op. cit., 1977; UN Secretariat, "The Participation of Women in the Development of Latin America," ESA/SKHA/AC.10/Rev. 1, 1976; Kate Young, "Modes of Appropriation and the Sexual Division of Labour: A Case Study from Oaxaca, Mexico" (mimeo).

14. Asok Kumar Chakrabarti, "The Causes of Women's Unemployment in India," *Economic Affairs,* Vol. 22, No. 5, 1977, pp. 177–183; and Maria Mies, "Consequences of Capitalist Penetration for Women's Subsistence in Rural India," 1978. Document presented to the Seminar on Underdeveloped and Subsistence Reproduction in Southeast Asia.

15. UNECA, "Women: The Neglected Human Resource for African Development," *Canadian Journal of African Studies,* Vol. 6, No. 2, 1972.

16. UN Economic and Social Council, Commission on the Status of Women, "Status of Rural Women, Especially Agricultural Workers," E/CN 6/587/Add.1, 1973; Ester Boserup, *Women's Role in Economic Development* (London: George Allen and Unwin, 1970); Elise Boulding and Dorothy Carson, *Handbook of International Data on Women* (New York: Halsted Press, 1976); and Elise Boulding, *Women in the Twentieth Century World Community* (New York: Halsted Press, 1977).

17. Carmen Diana Deere, "The Agricultural Division of Labour by Sex: Myths, Facts and Contradictions: The Northern Peruvian Sierra" (mimeo), 1977.

18. Charles Edquist and Olle Edquist, *Social Carriers of Technology for Development,* Research Policy Studies, Lund University, Discussion Paper Series 123, 1978.

19. Glaura Vasques de Miranda, "Women's Labor Force Participation in the Developing Society: The Case of Brazil," *Signs,* Vol. 3, No. 1, 1977, p. 266.

20. Ibid.

21. Martin H. Billings and Arjun Singh, "Mechanization and the Wheat Revolution Effects on Female Labor in Punjab," *Economic and Political Weekly,* December 1970, A-169, A-173.

22. National Committee on the Status of Women in India, *Status of Women in India* (New Delhi: Indian Council of Social Science Research, 1975).

23. Ibid., Vasques de Miranda, op. cit.

24. Beneria, op. cit.

25. Stoler, op. cit.

26. UNECA, *The Role of Women in Population Dynamics Related to Food and Agriculture and Rural Development in Africa* (Addis Ababa: ECA/FAO Women's Programme Unit, 1974).

27. See D. Vallenga, "Differentiation Among Women Farmers in Two Rural Areas in Ghana," *Labour and Society,* Vol. 2, No. 2, 1977.

28. German Foundation for International Development/FAO, Seminar on "Involvement of Women in Cooperatives and Other Self-Help Organizations in English-speaking African Countries," Nairobi, Kenya, 1–15 October 1975.

29. C.A. Bond, *Women's Involvement in Agriculture in Botswana* (Gaborone, Botswana: Ministry of Agriculture, 1974).

30. UNECA, "Women: The Neglected Human Resource for African Development." Also Barbara A. Clark, "The Work Done by Rural Women in Malawi," *Journal of Rural Development,* Vol. 8, No. 1-2, 1975.

31. Maude Muntemba, "The Underdevelopment of Peasant Agriculture in Zambia," *Journal of Southern African Studies,* Vol. 5, No. 1, 1978, pp. 58–85.

32. Ibid., p. 83.

33. Susan Abbott, "Women's Importance for Kenyan Rural Development," *Community Development Journal,* Vol. 10, No. 3, 1975.

34. Ester Boserup, *Women's Role in Economic Development.*

35. Irene Tinker, "The Adverse Impact of Development on Women," in Irene Tinker et al., eds., *Women and World Development* (New York: Praeger Publishers, 1976).

36. Beverly Chinas, quoted in ibid., p. 27

37. Tinker, op. cit., p. 27.

38. Deere, "Agricultural Division of Labour."

39. Kathleen Staudt, "Agricultural Productivity Gaps: A Case Study of Male Preference in Government Policy Implementation," *Development and Change,* Vol. 9, No. 3, July 1978.

40. Susan Abbott, "A Seven Country Survey on the Roles of Women in Rural Development" (Washington, D.C.: A Report for USAID, Development Alternatives, Inc., 1974).

41. Martha Mueller, "Women and Men, Power and Powerlessness in Lesotho," *Signs,* Vol. 3, No. 1, Autumn 1977.

42. Meillassoux, op. cit.; Deere, "Rural Women's Subsistence Production."

43. Jette Bukh, *The Village Woman in Ghana* (Uppsala: Scandinavian Institute of African Studies, 1979).

44. H.P. Burn, "A Truly African Green Revolution," *UNICEF News,* Vol. 4, 1976, p. 18.

45. International Labour Office, *Conditions of Work on Women and Young Workers on Plantations,* Report 111, Geneva, 1970.

46. Barbara Clark, "The Work Done by Rural Women in Malawi," *Journal of Rural Development,* Vol. 8, No. 1-2, 1975.

47. Deere et. al., op. cit.

48. Beneria, op. cit. See also International Labour Office, op. cit.

49. See Beneria, op. cit. and International Labour Office, op. cit.

50. William L. Collier, "Choice of Technique in Rice Milling on Java: A Comment," *Bulletin of Indonesian Economic Studies*, Vol. 10, No. 2, 1974.

51. Stoler, op. cit., p. 88.

52. Ibid., p. 89.

53. UNECA, "Women: The Neglected Human Resource for African Development."

54. International Union for Child Welfare, Southern Sudan, *Final Report on the Programme of Vagrant and "Unattached" Children*, 1973.

55. UNECA, *The Role of Women in Population Dynamics.*

56. UNECA, "Women: The Neglected Human Resource for African Development," p. 362.

57. David A. Mitchnik, "The Role of Women in Rural Development in the Zaire" (mimeo, Oxfam), 1972.

58. A.K.N. Reddy, "Problems in the Generation of Appropriate Technologies: An Indian Experiment," paper presented at International Economic Conference on Economic Choice of Technologies in Developing Countries, Teheran, 1976.

59. B. White, "The Economic Importance of Children in a Javanese Village, Kulun Progo, Indonesia" (mimeo), 1973.

60. Subregional Consultation on Increasing Food Availability Through Waste Reduction and Improving the Marketing System in West Africa, Background Information, FAO/ECA, 1976, p. 4.

61. UNECA, "The Role of Women in the Utilization of Technology for Development." An ECA contribution to the African Regional Meeting on United Nations Conference on Science and Technology for Development (UNCSTD), Cairo, 24–29 July 1978.

62. Kenneth Little, *African Women in Towns: An Aspect of Africa's Social Revolution* (Cambridge: Cambridge University Press, 1974.)

63. Abbott, "A Seven Country Survey."

64. Lourdes Arizpe, "Women in the Informal Sector: The Case of Mexico City," *Signs*, Vol. 3, No. 1, 1977, pp. 25–38.

65. Laurel Bossen, "Women in Modernizing Societies," *American Ethnologist*, Vol. 2, No. 5, 1975, pp. 87–101.

66. UNECA, "Women: The Neglected Human Resource for African Development."

67. Sidney Mintz, "Men, Women and Trade," *Comparative Studies in Society and History*, Vol. 13, No. 3, 1971, pp. 247–269.

68. Report of the National Committee, *Status of Women in India* (New Delhi: Indian Council of Social Science Research, 1975).

69. Muntemba, op. cit. Also ILO, *Appropriate Technology for Employment Generation in the Food Processing and Drink Industries of Developing Countries*, Second Tripartite Technical Meeting for the Food Prods. and Drink Industries, Geneva, 1978.

70. Tinker, op. cit.

71. Emmy Simmons, "Economic Research on Women in Rural Development in Northern Nigeria" (Washington, D.C.: Overseas Liaison, American Council of Education, OLC Paper No. 10, 1976).

72. Arizpe, op. cit.

73. Marianne Schmink, "Dependent Development and the Division of Labour by Sex: Venezuela," *Perspectives,* Vol. 10, Nos. 1 and 2, 1977, p. 162.

74. Arizpe, op. cit.

75. Chinchilla, op. cit.

76. Boserup, *Women's Role in Economic Development,* and *Status of Women in India.*

77. Schmink, op. cit.

78. Beneria, op. cit.

79. Arizpe, op. cit.

80. Gloria Lowenthal, "Women Factory Workers in Ethiopia," unpublished paper, Addis Ababa, 1975; also Zenebeworke Tadesse, "Condition of Women in Ethiopia," unpublished paper, Addis Ababa, Swedish International Development Authority, 1976.

81. *Status of Women in India.*

82. Schmink, op. cit.

83. Francine Blau Weisskoff, "Women's Place in the Labour Market," *American Economic Review,* Vol. 62, September 1970.

84. June Nash, "Women in Development: Dependency and Exploitation," *Development and Change,* Vol. 8, No. 2, 1977.

85. Chinchilla, op. cit.

86. *Status of Women in India.*

87. Arizpe, op. cit.

88. Vasques de Miranda, op. cit.

89. ILO, *General Report and Training Requirements in the Textile Industry in the Light of Changes in the Occupational Structure,* Tenth Session, Geneva, 1978.

90. ILO, *Effects of Technological Changes on Conditions of Work and Employment in Postal and Telecommunication Services,* Joint meeting on Conditions of Work and Employment in Postal and Telecommunication Services, Geneva, 1977.

91. ECOSOC, *Repercussions of Scientific and Technological Progress on The Status of Women Workers,* 1968.

92. *Status of Women in India.*

93. Arizpe, op. cit.

94. Martha Tienda, "Regional Differentiation and the Sector Transformation of the Female Labor Force in Mexico, 1970," Ph.D. Dissertation, University of Texas, 1974, cited by Arizpe, op. cit.

95. Vasques de Miranda, op. cit.

96. Ibid., p. 268.

97. *Status of Women in India.*

98. Mere Nakateregga Kisseka, "The Politics of Culture and Tradition: Issues in African Women's Liberation," paper presented at the Ninth World Congress of Sociology, 1978.

99. Remi Clignet, "Social Change and Sexual Differentiation in the Cameroun and the Ivory Coast," *Signs,* Vol. 3, No. 1, 1977.

100. Diana Barthel, "The Rise of a Female Professional Elite: The Case of Senegal," *African Studies Review,* Vol. 18, No. 3, 1975.

101. Vasques de Miranda, op. cit.

102. *Status of Women in India.*

103. Folker Frobel, Jurgen Heinrichs, and Otto Kreye, "The World Market for Labor and the World Market for Industrial Sites," *Journal of Economic Issues,* Vol. 12, No. 4, 1978.

104. Ibid., p. 853.

105. Ibid., p. 856.

106. See UNESCO, *Women, Education, Equality,* Paris: UNESCO Press, 1975.

107. S. Blumenfield, "Women in Education," in USAID-Ghana, ed., *Women in National Development in Ghana* (Accra, 1975), pp. 100–130.

108. *Status of Women in India.*

109. Kisseka, op. cit.

110. Clignet, op. cit.

111. ILO, *Equality of Opportunity and Treatment of Women Workers,* 60th Session, Geneva, 1975, Report VII, and ECOSOC, *Access of Women in Education,* 1968. Resolution 1327 (XLIV).

112. E. Boserup and C. Liljencrantz, "Integration of Women in Development: Why, When, How?" UNDP, 1975.

113. *Status of Women in India.*

114. See, for instance, Protein Calorie Advisory Group, "Women in Food Production, Food Handling and Nutrition with Special Emphasis on Africa," United Nations, 1977.

4

The Impact of Science and Technology and the Role of Women in Science in Mexico

Mangalam Srinivasan

Contents

1. An Overview

It is probably correct to say that *in toto* science and technology in Mexico have been indifferent and frequently detrimental to the needs of women in that country. The available data seem like *prima facie* evidence that such is the case and suggest that when we add benefits to adverse impacts the resultant sum is negative. This fact notwithstanding, the defence of technology is plausible, even necessary, when we realize that technology has the capacity to emancipate women from drudge labour, offers them employment, and can even help them in achieving fuller and more creative lives. The question posed is no longer *whether* technology can help but *how* to use it to our best advantage.

At present relatively little research has been undertaken to evaluate the impact of technology in terms of its consequences for society. Nor has there been a significant effort to identify the parties who have a stake in technology and the groups and subgroups affected by it. The data are scarce, and the situation has not been empirically determined.

There exists a definite and fundamental inconsistency in the Mexican perception of the role of science and technology in development. In world forums, Mexico's position is consistent with that of the Group of 77, that technology serves the interests of those who control it. Mexico, along with many other developing countries, is aware that technology has the capacity to liberate as well as to exploit and oppress. Internally, however, policy planners deny that science and technology have helped to widen the gap between the rich and the poor, men and women. They consider technological choices neutral and therefore see no reason for a deliberate and cautious approach toward either introducing technologies that do not have adverse impacts on women or ensuring equitable distribution of the benefits of technology between men and women. Hence the omission of the subject of women and science in the national paper of Mexico prepared for the United Nations Conference on Science and Technology for Development.[1]

The sun-drenched history of Mexico is intricately interwoven with layers of civilizations, cultures, peoples, and religious influences. Despite its total conversion to Christianity, the country's religious psyche has undergone a synthesis of the old and the new, the native and the occidental. The Bleeding Christ on the Crucifix and the Mother of God – the Virgin of Guadalupe – arrived in the human world of the gods and goddesses of the Mayans and the Aztecs, and having failed to eliminate them, coexist with them. The religious archetypes and stereotypes are ever-present in the everyday world of life, work, education, social action, and human interactions. Art and science are organized accordingly. On the social scene, the Indians of Mexico, the Spaniards who came there, the child of the Indian (the *mestizo*), and the child of the Spaniards (the creole) are all still present in the minds of the people and exist quite distinct from one another despite assimilation. The position of things occidental in Mexican society is a very important orientation in understanding the role of women in science in Mexico, because it tells us *who is making things happen, who has the intelligence for survival, who are authorized to con-*

ceptualize (and therefore manipulate) ideas and tools, who can create, and who can sustain. The "ideas and tools" in the Mexican culture belong to creole men, which explains why few women have anything to do with science and technology in that country.

The role of women in science in Mexico is not inconsistent with their role in government and the family. Less than 7 percent of those involved in hard sciences are women. The percentage approaches 25 in the combined areas of medical, biological, and social sciences. In the area of fundamental sciences and research, Mexican women's contribution will have to be evaluated against where the women were when they entered the career, who their teachers were (role models), and the status of science in the country. Trained women engineers and technicians work in office administration and secretarial jobs because careers in science and engineering are not considered appropriate for females. Women have been systematically excluded from jobs with relatively high productivity and from hard science (policy and operation) on the basis of their "intellectual inferiority," "incapacity for independence," biological make-up, child-bearing and -rearing responsibilities, and wifely duties. When they are hired they are hired because they are "patient," "their fingers are long and delicate" (for electronic assemblies), and they "do not complain."

The task of making a career in science is particularly complicated because of the lack of role models and the limited career training and suggestions that women receive from schools, families, peers, and government. Dr. Tomas Garza, the Director of the Department of Applied Mathematics at the National Autonomous University of Mexico, points out that the problem of women in science is an integral part of the overall problems of science in Mexico. He considers the lack of tradition in theoretical and experimental sciences to be the chief factor inhibiting scientific and technological advancements in general and contributing to the problems of scientists in particular. He readily concedes that women are far behind in science due to the lack of education, specialized training, and support on the one hand, and the lack of policies to utilize their individual abilities and specific qualities to the best advantage of the nation on the other.

The general position of women in industry is determined, in great part, by the level of technology, the degree of mechanization, the scale of pay, and the magnitude and intensity of capital, as well as by how tasks are divided. The employment of women in manufacturing is about 20 percent of the total number of persons employed in these industries.[2] Most of the women are employed in industries that have some "craft" connection. The idea that women have to work in food, clothing, child care, crafts, and home-related tasks is intrinsic to the

industries that work with leather, wood, metal, chemicals, iron and
steel, heavy machinery, machine tools, and automobiles, which have
traditionally excluded them. In these industries we find women in the
first and last stages of industrial production. Their work involves
primarily preparing the raw materials, selecting and arranging items
in the first stages, and assembling parts (as in the case of
maquiladoras), and packaging the finished goods in the last stages of
production. The in-between stages are permeated with technology,
which requires technical skills. No matter how modern the
technology deployed in the particular industry is, women are mostly
engaged in nontechnological activities, such as gathering, assembling,
arranging, and packaging, and therefore, technical skills are not being
transferred equally to women.

This research effort has led us to some generalizations about the implications of technological changes for women. In a country where
having a job is a privilege, women do not think they have a right to
good working conditions, adequate pay, and access to training and
skills. In the more capital-intensive industries, women do not find
work except in packaging stages (in fat and oil industries) and
unautomated stages (vegetables and fruits).[3] Large companies have
fewer tendencies to employ women than do small ones unless they
have sections where tasks are performed by hand. Capital-intensive
and high-technology companies pay good salaries to women, even if
they are still being paid less than men. Women are underpaid in these
high-technology companies because women are considered only for
relatively low-paying labour-intensive sections and tasks and because
there are so many women competing for these jobs that the wage is
kept low for women.

Science, technology, and their mutual link with industry have
brought benefits to certain sections of Mexican society, but those
benefits are being coordinated by the dominant urban, rich, elite, and
male sections of the country, which have assigned disproportionate
benefits to themselves at the cost of widening social and economic
gaps between urban and rural rich and poor, and men and women.

Technology is a variable dependent upon the overriding social and
economic configuration of the country. Trying to examine science and
technology without giving simultaneous attention to unequal social
and economic development among the various sections of society and
trying to develop resource personnel without paying much attention
to more than half the human resources lead only to partial solutions.

To the proponents of economic development at all costs, technology
based on modern science is one definite bridge in the physical construction of a higher stage of economic evolution of a nation. They are

convinced that in economic development, as in algebra, the equation is the ultimate truth and the terms may stand for anything. To them, when science and technology achieve economic growth, all distinctions will be resolved and all economic and social tensions will have been removed. This position has conditioned the status of women in technology and society in Mexico today. But the problems of science and technology are more "human" than they are "technical."

2. Methodological Note

The study of the impact of science and technology on any part of Mexico or any section of its population is a highly complex task for reasons that are directly attributable to the many and vastly different layers of culture, all of which remain as parts of the country's present-day civilization. The vast differences in ethnic, cultural, socioeconomic, and regional characteristics account for the ambivalent attitude toward technology prevalent in Mexico. Technology has arrived in an ambiguous setting with the promise of modernizing Mexico, resulting in greater economic and social benefits for its people. Technological change is expected to achieve for Mexico liberation from drudge labour and from abject living conditions and to provide skills and tools for building a modern nation.

Whether technology is proceeding in the human interest in Mexico depends on whether the political elite has been able to create an environment for men and women enabling them to take advantage of the benefits and processes of science. The question therefore is not how much technology or even what level of technology, but the relatively ignored aspects of *social quality* of technology in Mexico. Therefore, in assessing the impact of technology on women we must not only examine the peculiar model of technology deployed, which at best tells us whether the impacts are technology-derived and/or technology-directed. We must also investigate where, how, and in what form, size, and shape technology has arrived. This method enables us to understand technological-human interaction under the conditions of developing economies and transitional societies. It enables us to understand technological *relevance*, its *tendencies*, how it *acts in response* to external influence, and how it controls action for its own purposes. These are particularly important considerations in Mexico, a country that shares its entire long northern border with the world's technologically most advanced country. This condition has unleashed problems of its own apart from those already present from unequal and disparate regional developments due to "modernization."

The Mexican government has objectively allied itself with the technology corporations and uses wage and skill differentials between Mexico and the United States to achieve its employment goals and economic growth. In selling labour the government has forgotten the labourers – the men and women who work in these companies. A case in point is the *maquiladoras* program of the Mexican government in the northern border towns, which are in fact offshore units and runaway plants of the multinational corporations from across the border in the United States. Mexico also imports hazardous factories and discarded machinery from the United States that have been declared unsafe for public health and consequently have been discontinued in the United States. The multinational offshore plants employ *only* women. The consequences of this "advantage" of having jobs *instead* of, and *at the expense* of their fathers, brothers, and husbands are not happy ones in a *machista* society.

3. Definitions

How we define science and technology influences what conclusions we reach. Science in this study refers to life sciences, physical sciences, and social sciences. Life sciences are those directed primarily toward understanding and improving agricultural productivity, forestry, soil conditions, animal health and breeding (agricultural sciences), and those that deal with life processes (biological sciences). Life sciences include medical sciences, which have to do with the understanding of human diseases and human health. Physical sciences include sciences dealing with matter, natural phenomena, pure and applied mathematics, mechanics, statistics, computer science, and engineering. Social sciences encompass economics, history, anthropology, political science, sociology, and psychology. Science also refers to the creation of new knowledge and new applications of knowledge to useful purposes. Technology means the practical application of knowledge, systematic use of scientific information, training of scientific and technological resource personnel, planning and administration of research and development, and testing and standardization.[4]

4. Scope of the Investigation

This research effort does not seek to advocate one kind of technology over another or to evaluate the levels of technology that are appropriate for particular stages in the economic and social evolution of a nation. The study is strictly limited to the investigation of the role of women in science and the impact of science and technology on women in Mexico. Modern technology has permeated every aspect of life, and its effects are being felt by wide sections of the Mexican population. The introduction of many new medical, chemical, drug, food, and other technologies has changed the ways of life of both men and women in Mexico. Consumer habits have undergone radical changes due to aggressive marketing by multinational corporations and their local affiliates or subsidiaries. The excessive use of paper products, processed goods, bottled drinks, cosmetics, substitute foods, synthetic milk in place of mother's milk for infants, and the personal automobile are some of the outstanding gifts of technology in Mexico that cater to wasteful habits, luxury expenditures, unhealthy and non-nutritional habits, and harmful association with hazardous chemicals. As important as these impacts of technology are, this investigation is limited to determining the role of women in science and the impact of industrial technology on women in Mexico.

The findings of this research effort are organized in two parts. The first part deals with the position of women in basic and applied science and the general position of women in science policy. The second part is an analysis of the place of women in selected technology-based industries as well as the impact of these technologies on women. There is scope for further research in all of the subject areas of investigation. The size and scope of this research undertaking have been dictated by time and resource constraints.

5. Constraints and Limitations

The Mexican economy suffers from disparate regional development and from extremes of technological unevenness in the industrial sectors. The disparities are notable in incomes, individual sectors, and product lines. Any measurement of know-how and employment gaps between men and women and within and between the various sectors demand clear definition of what is meant by technology and the extent of its differential impact on men and women. There are also distinctions as to consumer and producer goods, design and production technology, and light and heavy industry.

The literature on the impact of technology on the people of Mexico has provided us with some general conclusions that have been tested in this research effort. It is a generally accepted proposition that domination has come to Mexico not only *through* technology but *as* technology. "Modernization" and technology have assigned a limited, residual role to women in work. Changes in the distribution of work and production responsibilities brought on by technology have threatened the family structure in Mexico. The technological vision and policy of the government has been "making machines for more machines,"[5] which has allowed science to evolve into an activity unconnected to human needs.

These propositions have been examined in light of the evidence obtained through empirical research and through direct investigation of selected areas of technology in Mexico. The problem of the overlap between the effects of many other processes of development and those of technology is acknowledged, but it has not been studied within the framework of this research for lack of time and resources.

Although the position of the woman in the class structure does not liberate her from religious and social archetypes, the harshness of life is considerably less and drudge labour chores almost nil for the women in the higher social strata. Class, religion, and region, the degree of indigenous influences, and shades of color all divide women into various substrata. Statistical conclusions on this subject are not easily reached because of the serious difficulties connected with obtaining and processing relevant information on women in Mexico.

Yet another obstacle is one pertaining to the nature of available research itself. There is considerable pressure, in most part internally derived, to write research papers for scholarly audiences across the border and across the Atlantic rather than in the interest of policy in Mexico. Dr. Tomas Garza has pointed out that the problems that science undertakes to explore and evaluate are largely problems of interest to world science, which, according to him, explains why science and technology stay separated from the interests of people in general and of women in particular.

6. The Role of Women in Science and in Society in Mexico

The problem of women in science and technology is a problem of discrimination, which in fact is a worldwide problem. There are few women in science and technology on the Mexican scene. The organization of science and its technologies does not even peripherally affect the lives of the majority of the people in Mexico. Science there is elitist, urban, exclusive, and mostly in the hands of men. It is esoteric knowledge meant entirely for the initiated. Statistics concerning women appear in aggregates. According to the Consejo Nacional de Ciencia y Tecnología (CONACYT), 15 persons out of every 100,000 in the country are involved in activities related to science and technology. The same source puts the figure of female participation in science related to research and development at 3 persons per 100,000. Participation of women in various branches of science for the year

TABLE 4.1
Participation of Women in Research and Development Activities, 1974

Branch of Science	Total number of Persons	Number of Women	%
Natural and exact sciences	2,372	513	21.6
Agriculture and fisheries	1,149	71	6.2
Engineering sciences	1,248	83	6.7
Medical sciences	1,269	440	34.7
Social sciences	2,918	921	31.6

Source: CONACYT

1974 is shown in Table 4.1. Further categorization is shown in Table 4.2.

Women's participation in science and technology is also indicated significantly by their membership in professional societies and academies of science, by their participation in and contribution to national and international conferences, and by the awards, distinctions, and recognition that women receive for achievements in science and technology. In Mexico, only 9 percent of the women engaged in scientific and technological work belong to any professional organization, and out of the sixty-five prizes and distinctions awarded between 1948 and 1975 for achievements in science only one went to a woman.

Mexico's program for science prepared by CONACYT promises to "make an analysis of the relation between the quality of education and the demand for human resources, studying the adaptation of educational cycles to integration in the employment markets."[6] The program for human resources training talks about instituting scholarships and allocating funds to develop technical know-how and skills but does not specify how it plans to equally integrate women in the development process through the efforts of science and technology; nor does it include plans for the special efforts that are needed to equally integrate women into the inner circle of science. The program also fails to adequately explain how it plans to evaluate the impact of existing technology on women and other marginalized sections of the population.

The government's employment policies do not promote exemplary actions in employing female technicians and scientists. The few

TABLE 4.2
Number of Men and Women in Scientific and Technical Disciplines, 1975

Discipline	Men	Women	Total	Percentage of Women
Agriculture and fisheries	1,078	71	1,149	6.2
Engineering	1,165	83	1,248	6.7
Physics	299	28	327	8.6
Earth sciences	526	58	584	9.9
Mathematics	255	38	293	12.3
Political science and public administration	39	12	51	23.5
Chemistry	381	158	539	29.3
Astronomy	30	11	41	26.8
Biology	364	215	579	37.1
Medicine	829	440	1,269	34.7
Education	237	181	418	43.3
Sociology, population anthropology	371	285	656	43.4
Physiology	83	68	151	45.0

Source: Dr. Ruth Gall, Autonomous University of Mexico, and CONACYT.

women in the higher echelons of government are mostly in administration and statistical operations.

Careful analysis of the place of women in science in Mexico revealed that the scientific disciplines where most women are located are those that are clear extensions of their place in society. Primary and secondary school teaching, medicine, nutrition, and social sciences tend to attract women, and women find that they have better chances of finding employment in these areas rather than in hard-core science and technology. Direct investigations revealed that many women with engineering training were managing offices; some scientists were working in support services; and chemists were working in cosmetics and soap factories in subordinate positions. The government can deal with discrimination in employment by exemplary action, by seeking legal sanctions against the violators, by obtaining employer-worker cooperation in the case of private industries and by developing educational programs. Both education and employment in the fields of science and technology are perhaps the hardest domain for women in Mexico to penetrate. The science policy apparatus needs more women analysts, scientists, and advisers, but more importantly, it needs more women in policy positions in order that the science policy for development may be enriched by means of special points of view, particular knowledge as to the depressed situation of women in relation to science, and the special steps necessary to draw women into both educational programs and occupational training related to science and technology.

The differential sex roles instilled early in childhood accounts in great part for the social discrimination prevalent and for the continuing discrimination in education and training for women in Mexico. Despite the increasing proportion of women in employment, careers in science and technology are not considered appropriate and are seen as being contrary to and incompatible with women's roles as wives and mothers. The educational programs in Mexico purportedly offer the same opportunities for progress for both men and women. However, there are no specific programs to promote greater participation of women in vocational, technical, and professional education and career training. The primary and secondary schools actively cater to differential achievement by girls and boys. Boys are encouraged to ask questions, explore, analyze, doubt, and expose theories to fact; girls get good-conduct awards for passivity, submissiveness, silence, and refraining from asking questions. These are of course archetypes and are not clearly delimited in scope since they continue to influence the individuals in the selection of, preparation for, and performance in work, as well as in the ensuing work relationships.[7] This contention is adequately borne out by the following enumeration of the participation of women in scientific and technological careers in Mexico: Although women's participation in agriculture and related activities has been and continues to be important, only 5 percent of the scientists and technicians working in these areas are women; the number of women mathematicians and physicists make up 7 percent of the total; and in the combined area of medical, biological, and social sciences, the percentage approaches 25 percent of the total scientific and technical personnel.

The process of socialization is set in the unequal worlds of yesteryear and is grounded in the religious stereotypes carefully preserved by the church of today in Mexico. To the Indians of Mexico, when the Spaniard arrived with his "God-like" mission and manner to conquer Mexico, it was the return of Quetzalcoatl,[8] only this time Quetzalcoatl was more man – more able and presiding over larger and forever expanding horizons of conquest of the earth and heaven. From then on, being a man meant being inventive, creative, subduing, and conquering.

The Spaniards also brought with them the "Mother of God" and she, unlike the goddesses of the Mayans and other Indians of the Americas, was enduring, pious, and silent. The missionaries further instilled in the minds of men and women alike the message that woman "will be saved through bearing children, if she continues in faith and love, and holiness, with modesty" (Tim. I: 2–15). This gentle condemnation of women to archetypes of passivity and creative nonaction, combined with the indigenous belief and conception of "personal salvation only as part of the salvation of society and the cosmos,"[9] has posited in women a reality of their own that is separate and distinct from those of the material world and the tools required to negotiate a meaningful and fulfilling life in that world.

This mentality has assigned the understanding of the physical laws of the universe and therefore science and technology to men who are "able" and "intelligent" and who have the mediate "knowledge" to apprehend and take charge of the world of concepts and tools.

As women do not make a target group in themselves without specific categorization as to the area, sections of the population (age, groups, etc.), and economic and social stratification, a general knowledge about the country and its socioeconomic system is a basic minimum for a project of this type. Comprehending the role of science and technology in the material and intellectual progress of Mexican women involves consideration of the ruling ideology, the socioeconomic structure of Mexican society, administrative and infrastructural obstacles, educational policies and programs, the labour market and work conditions, and cultural and philosophical notions as to what is science, what is progress, and what is national development.

7. The Impact of Industrial Technologies on Women in Mexico

The Impact of Selected Manufacturing Industries and Their Technologies on Women

General comments and criteria for selection. Textile, electronics, oil refinery, and related technologies were studied in relation to their impact on women. These vastly different and unrelated technologies from widely separated regions of Mexico were chosen for the following reasons: textiles and food processing are traditional Mexican industries that have employed and sustained women throughout history. The activities in the textile industry extend to every region of the country, both rural and urban, involve nearly every section of the population, and employ a wide range of traditional and modern methods of production and types of technology. In recent years the textile assembly plants (*maquiladoras de ropa*) have been multiplying both alongside of the border and in the interior. Mexico also has some of the most automated and modern textile factories in Latin America. Women's involvement in the industry ranges from making a complete item – such as a poncho, dress, shawl, sweater, or coat – to putting dots on dresses for ten hours a day, five days a week for a whole year in the *maquiladoras*.

Food processing industries, also traditional work sources in Mexico, offer a valuable base from which to judge the impact of technology on women. Food processing is a dynamic and continually changing sector where technical changes and supply characteristics affect the demand patterns. In small industries and family-based operations women make the items for sale, whereas in large industries, as the level of automation increases, women's work roles change from making the entire item to that of simply packaging items already made. In addition, whenever modern technology replaces a traditional food item with new substitutes, immediate effects are manifest in terms of unemployment for women.[10] Although the initial investigations revealed excellent research possibilities in the area of women in food processing and technical changes, lack of time has precluded any in-depth investigation at the present time.

Electronics and its "offshore-sourcing" assembly plants offer perhaps the most unique opportunity to analyze the impact of technology on women from a situation in which women are the predominant employees in a modern factory. The runaway plants from Texas and California have established themselves inside the Mexican border to court and engage female labour. Lastly, oil and refinery technologies are affecting women in extraordinary ways hitherto unknown. All four modernizing sectors have been researched and investigated in varying degrees. The data from several previous missions to Mexico have been carefully studied in conjunction with the present investigation; the results are discussed in the following pages. The vast range of regions, peoples, occupations, technologies, products, and issues these industries represent allows for some generalization as to the impact of technology on women in Mexico.

There were methodological problems in the execution of this research project that pertained to the difficulties of examining the situation of women in technology as a historical development, and there were areas where it was difficult to have a short focus. Also, the impact of technology is not always related to the work situation only. New chemical technologies have an immediate and direct impact on the environment and the health of people; nuclear and pharmaceutical technologies have both short-term and long-term impacts. The scope of this project is limited to industrial technologies and mechanization and therefore does not directly deal with all aspects of the impact of technology.

The Electronics Industries. Electronics is one nontraditional, high-technology-based industry that hires women in large numbers. This of course is the aggregate position. Within the industry, however, there are large areas of work and challenges that are completely closed to women. At present there are 364 establishments registered with the Mexican government under electronics, but of this number, 35, or approximately 10 percent, are involved in building, importing, and distributing discs, cassette tapes, and auto stereos. Seven establishments are rental service companies. In these establishments, women are involved only as secretaries and bookkeepers. Out of the remaining 322 establishments, 63 register themselves as companies whose principal business is electronics; 180 as manufacturers of electrical items and parts; 75 as distributors; and 5 offer technical assistance and sell electronic accessories.[11] The electronics industry had 23,677 women on its payroll in 1970. Although this is 27.5 percent of the total number of persons employed by the industry, the complex differentiations present in the industry will have to be learned and understood to appreciate the real meaning of women's participation. Women are not employed in technical or managerial-level jobs in the industry. The electronic media, radio communications, and telex employ women in middle- and low-level jobs; these jobs amount to about 40 percent of the total employment. Out of 36,501 persons involved in repair, maintenance, and service operations connected with electronics, only 1,959, or 5 percent, are women. These numbers do not include women working with the government or in academia. Government departments such as the secretariat of statistics, PEMEX (the petroleum corporation of Mexico), CONACYT, and universities are considerably involved in electronic and computer operations. The estimates of women's participation in both sectors are between 5 and 7 percent.

The largest number of women in the electronics industry are employed in the *maquiladoras,* which number 157, and *all* of which are located in the border municipalities. Women make up 90 percent of the total employed; the implications of this situation are discussed in a later section. The reasons for employing women *instead* of men range from "they work well"; "their attention span is longer"; "they do not make trouble for the company" to "they have delicate ways of handling minute electronic components with their small delicate fingers"—all of which are excellent qualifications for a surgeon. The answers are obvious when one wonders why with such advantages women are not functioning as surgeons in any significant number!

The Textile Industry. The art of textiles in Mexico has vividly preserved native talents, sense of color and patterns, and represents Mexican civilization in all of its most striking aspects: its worship of the sun, its love of nature, its quintessential symmetry and beauty of proportions, and its technological abilities. Today's Mexican textile industry ranges from hand-made items painstakingly constructed in the individual homes of the Indians of Mexico to the making of synthetic yarn and clothing in the most automated textile factories. A very high proportion of women find work in textiles, and like the electronic *maquiladoras,* the textile offshore assemblies prefer women workers to men. The employment picture with the textile industries appears in Table 4.3

Thirty-six percent of all working women are employed in the textile industry. In this industry the number of women employed is inversely proportional to the increase in automation but directly proportional to the extreme division of tasks. Therefore, we find a high proportion of women employed in modern *maquiladoras de ropa* (clothing factories) and thus there are women in modern textile factories that are both capital- and technology-intensive.

According to one Mexican entrepreneur whose factory is considered the most automated textile unit in Latin America, automated factories usually do not employ women owing to the nature of the work, place, and type of machines used. Textile manufacturers acknowledge that women are good workers and that they have great abilities for yarn preparation and weaving. According to the manufacturers, weaving with synthetic yarn presents special problems because of the high degree of mechanization. The high level of noise (90 decibels over the standard permitted in the United States), high speed of the looms (six or seven operating at the same time), and the high temperature and humidity (26 C. [79F.] and 70 percent relative humidity respectively) inside the factories are unsuitable for women. Another entrepreneur commented that his automated factory does not employ women because he is not prepared to finance the yearly pregnancies of the Mexican woman worker. Several of them gave the opinion that training the women to operate complicated and sophisticated machinery is an expensive proposition. The automated industry has less than 10 percent women workers, and none of these women work in technical, mechanical, or managerial operations. Few are in administrative areas; most of the women work as secretaries, bookkeepers, and clerks.

The intermediate factories of the textile industry are extremely vulnerable to the imports of hazardous factories and machines from the United States as companies in the United States gradually start to replace equipment considered dangerous to the health and safety of

TABLE 4.3
Distribution of Workers by Sex and by Percentage Participation, 1970

Type of Manufacturing	Total	Men	Women	Men %	Women %
Textile Manufacturing	135,151	115,246	19,905	85.3	14.7
Articles Made of Textiles	33,279	24,246	9,033	72.9	27.1
Manufactures of Clothing	206,401	76,272	130,129	37.0	63.0

Source: Dirección General de Estadística, IX, Censo General de
Población, 1970.

the people. Such imports of rejected technology, especially in the cotton factories, are causing much harm to the men and women who work in them, to the children and the aged, and in general to the whole community from cotton dust and the high level of noise and humidity.

In the countryside of Mexico, textile technology has yet to make its impact. In the villages women continue to weave, knit, embroider, and tie laces as in the olden days. The painstaking art is time-consuming; often it takes months to make one item. The incomes derived from these activities do not compare with the quality of the work nor are they commensurate with the time put in. In addition, the maker of these items cannot sell them directly to the buyers or take them to towns for better prices. The *mestizo* middleman in the villages procures the products from the villagers by every means, including bribing the policemen who in turn take care to see that the women do not leave the village on their own in search of buyers and better prices! By comparison, women who work in modern factories are assured of fixed pay, fixed hours of work, and fringe benefits.

Extraction of petroleum and technologies. The vast petroleum reserves of Mexico, estimated at about 37 billion barrels of crude, are causing considerable industrial awakening in states where oil is being found. Mexico's Program for Science and Technology (1978–1982), issued by the Consejo Nacional De Ciencia y Tecnología (CONACYT), discusses present energy consumption, future energy needs, development of needed technologies, and so on, but it ignores the impact of existing technological activities connected with the recovery, processing, refining, and distribution of oil on the people of Mexico and does not mention how it plans to avoid adverse impacts.

Even though PEMEX, the petroleum corporation of Mexico, has been around for sometime, it is only of late that activities connected with the extraction and refining of petroleum have been intensified.

The effects of the discovery of vast resources of petroleum are being felt throughout Mexico, and activities related to crude oil production are adversely affecting the population of the area, women in particular. Veracruz and Tabasco, the oldest and the newest PEMEX operational areas respectively, were chosen for investigation and the results are as follows.

Inside sources in PEMEX estimate that out of the 100,000 employees working for the corporation, less than 5 percent are women. Most women who work for PEMEX are engaged in secretarial, administrative, and janitorial jobs; few women work as chemists, doctors, and engineers. Energy, one of the most vital sectors in economic and social development, receives practically no policy participation from women. "The annual consumption of energy resources per capita in Mexico," according to CONACYT, is the "equivalent of approximately 7.8 barrels of crude petroleum."[12] This figure is lower than the corresponding statistic from the industrially developed countries, but it is considerably higher than those of most developing countries. This growth in energy consumption (between 1965 and 1977 the consumption of energy increased 6.7 percent per annum[13]) and therefore, the growth in economic development activities[14] has not significantly increased the share of women in the income growth the country is experiencing.

Oil technology is entirely male dominated and women are not employed in any activity connected with exploration, extraction, refining, or distribution. There are a few women working in the petrochemical area, mostly as research chemists and laboratory assistants, and PEMEX has no firm figures on the number of such women.

But the most important adverse effects of the technology of recovering and processing oil and natural gas are occurring on sites where petroleum is being extracted and refined.

According to a PEMEX study on Veracruz, the share of the labour force employed by the petroleum industries has steadily risen from 1.7 percent in the year 1940 to 3.4 percent in 1976. In the same period the urban population of the state of Veracruz increased more than sixfold.[15] The rural population, which accounted for 72 percent of the total population in the state in 1930, now stands at 40 percent of the total. Veracruz, situated on the Gulf of Mexico coast, is predominantly an agricultural state, with milk and other dairy products and meat as its most important produce. The Department of Commerce and Industry of Mexico reported that in Veracruz activities in the primary sector declined considerably between 1940 and 1970. In 1940 nearly 72 percent of all workers in this state engaged in activities related to agriculture; in 1970 the figure was 53 percent, and it is expected to further decrease and reach 45 percent by 1980. The tertiary sector recorded a notable increase and so did the secondary sector, led by petroleum-related activities.[16]

Tabasco, another gulf state, is the newest PEMEX domain. Tabasco is rich in agricultural assets and grows a variety of tropical and semitropical crops. The state is largely rural and cultivates plantain, bananas, cocoa, sugarcane, and aquatic products. Sixty-three percent of the total economically active population in the state is involved in agriculture-related activities; 13.6 percent engage in secondary and 23.3 percent in tertiary sector activities.[17] By 1975 the state had nearly 8,000 petroleum-related industries, a 25 percent increase over 1965. At the time of the 1970 census, 80 percent of the state was rural in character.

In these two states, the female labour force recorded a decrease in size between 1960 and 1970. Much of this decline occurred in agricultural states like Tabasco and Veracruz. The dates are significant in that they correspond to the years of increased activity by PEMEX, to the establishment of the *maquiladoras* (mostly textiles and electronics) as well as to the great migration toward the *Distrito Federal* (Mexico City). Female labour in the total agriculture and fisheries labour force accounted for 11 percent nationwide in 1960; by 1970 the proportion was reduced to 5 percent. In areas where petroleum industries are established female labour turned to the service sector and sought employment in domestic work, street vending, and even prostitution. Yet another traditional sector that has suffered due to increased activity in the petroleum industries is the craft industry, which is mostly home-based and uses clay, parchment, textiles, dyes, and folk items. Even though no accurate statistics exist, it is safe to assume that one-fourth of all rural women participate in handicrafts and cottage industries of one kind or another.

The history of PEMEX in Tabasco is important because of the social and economic consequences of its presence for the people of the region. The prime agricultural lands of Tabasco have been bought by PEMEX from peasants at prices that are considerably below the market value. The exciting discoveries, the arrival of technology, and the subsequent industrialization have adversely affected the local people, their abilities to earn income, their environment, and their families. The arrival of petroleum technology first deprives men and women of their land and therefore, their sustenance, and second, relegates them to the ranks of the unemployed. PEMEX usually takes its men and its equipment wherever it goes. The purpose of this is to maintain political as well as technological control. In addition, the sudden spurt of activities (both technological and construction) and the super-salaries that PEMEX pays for site jobs have driven the cost of living far above the reach of the people of the region: The prices of essential items, such as food, clothing, housing, heating, lighting, etc., tripled in the case of Veracruz and doubled in the case of Tabasco between 1966 and 1976. This situation has put women in Tabasco in a triple bind. They have lost their land to PEMEX, which will not hire them and whose presence has caused the prices of necessities to rise beyond their reach. According to a uniquely Mexican tradition, whose roots are to be sought in the *machismo* mentality, men, when they find that they are unable to support their families, often simply desert them. The number of women-headed families has increased since the arrival of technology in Tabasco, though there are no hard data available, mostly because women are unwilling to admit that their husbands have left them. Women and girls find employment selling wares—including their bodies—to men who come with PEMEX leaving their families elsewhere and who have surplus funds to indulge in whatever pleases them. PEMEX admits in its internal studies that these types of social and economic distress have occurred; however, it tries to defend its activities to the public. In recent months disputes between the people of Tabasco and PEMEX have brought several adverse effects of the presence of oil recovery, processing, and refining technologies out in the open. The environmental damage has yet to be assessed; in the meantime, sulphur is accumulating on the surface of the awakening oil land, and its effect on human health and ecology awaits manifestation.

Despite the claim made by PEMEX and supported by statistics, spot surveys indicated that there has been a drop in female literacy in Tabasco as more and more children are suffering the consequences of their families' becoming increasingly despondent and dislocated. To the proponents of growth through oil these troubles and distresses have the function of a Greek chorus, with its antiphons and laments on the side, while economic development will emerge as the ultimate truth.

The Impact of Offshore Assembly Plants (Maquiladoras) on Women in Mexico

The *maquiladoras* are the direct outcome of the Border Industrialization Program (BIP), which was initiated by the Mexican government in 1965 and began operating in 1971 with the following objectives:

- to create new and more jobs;
- to create better incomes;

- to raise the levels of industrial skills; and
- to reduce the country's trade deficit by supplying locally produced components for assembly plants.

The *maquiladora* operations aim at the exportation of assembled consumer products. It was hoped that the wage differentials on either side of the border and export duty exemptions would act to pull U.S. investments and modern technologies into Mexico.

The results of the program have yet to be studied for their full implications for the Mexican people. Obvious trends, such as migration, growth of service industries, and the worsening employment situation, are more readily analyzed than the widespread social consequences of these programs, not only for the border *municipios* but for the country as a whole. There is an urgent need to empirically determine the implications of the *maquiladoras* program. The industrial expansion has contributed to the considerable population growth of the Mexican border municipalities. The population growth rates in the border cities are higher than the national average.[18] (See Table 4.4.)

At this juncture, it is important to explain the outbreak of the *maquiladora* phenomenon in Mexico. The Spanish term *maquiladora* has been translated to mean "offshore" assembly plants located at some distance from the main operating unit of an industrial enterprise. According to the Mexican customs code, a *maquiladora* is an industrial operation whose machinery is imported and that exports its total production.[19] The Mexican government came up with the idea of the Border Industrialization Program (BIP) to create industrial jobs, improve labour skills, and help the country with its trade deficits.[20]

The offshore plants, which are always in search of cheaper labour elsewhere, are not stable aspects of the Mexican technological and economic evolution. They create a sporadic and seasonal demand for female labour through technological changes. The net effect of these offshore plants on women is negative. The disadvantages stemming from destitution, disorientation, the breakup of families, and the penury of migratory workers looking for jobs and not finding them, as well as losing the jobs they get every two months according to the whims and fancies of the runaway *maquiladoras* far outweigh any financial benefits of having jobs in these factories. The aggregate net picture for the area is even more severe when we consider the extravagant and wasteful consumer habits, the environmental damage due to sudden migratory pressures, male and female prostitution, gambling, alcohol, and drug abuse in the northern cities.

The arrival of the assembly plants has adversely affected agriculture and related activities in the border *municipios,* creating considerable

TABLE 4.4
Population of Border States and Border *Municipios* -- 1950,
1960, and 1970

	1950	1960	1970	Rates of Growth 1950-60	Rates of Growth 1960-70
Mexican Republic	25,791,071	34,923,129	48,313,438	3.1	3.3
Border States	3,762,963	5,541,100	7,912,930	4.0	3.6
Border *Municipios*	849,135	1,508,187	2,274,085	5.9	4.2

Source: Secretaría de Industria y Comercio, Dirección General de Estadística, Government of Mexico; Jorge A. Bustamante, "Maquiladoras: A New Phase of International Capitalism in Mexico's Northern Frontier" (paper presented at the Sixth National Meeting of the Latin American Studies Association, held in Atlanta, March 1976).

unemployment among older women. In the years between 1950 and 1970 there have been a steady decline of the economically active population involved in agriculture, some increase in industrial employment, and considerable increase in service-related activities. In other words, those who have left agriculture on account of one pressure or another are not absorbed in *maquiladoras* but rather are forced to get into service industries – the particular categories of which are described in a later section at some length. The decrease in primary activities and the increase in secondary and tertiary activities of the border industrial towns are higher than the respective national averages. (See Table 4.5.)

The *maquiladoras* hire mostly female labour and in some industries, such as electronics, 90 percent of the employees are women. This special situation offers rather unique insights into the social and economic environment in which women find themselves in a rapidly industrializing area that offers them more than equal opportunities for employment.

The facts about the plight of women in the *maquiladoras* are just beginning to emerge. The analysis of the situation is rendered especially difficult due to the lack of any kind of concepts, hypotheses, or theories on the question of women in production. Finding a job and holding it are in themselves such accomplishments that the question of working conditions is never raised by female employees.

Contrary to the great expectations of the host country, the *maquiladoras* have turned out to be the production arms of high-technology companies from across the border producing consumer goods for exportation only. They indulge in little or no dialogue as to

TABLE 4.5
Percentage of Economically Active Population of Border *Municipios*
-- 1950, 1960, and 1970

		1950	1960	1970
Republic of Mexico				
Agriculture		58.4	54.2	39.5
Industry		16.0	19.0	22.9
Services		21.4	26.1	31.8
Unspecified		4.2	.7	5.8
	Totals	100.0	100.0	100.0
Border Municipalities				
Agriculture		45.5	39.4	22.2
Industry		16.6	20.2	24.5
Services		31.5	37.6	46.1
Unspecified		6.4	2.8	7.2
	Totals	100.0	100.0	100.0

Source: Secretaría de Industria y Comercio, Dirección General de Estadística, Government of Mexico.

the social benefits of any of their projects for Mexico, effect little or no technology transfer, and clearly demonstrate their motives for being where they are to be purely financial. In other words, they are there merely to take advantage of the wage differentials between the two countries. Many *maquiladoras* at the border towns pay as low a wage as $3 per day, compared to the nearly $30 per day wage that they pay in the United States.[21] The facts that women in these plants are reluctant to unionize and are not adequately initiated to trade union bargaining methods are of very great interest to the *maquiladoras*—hence the preeminence in these factories of women, who are an "inexhaustible labour supply at 30 cents an hour."[22]

The government has not conceded that the economic impacts of the *maquiladoras* program have not been as predicted. The government had expected to promote employment through the creation of industrial jobs. Despite the new jobs, in the decade between 1960 and 1970 the border municipalities suffered from higher unemployment than the rest of the country. Nearly 54 percent of the total unemployed among the economically active population in the nation is to be found in Tijuana, Mexicali, and Ciudad Juarez—all border *municipios*. Both the employed and the unemployed in these regions are mostly migrants who have relinquished their work in the primary sector in favour of work in modern factories.

Women come to border towns from every state of the union, looking for jobs in modern industrial factories; men come mostly from Tabasco. This in itself is a very interesting fact, as Tabasco is experiencing a great economic boom through oil activities. Yet the men in that state, unable to find jobs with PEMEX, are moving northward.

According to 1970 Mexican census data, in the border municipalities the share of agricultural workers in the economically active population declined from 45.5 percent in 1950 to 22.2 percent in 1970 and is still declining. (See Table 4.5.) In the same years industry's share has increased, from 16.6 percent to 24 percent, as has that of services. Men and women have left agriculture for jobs in the assembly plants, and when they fail to find these jobs they turn to service jobs in the commercial, government, and domestic sectors rather than go back to their villages. This finding is supported by Uniquel et al[23] who pointed out that unlike the case of the industrially developed countries, in Mexico the increase in service industries indicates unemployment and underemployment as well as marginal employment. Although 90 percent of the assembly plant workers are women, there are more of them unemployed and underemployed as a result of the increased migration.

Mexican women have always worked to produce income and goods for the family and the community. In the rural areas, in agriculture and in crafts, women have always worked alongside men. Work in modern technology corporations is different. It is competitive, highly specialized without requiring special skills on the part of the women who work, and is organized in such a way that changes in personnel occur daily. In fact, no one is allowed to acquire any special skill because specialized workers would mean better salaries and the employers are not prepared for that.

For women who left the land because of subsistence conditions and exploitation, urban technology work is not any better. Although the exploiters are different, the exploitation is the same; only the relationship of land to the means of production has changed. New troubles and problems have been substituted for ancient forms of oppression and suffering. The supportive family and the familiar and sympathetic community are absent in the new scene; instead, young women find their neighbors ready to subject them to every type of abuse, including prostitution.

Unlike other industrialization programs in the country, where technological changes have led to some form of permanent employment opportunities and raising of technical skills of the local population as well as those of migrants, the *maquiladoras* have a gossamer quality to their comings and goings. They suddenly light up the place with activities and labour comes like moths to scorch themselves by dashing at the lights. Dr. Bustamente raised the following pertinent question of whether in fact "the *maquiladoras* have the degree of permanency and stability that would generate economic development and absorb the labour force that the industry has attracted to the large industrial centers."[24] The disappearance of Magnovo's and Packard-Bell from the border scene is an example of the kind of instability founded on wage differentials and partial production processes catering to exportation only. When the plants folded and left for home and elsewhere (in search of cheaper labour) practically overnight, most of the people who lost their jobs and therefore their sustenance were women. It has been estimated that as many as 5,000 women lost their jobs when these two companies left Mexico.

When their employers leave, women find it very hard to locate another job, as they are lacking in skills. The women are employed in the *maquiladoras* for specific tasks that involve fine and minute divisions of labour that result in the women doing highly repetitive jobs. The specialization includes no career training and certainly requires no skills – simply the ability to recognize items as they come through the assembly line and after completing the part of the assembly assigned, to send the same for further assembly or for repackaging – jobs exclusively done by women. This type of specialization is precisely the obstacle to finding new jobs. Bustamante argued that "no matter how high the level of training obtained in the *maquiladora* industry, the degree of specialization by the greater part of the piecework operation makes the recuperation of that type of training very relative, taking into account the technological development that exists in the 'permanent' industry in the rest of the country."[25]

In the clothing industry (*maquiladoras de ropa*) for example, the division of work is so detailed and specialized that often women work just putting one dot on a dress, making buttonholes, doing the bottom seamline, and the like. In other words, the same woman does the same job of putting a single dot on a dress all day long and everyday.[26]

Textiles is an area where the Mexican women have shown extraordinary creativity throughout history. Their particular sense of appreciation of color, of patterns, and styles have included centuries of cumulative knowledge of weaving, dyeing, design, and garment technologies. The *maquiladoras* are reversing this process and rendering skilled workers unskilled and uncreative in their own art. The Mexican government has tried to argue that the *maquiladoras* carried the potential of generating a transfer of technology and of turning peasants into skilled technicians. But in fact the *maquiladoras* require much less creative skill than is required in subsistence farming. The assembly plants are there in Mexico for the same reason for which old feudal systems existed – because of the plentiful supply of unskilled and semi-skilled labour.

The distribution of women in the industrial labour market has yet to be empirically studied in Mexico. In a country where working is a privilege, it is not surprising that women, particularly those in the labour categories, have little to say about production methods. The production standards for the *maquiladoras* are set in the United States. The electronics *maquiladoras* are organized by quotas of production and clothing by numbers of items produced. The advantage of highly organized technology whose industrial arm has extreme divisions of labour is that women get jobs. In fact such jobs are rarely open to men. The advantages to the industry are manifold, where the labour force consists predominantly of untrained and semiskilled women who have left their home villages for these jobs. The companies are able to bust unions, reduce salaries, and set new production standards every two weeks. The incentive system is based on how many items are assembled or worked upon. The female labourers, eager to please the employer, often find themselves working nonstop on these jobs.

The *maquiladoras* offer yet another insight into the economies of hiring women *instead* of men. The assembly plants are basically labour intensive and there is considerable evidence now that in situations of capital intensity women will not find jobs – as in the case of oils and fats within food processing, automated textiles production, electronic design, and oil refineries, to name a few. It is true that production is carried out with the assistance of high technology–intensive and therefore capital-intensive methods, but technology has played its part in worsening the conditions of women in development. The lowest-paying jobs are usually reserved for women; men are in the low-paying jobs only if they require physical strength, quality control, new machines, and supervision of men.

The wages and salaries that are earned by the women in these factories are still being paid in cash,[27] which is either recovered by their fathers, husbands, or boyfriends or immediately spent by the women themselves for the purchase of clothes, perfumes, and entertainment to satisfy their newly acquired tastes and the expectations of the modern factories to have women who are well dressed and fashionable working for them.

Social Consequences. The Secretary of Industry and Commerce made a proclamation in April 1975 describing the benefits to Mexico due to the existence of the *maquiladoras* program.[28] This is the general position: Out of the 453 *maquiladoras* in the entire country 416, or 92 percent, are located in the border municipalities. As of March 1978, they employed a total of 83,993 persons, with women's participation ranging from 75 percent on a national basis to 90 percent in some types of *maquiladoras* in the border *municipios*. They paid salaries totalling 1,267,196,000 pesos. The number of employed persons increased from 56,253 in 1975 to 83,993 in 1978. In the same years, the number of unemployed persons increased to 30,000 persons. These numbers compiled by the government's Department of Labour point out that the *maquiladoras* have offered excellent opportunities for women to work in modern technology-based industries. This situation of women getting jobs *instead* of men getting them raises a very important question of whether this is an advantage. In addition to the severe unemployment, underemployment, and growth problems the North is facing, social problems of extraordinary magnitude – related to drinking, prostitution, divorce, alienation, destitution, drug addiction, breakup of the family structure, and children without parents – have been unleashed on the border municipalities with strong *maquiladoras* programs.

A recent study done by the researchers at the Universidad Autonoma de Baja California revealed that nearly 76 percent of the women employees in privately controlled *maquiladoras* and 70 percent in cooperatives were under the age of thirty. Women between the ages of twenty and twenty-five are the most sought after; men and women over the age of forty have practically no chance of finding work in these modern industries.[29]

The implications of this situation alone are beginning to manifest themselves in every walk of life in these border towns. The modern factories interpret modern with being youthful and attractive – virtues venerated above all others in the United States and imported into Mexico by the offshore sources! In agriculture, crafts, and other traditional industries, women worked without regard to their age and appearance. In fact, the *maquiladoras* do not pay any attention to the women's mind, her intelligence, educational qualifications, or skills.

The unemployed male population presents serious problems. Many of them work as pimps and as male prostitutes. Tijuana, Mexicali, Ciudad Juarez, and Nuevo Laredo all offer different facets of the same problem. The hotels in these cities have become centers of prostitution and cater to the exploitation of women and men as prostitutes by tourists from both sides of the border. Women from the ages of eight to eighty are drawn into the prostitution industry in order to sustain themselves. The Mexican government, overwhelmed by the employment statistics and so-called economic growth indicators, has yet to take a look at this devastation of the human body, mind, and dignity in the name of "modernization."

Modern industry has effectively destroyed the traditional family structure and has offered nothing in its place. Alien values of each for himself/herself, supreme faith in the power of money, and the worship of youth and physical attractiveness have suddenly confronted the peasantry of Mexico in these big border towns; the result is degeneration of spirit, demoralization of values, loss of self respect, and suicides.

The working conditions prevailing in these *maquiladoras* have not been adequately investigated by the government. Even though we are in the twentieth century, the bitter realities of technological awakening in Mexico are quite reminiscent of conditions in Victorian England. The "song of spirit" heard in the Mexican northern border is not "ringing grooves of change" of better social and economic opportunities for women, because when we ask the questions "How much intellect represented, How much imagination, How much learning, How much express the great progress of the country, And what sort of conclusion to human happiness and self expression?"[30] The answers tell us negative stories. The work in these factories is often exploitative and repetitive and entails boredom due to the extreme division of labour. The companies explain that they employ women "because they work well," "they are patient," "they are attentive," "they do not join unions," and "they have delicate fingers for assembling minute electronic parts." In other words, the reasons for employing them in modern high technology companies are the same reasons for which they are excluded from training, technical responsibilities, and high-paying jobs. The women who work in the *maquiladoras* do not grow into progressively responsible positions or accumulate technical and administrative skills. In the textile *maquiladoras*, the average time that women hold these jobs is estimated to be about two months.[31]

Although piecemeal research is going on, an organized and well-articulated effort toward empirically determining the role of *maquiladoras* in migration and the unemployment situation, and its impact on women, cultural values, sex roles, family structure, and identity has long been needed. How much blame is due to technology in all of this will depend on how and under what conditions technology has come in and how it is being *controlled. The shape rather than the size of technological investments* needs to become the central aspect of any investigation of the impact of technology on women. Machines being the chief technological input, the study of design and manufacturing processes is an equally important aspect of the investigation.

8. Some General Conclusions

In general terms finding jobs in modern industries for women depends on the size of the male labour force and the availability of child care facilities.[32] But in Mexico's northern bordertowns, women's employment has not depended on these factors because women are employed *instead* of men and the day care situation of the children is carefully avoided by industries that prefer to hire unmarried young women and constantly keep their labour force in a state of perpetual youth by changing workers quite often.

Despite the general ill effects of the *maquiladoras,* direct investigation revealed that the women who are working in these plants are happy to have their jobs. The young women in these factories enjoy the money they get, which is considerably more than the monthly wages of 500 to 1,000 pesos that most of these women are used to making. In traditional textile industries a woman often spends a whole month to make one item that is sold for less than 150 pesos – making that sum their monthly earnings. The same woman has the opportunity to make as much as 3,000 pesos per month in a modern textile *maquiladora.* The peasant girls seem to like the new style of living, which caters to their fanciful spending on consumer goods. More importantly they like having jobs that are not home-based[33] and therefore have a certain "status" attached to them. The image of working in a modern technology-based industry is greatly pleasing to them *even though the job has all the trappings of a traditional industry without its benefits.* The migration to the north as well as the preference by women for factory jobs in all urban centers in Mexico has had an important effect on the domestic service market. The few who remain to be maids are in a better bargaining position and their salaries have doubled in the last five years.

Although there is reason to believe that the celebration of the International Women's Year in Mexico raised the level of consciousness as to the place of women in society, the government seems to have relegated the normative dimensions of needed change entirely to the individual consciousness of the people rather than through deliberate and well-articulated policy measures. At the time of this writing Mexican public policy toward technology is mostly concerned with technology investments, expenditures, and employment, and little concern is being shown for the impact of technology and technical changes on people. The government seems so concerned about its economic goals and so devoted to the idea of work that it has hardly noticed the worker who, with the arrival of technology, is fast turning into a mere wage-slave entirely at the mercy of industries.

9. Policy Considerations

Based on the analysis of the impact of selected technologies on women as well as the role of women in science in Mexico, this study concludes that:

- Technological change can be important in improving the status of women and facilitating their equal integration in development. Integration of women in technological development would be a qualitative step, which does not merely domesticate women in economic activities, but helps them to attain a scientific world view and a share in conceptualizing ideas and tools for human progress.

- The specific issues related to women and science are parts of the general question of class, subgroup, and individual involvement in policies and practices of science and technology for development. How the benefits due to technology are distributed depends on how technology is conceived in relation to classes, subgroups, and individuals and is directly proportional to the degree and nature of their acceptance and participation.

- At present there are no set goals, no stated objectives, no plans of action, and no enumeration of resource allocations specifically linked to institutional arrangements to facilitate adequate and equitable distribution of the benefits of science to women in Mexico. There are no specific policies and programs which seek to *increase* the number of women in science, to *raise* their level of participation in policy, or to *improve* the qualifications of women in scientific and technological professions.

- Mexican science policy shows too much concern for the benefits of technologies to be introduced and too little concern for the impact of already existing technologies (local, imported, and offshore) on the various classes and subgroups in the Mexican economy and society.

- The linkages among variables, such as investment in science and technology and the institutional arrangements for solving the critical social and economic problems of the vast majority of the people in Mexico, are not clearly identified as of now and therefore, how technology affects women in raising their real income and improving their participation in productive labour has yet to be studied empirically.

- The Mexican government fully recognizes the role of technology in creating employment opportunities for all its people. The basis of the government's belief is the capital-oriented labour market theory, which traditionally has severely and adversely affected the interests of semi-skilled and low-skilled workers and women. Humanization of work and the equitable distribution of the "results of work"[34] do not receive much attention from policy planners.

- Investments—both domestic and those of transnational corporations—have resulted in the production of consumer goods, capital-intensive, and other technologies that are not responsive to the needs of the vast majority of the people, especially women. Consequently, planning for change with the help of technology has further exacerbated the development gap between men and women and has allowed special interest groups to consolidate their already powerful social and economic position in Mexican society. The international investments in the border towns of Mexico in the *maquiladoras* have not been realistically evaluated with regard to their social impact and to their employment policies of hiring women *instead* of men.

- How we define science and technology affects what conclusions are reached about their impacts on society. If technology is understood as a body of systematized, variable information that can be transferred, women who work in technology-based industries in Mexico are not the recipients of engineering know-how connected to design and manufacturing process.

- Special turn-key projects that are conducive to extensive transfer of design and manufacturing instructions, training, and management information to facilitate participation by Mexican women in control and production decisions are necessary. At this time training is not being equally channeled to all workers but only to men.

- National research policy continues to be a traditional, somewhat esoteric science and technology policy. Research is often evaluated on the basis of where and how it is being conducted rather than what its social purposes are; hence the failure to deal with the question of women's role in science as an integral part of the general human resources question in science and technology policy.

- Mexican women have received limited career suggestions. To counteract this trend, preparation for careers must take place early in life. Continuing education, re-education and work-time education, improving infrastructure vitality and effectiveness by increasing understanding of the meaning of work redefined on the basis of constantly improving technology of process and production are urgently needed.

- The question of what is the appropriate mix of policies, technologies, and development planning that will lessen the country's socioeconomic stresses and afford opportunities for equitable achievements in skills and income between men and women needs immediate attention.

- Major theoretical and practical efforts are needed to delineate responsibilities to be assumed by public policy and to identify the instruments by which institutional arrangements are reorganized to include women in the processes and benefits of science in the evaluation of technology – its appropriateness, design and processes, methods and controls.

- Outside the government, appraisal of existing scientific advancements and technological processes is limited to a few sociological research studies, which are few and far between. No attempt is being made to systematically study the impact of industrial work on women, the susceptibility to monotony in high-technology assembly plants, and the double bind that women face by being speed-workers in modern factories combined with child-bearing, child-rearing, food-gathering, and food-maintenance tasks at home.

- There are special methodological and statistical difficulties that inhibit the utilization of empirical social research. The information and issues encountered by public policy concerned with women and science are at present "circumstantial" rather than "analytic."[35] There is also the problem of the scale of analysis, which deals with aggregates and indicates that trade-offs are present but does not differentiate as to the groups, subgroups, institutions, and individuals involved or who is trading what for what.

- The aggregate and average measures tell us that shifts are occurring in the female labour market but they do not highlight the trends in the interface between industrial technology-based and traditional sources of employment for women. Thus agriculture, a significant domestic and export industry with tremendous possibilities for the deployment of the "genius" of Mexican labour technologies and innovation, is increasingly the recipient of residual labour that is unable to find jobs in a modern factory.

- The factories' antiquated custom of paying salaries in cash places women in a position in which their pay is taken by the men in the family. Women have little opportunity to save, invest, or even make decisions as to how their pay is to be expended.

- The few studies that are being undertaken on the effect of industrial work and modern technologies on women are relegated entirely to social science research and are almost never included in technology assessment. This kind of inner logic present among decision makers has allowed public policy to define development programmes in terms of mechanical increases of technology without regard to its impact on women, whether they relate to birth control, packaged foods, chemical fertilizers, household appliances, or industrial employment.

- At present, no mechanism exists that orients science policy processes toward planned observations, changes in institutional practices, feedback information, innovative action programs, and creative interventions to achieve greater participation by women in the benefits and processes of science and technology.

Notes

The information on PEMEX Mexico was in part derived from an earlier study undertaken while holding an appointment as a Fellow at the Center for International Affairs, Harvard University, 1977–1978.

1. Consejo Nacional de Ciencia y Tecnología, *Mexico's Program for Science and Technology 1978–1982*, October 1978.

2. Dirección General de Población 1970.

3. These conclusions were reached based on extensive interviews with Viviane de Marquez from El Colegio de México, who has researched data in connection with her empirical study of firms.

4. Definitions adopted from the U.S. National Science Foundation Document No. NSF 58-24.

5. The phrase is from a poem entitled, "To Irons Founders and Others," by Gordon Bottomely (1874).

6. *Mexico's Program for Science and Technology 1978–1982.*

7. Jorge Crisse B. in his paper "Mitología de la Feminidad" in the book *Opresión y Marginalidad de la Mujer en el orden Social Machista*, ed. by Ander Egg et al. (Humanities Argentina, 1976), pp. 115–117; Evelyn P. Stevens, "Mexican Machista Politics and Value Orientation," *Western Political Quarterly*, Vol.

28, No. 3. September 1965, pp. 848–857; Samuel Ramos, *Profile of Men and Culture in Mexico*, translated by Peter G. Earl (Austin: University of Texas Press, 1962).

8. For a succinct analysis of religious stereotypes in Mexican society see Aurelia Gpe. Sanchez M.: "Archetypes and Religious Stereotypes: Their Impact on Man-Woman Relations," *Boletin Documental Sobre Las Mujeres* (Coordinación de Iniciativas Para el Desarrollo Humano de America Latina [CIDAL], Cuerna Vaca), October 1974.

9. Octavio Paz, *The Labyrinth of Solitude* (New York: Grove Press, 1961), p. 108.

10. See Kurt Unger, "Food Manufacturing in Mexico and Technological Dimension for Policy Making: Some Observations and Suggestions," paper sponsored by the International Development Research Center (Canada) and the Instituto Tecnología y de Estudios Superiores de Monterrey, January 1979.

11. A.F. Albarran N., J. Gil M., A. Guarda et al, *La Electrónica en México: El Sector Privado*, National Autonomous University of Mexico, November 1976.

12. *Mexico's Program for Science and Technology 1978–1982.*

13. Ibid.

14. A number of studies have established the dynamic relationship between economic growth and per capita energy consumption. See R. Krishna Prasad and A.K.N. Reddy, "Technology Alternatives and the Indian Energy Crisis," National Seminar on Energy, March 1976. Also, M. Srinivasan, "Shifts in Energy Consumption and Policy for Energy Development," unpublished paper prepared while at Center for International Affairs, Harvard University, 1978.

15. Repercusiones Socioeconomicas de la Expanción de la Indústria Petrólea; and Government of Mexico, *Censo de población 1960–1970.*

16. Ibid.

17. Government of Mexico, *Censo de población 1960–1970.*

18. According to Luis Uniquel et al. (*Desarrollo Urbano de México*, 1974), the growth is the outcome of external rather than internal factors. The authors point out that the border cities, where the tertiary sector is predominant, have recorded the highest rate of growth of 5.23 percent as opposed to the national average rate of 3.04 percent.

19. Article 321, Mexican Customs Code, Regulation of October 31, 1972.

20. The *Wall Street Journal* of May 25, 1976 quoted Mr. Octaviano Campos Salas, the Minister of Industry and Commerce, as saying the following: "The idea is to offer an alternative to Hong King, Japan and Puerto Rico for free enterprise."

21. Jorge A. Bustamente: "Maquiladoras: A New Face of International Capitalism in Mexico's Northern Frontier," paper presented at the Sixth National Meeting of the Latin American Studies Association, Atlanta, Georgia, March 1976, p. 23.

22. Ibid.

23. Uniquel et al., op. cit.

24. Bustamente, op. cit., p. 17.

25. Ibid., p. 17.

26. Monica Gambrill, a researcher working in this area with El Colegio de Mexico, points out that of all the textile industries in the border states only one *maquiladora* in Tijuana produces the entire item; all the others work to produce parts of garments.

27. According to the ancient law still on the books, which states," Hay que pagar con dinero contante y sonante" (Money Must Sound), workers in factories are being paid by cash rather than by check.

28. Secretaria de Indústria Comercio, *La Frontera Norte: Diagnóstico y Perspectivas,* April 1975, pp. 112–113.

29. Maria Antonieta Vigorita Parente and Norma A. Escamilla Moreno, "La Condición Actual de las Oberas en las Maquiladoras de Ropa," Universidad Autonomía de Baja California, Mexicali, June 1978.

30. *Letters of Charles Dickens,* ed. by Walter Dexter (Nonesuch Press, 1938). The questions are somewhat taken out of context but they are pertinent to any technology.

31. Estimates obtained through direct investigation.

32. Irene Tinker, "The Adverse Impact of Development on Women," in *Women and World Development,* ed. by Irene Tinker and Michele Bo Bramsen (Washington, D.C.: Overseas Development Council, 1976).

33. Vladimir Lenin has argued in many of his writings on women's place in world development that so long as women are excluded from socially productive work and are restricted to housework, which is private, women can never be emancipated. Lenin generally held cottage industries to be one of the outstanding causes for the lack of progress in women's status in prerevolutionary Russia.

34. See U. Engelen-Kefer, "Arbeitsorientierte Interessen als Grundlegung gewerkschaftlicher Strategien im Rahmen einer emanzipatorischen Gesellschaftspolitik," *WSI Mitteilungen (Cologne),* April 1973.

35. The concept is borrowed from Harold D. Lasswell's "Some Perplexities of Police Theory," *Social Research,* Volume 41, No. 1, Spring 1974, p. 183. The phrases are taken somewhat out of context but all the same they explain the important difference between what are central issues and what are not.

APPENDIX

Like most cultures, Mexican culture considers decency, honesty, modesty, chastity, piety, and endurance as exemplary qualifications for its women. In addition, the ancient Mexicans also saw *strength* as an important quality for women. In the matriarchical society of pre-Spanish Mexico, the art and science of plant breeding and animal domestication rested with women. Early in history, women became the sustainers of Mexican society, a role in which they continue now in many instances. The Spanish conquest of the country superimposed the patriarchical, male-dominated culture of the conquerors, whose *machista* values took away women's honoured role as the sustainer, substituting in its place the role of an appendage whose duties largely consisted of pleasing their husbands and rearing children at the upper levels of society and in addition to the above, of working as drudge labourers inside and outside their homes at the lower levels.

In order to determine how technology affects the women of Mexico it is important to assess how it is affecting these individual layers as well as the collective and cumulative psyche of the nation with respect to women. An important orientation is the understanding of the position of occidental culture and its overlap in Mexican society. This orientation is especially important because the process of assimilation is incomplete and is still proceeding in the set patterns of yesteryear, now with the assistance of technology. The occidental is patriarchical, male-oriented, dominant; the other one is completely silent and passive. The modern organization of Mexican society is very much the sociopolitical *cacicazgo* system in which the Spaniards made local arrangements and concluded informal contractual agreements, giving recognition to the *cacicazgo* and assurances of noninterference in the indigenous status quo in return for recognition as the ruler and power-in-charge of the resources—human and natural—of the country. Despite the noninterference agreement, Spanish culture came to be looked upon as a superior culture to be imitated by the Indians. The constantly evolving social acculturation involves (1) the Indians of Mexico, (2) the *mestizo* (the child of the Indian), (3) the creole (the child of the Spaniard), and (4) the Spaniard. To the indigenous people, females represented the origin of the species; to the conquerors males meant potential and power. The *mestizo*, the child of the Indian through the Spaniard, venerated his/her father as power and authority while looking to the mother for education in the ways of art, craft, and survival.

On the other hand, the creole, the child of the Spaniard through the Indian, dominated the political power spectrum and promoted and maintained the institutions, systems, and values of the Spaniard. The church became the protector of the Indians and the mediator between the Spaniards and the Indians, now playing the role of the peacemaker, now that of the intimidator of both sides by striking awe and fear into the hearts of the followers.

The missionaries brought the bleeding Christ forever on the crucifix, striking at once violence and awe in the men; and the missionaries also brought along the Virgin Mary – the Mother of God who was forever silent, serene, enduring, and suffering. The Virgin of Guadalupe, the very picture of passive nonviolence, always holding her child in her hand, is perhaps the best explanation of the supreme duties of women in Mexico, namely, child bearing and rearing. The church became the protector of the weak and the destitute against the oppressor and in the process further confirmed the woman's position in society as a weak (nevertheless virtuous) damsel needing protection for life and charged her with the sacred duty of child bearing and rearing, keeping the family together at all costs, and educating her sons in the *machista* tradition.

This multiplicity of philosophies, values, notions, and practices has successfully fixed her position in society, work, family, and politics. The intelligence for survival and the consequent genius for adaptation that Mexican women always had have been compromised to their low position in society. Women's ancient roles as creative and innovative members of the family and community who made things happen are principles vastly understated not only by outsiders doing research on Mexican women, but by Mexicans themselves. This is the backdrop against which science and technology and their impact on women have to be evaluated.

5
The Power of Persistence: Consciousness Raising at International Fora—The Case of UNCSTD

Mildred Robbins Leet

Persistence—perseverance—pertinacity. They all start with the prefix "per", meaning "through," meaning "the route by which." This chapter will recount a year's effort to raise the consciousness of women and men to the imperative to integrate women into the planning and decision-making processes of development, most particularly in regard to the utilization of science and technology.

It all started when the nongovernmental organizations (NGOs) in consultative status with the United Nations Economic and Social Council (ECOSOC) set up a committee for the UN Conference on Science and Technology for Development (UNCSTD) with task forces to consider items not adequately dealt with in the UNCSTD preparatory papers. Asked to form the Task Force on the Roles of Women in Science and Technology for Development, I called on many professionals—scientists, technologists, economists, sociologists, and anthropologists—and the first meeting of the Task Force[1] was convened on August 1, 1978.

It was agreed after much discussion that a priority of the Task Force would be to add an item on women to the UNCSTD agenda. This decision did not come easily, as there were differing opinions as to whether emphasis should be put on the ultimate goal of the integration of women and men into developmental projects, or on the immediate need to introduce the aspirations, rights, and expectations of women into the consciousness and priorities of decision makers. The importance of having an item on the agenda is that it may trigger new thinking and discussions in many countries and may affect the preparation of national position papers.

In order to further the consideration of an agenda item on women, the following letter was sent by the Task Force on August 14 to UN delegations, 130 UNCSTD national focal points, national women's groups, NGOs, UN Secretariat members, and other parties:

> Because women play a pivotal role in the agricultural and trade activities of many countries; because they have more recently been displaced by technology with unfortunate social and economic effects; because often women have not had ready access to education, training, or involvement in the various decisionmaking processes, it was felt that a specific item on women should be considered at the UNCSTD Conference in order to develop a more realistic program for the third development decade, for the scientific and technological input into a new international economic order, and for consideration at the World Conference of the UN Decade for Women – 1980.
>
> At the first Task Force meeting, we developed the following suggested item for the agenda:
>
> "Methods of creating social-economic environments in which science and technology policies will actively and equally involve and benefit women. . ."
>
> We await your comments and would welcome your assistance in bringing it to the attention of interested parties so that the hope for an agenda item on women becomes a reality.

There were encouraging responses from various women's groups around the world. Affirmative responses were received from many delegations, with three countries – Norway, Nigeria, and Zambia – offering to introduce the item at the Third Preparatory Conference that was scheduled for September.

These responses raised our expectations, for only national delegates may introduce items on the conference floor. In order to reinforce the possibility, forty members of various voting blocs, including the Group of 77, the Nordic bloc, the European bloc, and the socialist bloc, were personally contacted. Meeting pivotal delegates prior to group meetings can make acceptance easier.

Unfortunately, things didn't progress that smoothly for long. The Third Preparatory Conference was postponed until January. The UN's 33rd General Assembly convened, and UNCSTD was placed on the agenda of the Second Committee. More and more of the delegates became uneasy about introducing a new item in that forum. Calls for more specific documentation as to the need for the agenda item by delegates led to the preparation of a seven-page resolution that included these substantive points:

> . . .that ESCAP [Economic and Social Commission for Asia and the Pacific] and ECA [Economic Commission for Africa] estimate that women provide 60–80% of the agricultural labor in Asia and Africa; in

Latin America, according to ECLA [Economic Commission for Latin America], the figure is 40%.[2]

. . .that the extent to which women contribute to the economy of developing countries should be evaluated not only through their direct
• participation in the labour force, but also through their indirect labour input as offered free of cost within the family unit of production.[3]

. . .that the ECA Training and Research Centre for Women, UNICEF, UNDP, UNESCO, FAO [Food and Agriculture Organization], and the World Bank have planned activities and studies for the development, promotion, and improvement of village-level, low-cost technologies available to women, in order to enhance their contribution to economic life,[4] and

. . .that the ILO contribution[5] to the African Regional Meeting on UNCSTD stated: "Women and technology as a dimension in the development process has remained virtually an unexplored territory. That the subject is important as an 'issue' may be gathered from the fact that for the first time this item is appearing on the agenda of a preparatory UN Meeting, with a view to further investigation in UNCSTD in 1979."

This document was circulated to all delegations on October 17, 1978, and at the suggestion of another delegate, it was reduced to a succinct, one-page draft resolution[6] and recirculated on November 7.

Unfortunately, the idea of an agenda subitem on women did not seem as appealing in November as it had in August. The Group of 77 felt that "it would be opening up the Agenda to other extraneous items," that "it would be like opening up a Pandora's Box," and that "it would be inappropriate to bring it up at the Second Committee." Perhaps this feeling had already been verbalized in September when a South American delegate said, "the Group of 77 were not interested in the sectoral approach, but rather in a general approach; they did not want to talk about population, energy, environment, or women, but rather about how everything is inter-related. Their common interest is in the establishment of a new international economic order where they are not in a state of dependence, but in a state of equity."[7]

With little chance for the agenda item to be accepted, a mailing was sent on November 28, 1978, to all the permanent missions of the UN member nations in New York, stressing the need to integrate the issue of women in scientific-technological development into the Draft Programme of Action and expressing the hope that the respective governments shared the concern expressed by the governments of Denmark, Finland, Iceland, Norway, Sweden, and the United States and would communicate this concern to the Secretary-General of UNCSTD.

Attached to that mailing were the statements of the United

States Representative and the Norwegian Representative to the UN General Assembly's Second Committee regarding UNCSTD (both dated November 24, 1978) and the Cairo Statement of the ILO,[8] which made mention of three specific problems:

> First, reference has been made to the unequal access of women to the formal education and training, especially in scientific and technical skills in the modern sector, reinforced by the omission to incorporate women in agricultural training programmes, projects, and training schemes. Secondly, some evidence has been examined from the multi-dimensional activities that women continue to "manage" the subsistence economy (with or without skills) with "traditional" techniques (new technology frequently aiding men's work). Finally, it has been shown from examples of some industries – modern and traditional – that the introduction of new techniques, in a shifting occupational hierarchy, continues to displace women in low skill, low productivity jobs. This process deprives them of the opportunities of upgrading their skills and acquiring technological know-how.

Shortly after, on December 1, 1978, The Task Force decided to develop a Background Discussion Paper on the Roles of Women for UNCSTD – after determining that no one else was preparing one, and that there was a need to submit one at the third session of the Third Preparatory Committee. Preparation time was limited to two weeks; each member was asked to formulate a one-page paper focusing on a critical issue of concern. With the Task Force responding enthusiastically and promptly, and with Barbara Walton as editor, the document[9] was completed within the ten-page limitation. The paper was distributed on December 20.

While working with the UN delegates and the UN and UNCSTD secretariats, the Task Force also worked closely with the NGO Forum, whose first effort was a week-long meeting from September 25 to September 30, 1978. More than 250 women and men participated in the seminar on the "Roles of Women in Science and Technology for Development," and many ideas for future action surfaced.

The meeting was opened with a message from Margaret Mead, who was unable to attend, but who said,

> women should be particularly concerned with what role they can have in shaping decisions that affect all human beings – men, women, and children – not only with their own status. They should emphasize that it is a great loss for *everyone* when women, whether professionally, or experientially trained, are barred from participating meaningfully in the decision-making process, be it at the traditional historic locus of the

household and village or at international deliberations about global problems. It is important to pressure international agencies to include more women at every level of planning; to emphasize the importance of low and intermediate technology (which sometimes may need to be manufactured in developing countries); and to insist on a great deal more higher education in the country itself, rather than on sending young people abroad for inappropriate technical and scientific education.

Another speaker was Michaela Walsh, Chairperson of the Committee to Organize Women's World Banking, who stressed that we must find new technologies and new institutional processes that involve the shared responsibility of everyone who is affected by decisions about our global resources. She said that

> a group of us have been working to create a new mechanism which will encourage women's participation in money-generating activities of their societies. It is designed as an opportunity for all women to become directly involved in their economies by helping to support the development of enterprises and techniques which are compatible with their own values and those of their families. We believe this mechanism—Women's World Banking—can be one of the first steps toward encouraging women to take responsibility together and giving them a voice in the decisions concerning our futures.

The other speaker, Lindawe Vilakati, Manager of the Entonjeni Women's Project in Swaziland, had been educated in both the United States and England. She elected to return to her own country because, she said, "there is so much that has to be done." She said she has adapted her learning to the needs of the villagers, applying ingenuity and intuition to solve problems that the village women have expressed. Together they work out solutions—sometimes simply, as with a solar food dryer, at other times with a bit more trial and error, as with a new kind of stove or roof. She described these innovations graphically, stressing the importance of relating technology to the culture of the community.

At that same seminar, the four recommendations that had been developed by the Task Force were circulated with the hope that they would be brought to the attention of other international nongovernmental organizations for signature and that they could then serve as inputs into the UNCSTD Programme of Action.

Two were recommendations directed at the national level of policymaking: "Data Gathering and Distribution" and "Systems for Education and Training." One was a recommendation directed at the regional level of policymaking: "Arrangements for Common Training Centers." One was a recommendation directed at the international level of policymaking: "Research and Development Needs of Developing Countries." These four recommendations were ultimately sponsored by nineteen international NGOs[10] and by January 1979, they were circulated to the delegates at the third session of the Preparatory Committee together with the Background Discussion Paper on Women.

When the UNCSTD finally convened in August 1979 in Vienna, the Working Group on Science and Technology and the Future established by the plenary of the conference took these documents into account in its deliberations. They were also distributed as UN documents BP/NGO/18 and BP/NGO/17, respectively.

While the Preparatory Committee was meeting at UN headquarters in New York in January, a distinguished group of scientists was meeting in Singapore in cooperation with the Advisory Committee on the Application of Science and Technology to Development (ACAST) for the International Symposium on Science and Technology for Development. Having learned that a few women were to participate, I sent copies of the Task Force's Background Paper to them. Dr. Bolanle Awe of Nigeria provided the leadership, for she not only distributed the paper at all the meetings, but worked hard to ensure that the final conference report reflected the discussions about women that were held in the workshops.

After that meeting, Dr. Awe and I began a correspondence, and she was able to accept the invitation of the NGO Forum Planning Meeting and travel to Vienna in April 1979 to participate. Funds were raised to bring both men and women from developing countries to the forum. For example, ten women were sponsored by the Netherlands; selection was delegated to the International Association of University Women.

Again at the third session of the Preparatory Committee in January 1979, the need for constant vigilance was apparent: The resolution on "Women and Development and International Conferences,"[11] which had been adopted by the UN Economic and Social Council on May 25, 1978,[12] was being overlooked.

Persistent political action, however, brought about the inclusion of the substance of the ECOSOC resolution in the UNCSTD Annotated Agenda.[13] The ECOSOC called upon governments to ensure "(a) that women are involved in the planning stages of international conferences (including UNCSTD) and are included in the governmental delegations attending the conferences; (b) that the topic of women and development is included within the substantive discussions of the conferences (including UNCSTD) and, where appropriate, is considered as a separate agenda item," and requested that a report of the conference related to these items be communicated to the 1980 session of the ECOSOC Commission on the Status of Women and to the World Conference of the UN Decade for Women to be held in Copenhagen in 1980.

Two NGO statements were made to the delegates at that session of the Preparatory Committee, one by Chairman Karim Ahmed on behalf of the NGO subcommittee preparing for the NGO Forum, which drew attention to areas of concern missing from the Programme of Action, among them the roles of women. The other was an NGO Statement on the Roles of Women in Science and Technology for Development, which drew attention once again to the need for a subitem on women, as well as to the one place in the UNCSTD Secretariat's Programme of Action[14] where women were mentioned. A suggestion was made for improvement in that section dealing with policy for human resources and their utilization. Item 31 cited "women," but only in parentheses in the following statement: "Developing countries should, in their programmes for training the national labour force, make special provision to increase the productivity of low-income groups and enable people who have been prevented from exploiting their full potential (e.g. women) to play their full role in society." Elimination of the parentheses and the substitution of the word "particularly" for "e.g." was suggested. The Nordic countries also made this point in their statement.

When the revised Draft Programme of Action appeared for consideration before the fourth session of the Preparatory Committee in April/May 1979, we were delighted to see that the suggestion had been accepted. However, the entire paragraph was subsequently deleted because of the intervention of a woman delegate who questioned its need, as she said, "Women in the Third World are not discriminated upon. Look at me."

At the opening meeting of the third session of the Preparatory Committee, the Secretary-General of the conference expressed his personal view that pilot projects that were action-oriented and global in impact should be developed. We expressed the hope that one project would be developed to assess the impact of science and technology on women and their roles in the developmental process. This idea was pursued by the Task Force, as well as at a meeting convened by the American Association for the Advancement of Science in March 1979.[15] A number of suggested projects emerged, one of which was presented at an ACAST-sponsored symposium in Mexico City and subsequently circulated among the delegates to UNCSTD in Vienna.

During the third session of the Preparatory Committee we were able to suggest certain items for inclusion in the Programme of Action as a result of consultations with a number of delegations. Norway was particularly active. These suggestions were circulated and were subsequently included in country recommendations to the secretary-general of the conference.

The sections involved follow, with the changes italicized:

Target area I

1.9. Developing countries should also share among themselves information and experience in the most relevant fields such as agriculture, health and communications, *including the traditional technologies long practiced by women and men.*

1.12. The international community should promote personal contacts between the scientists and technologists of developed and developing countries through such means as conferences, meetings, visits and study tours, *through UN bodies, governments and non-governmental organizations.*

1.20. Research and development efforts of developed countries devoted to the problems of developing countries should be consistent with the priorities of developing countries and provide for the active participation and co-operative control of developing countries. *In this regard, special mechanisms should be developed to ensure the involvement of women in the setting of priority and in controlling those to be implemented.*

Target area II

Under I.25, new paragraph c. *Give particular attention to the need for strengthening or developing networks of women researchers in developing countries to promote research that can identify and enhance women's development priorities, and whenever desirable, facilitate contact between such networks and individuals and research institutions in developed countries and in international, regional and bilateral organizations who can promote their objectives and needs as identified by them.*

Target area III

New paragraph. *It is essential to think about transfer of technology in the context of the impact it will have on the cultural and socio-economic environment in which it will operate, since this environment will influence the lives of women and men and their families. More attention should be given to the relationship between technological choices and the environment, e.g. the technologies chosen for special economic goals such as increasing agricultural export, promoting industrialization, or providing employment, and the conse-*

quences of these choices for people, especially on women and thereby also on the conditions of children.

III.2 Developing countries should strengthen their capabilities for the assessment of technologies from the point of view of their national development objectives and having regard to social, cultural, environmental, and political aspects, *including the potential for and the constraints against the participation of women and men.* Such a screening process should ensure that technologies which are unnecessary or undesirable are not imported.

Target area IV

IV.3. Developing countries should establish and strengthen networks of research and development institutions and link them more closely to the productive system so as to enable them to meet the actual demand created *by the needs of the people,* by the dynamics of the economy and by governmental action. Such a network should include institutions with explicit responsibility for translating the results into commercial application. Governments should promote basic research as well as applied research and development in a balanced mix to expand knowledge. *Existing UN regional training and research centres for women in Asia, West Asia, Africa and Latin America, should be strengthened and expanded to focus on development issues more specifically, and their data should be integrated into plans nationally, regionally, and internationally. National institutions, including non-governmental organizations, should actively assess both indigenous and imported technology, and make appropriate information readily available to both men and women.*

IV.5. Developing countries should closely co-ordinate research and development work between the State, industry, university, and other institutions, *as well as at the village levels,* so as to achieve optimum utilization of the available national resources and skills in the interests of national development. *Participation in research at community level and identification with the people of the stock of technology already available at this level, should be seen as a tool in that part of the national planning process which should proceed from local level upwards, with women and men participating on equal terms in the setting of priorities.*

IV. 18. Developing countries should also establish adequate machinery for the evaluation of the social and cultural aspects of science and technology and of the cost-benefit ratio in technological innovation. *A revised data base for national planning should be established to measure the activities and needs of women as well as the impact of technological choices on them and their dependents. Data are needed on women's work in the informal sector in both urban and rural areas.*

IV.22. Developing countries should offer special incentives *to both women and men* to stimulate the small and medium-sized enterprises to undertake research and development activities either individually or collectively and to adopt more rational management and production methods.

IV.25, new section i. *National and transnational enterprises should, to ensure that technology transfer will be successfully implemented, make available appropriate education and training to women and men on an equal basis.*

IV.31. Developing countries should, in their programmes for training the national labour force, make special provisions to increase the productivity of low-income groups and enable people who have been prevented from exploiting their full potential, *particularly* women, to play their full role in society. [In the above "particularly women" replaced the existing phrase "e.g. women."]

Target area VI

F.1. (Added). *A specific project for women in rural sectors could be developed to involve ILO, FAO, UNESCO, UNDP, WHO, and UN regional training and research centres for women, together with national governmental agencies and non-governmental organizations.*

In addition to the above items, it is also suggested that the issue of women and their relationship to science and technology for development be included in the 50-page digest of issue papers to be produced by the UNCSTD Secretariat. [Background discussion paper on Roles of Women in Science and Technology for Development produced for the Third Preparatory Conference.]

In the Draft Report of the third session of the Preparatory Committee,[16] the suggested agenda item on women was noted and the involvement of women in development led a list of important subjects that many delegations felt should be given greater emphasis. Thus, the meeting proved to be another small step forward in raising the consciousness of the delegates to the roles of women.

Between the third and fourth sessions of the Preparatory Committee, in addition to meeting with members of the UNCSTD Secretariat, UNCSTD delegates, and NGOs, a continued outreach was being made to women around the world. Because national decisions on positions are made principally in the home capitals, pressure is most effective when exerted there. The impact of nationally organized groups of women on their governments' positions is a growing and significant factor. With this in mind, the following letter was sent to women leaders around the world.

If we can agree that conferences are the fora for raising political consciousness, then the forthcoming preparatory meetings for the United Nations Conference on Science and Technology for Development, as well as the Conference itself, should be a focus of our attention. I would

hope that it might be possible for you to draw the attention of your
government to the need 1) to stress the roles of women in science and
technology for development, and 2) to include women in your national
delegation to the Conference.

Enthusiastic responses were received from New Zealand, Austria,
Mozambique, Sweden, Australia, Nigeria, Denmark, Ghana, Argentina, and others.

Realizing that I should not fail to do myself what I had urged other
women to do, I submitted testimony to the Joint Hearing on U.S.
Policies and Initiatives for UNCSTD of the Senate Committee on Commerce, Science and Transportation, Subcommittee on Science,
Technology and Space, and the House Committee on Science and
Technology, Subcommittee on Science, Research and Space. In it I
suggested that women be included in the delegation and urged that
the United States's position should recognize the roles of women in
development.[17]

The Secretary-General of UNCSTD expressed the hope that the Programme of Action would reflect the contents of the national papers, as
well as the findings of the numerous regional conferences and
meetings of United Nations agencies and nongovernmental organizations. At three such meetings, women were the subject of papers and
discussions, but the final report did not adequately reflect these concerns. These meetings were:

1. *The Workshop on Public/Private Collaboration and Third World Food
Systems.*[18] The report of this workshop noted in its post-workshop
reflections that, "Specifically, the workshop evinced a special concern
that the needs and roles of women be given special attention as
businesses undertake nutritional improvement and education programs and in all food-related training efforts. . . . The report does not
give this concern the emphasis demonstrated in the workshop discussions." This last sentence is reminiscent of many final reports. At the
third session of the Preparatory Committee, the delegate from Tanzania made this comment, calling attention to "the almost total omission in the Programme of Action of the role of women in the application of science and technology for development and their contribution
to the development process. This is surprising in view of the many
contributions made on the subject by national and regional papers."
The Tanzanian delegate knew of many papers that had been
presented, including the one by the ILO and one prepared by the
African Training and Research Centre for Women, May 1978. The latter had carefully developed eight recommendations.

2. *The ECA Regional Meeting.* The report of this meeting arrived after the third session of the Preparatory Committee and ran to 105 pages.[19] The slight references to women included the following: "encouraging more women to pursue careers in science and technology; . . . Provision of gainful and productive employment, especially for women, in the agricultural sector; . . . Greater emphasis should be placed on intensive research designed to examine the role of women, particularly in agriculture and the home with a view to introducing improved technologies to assist in their work."

3. *The International Forum on Appropriate Industrial Technology of the United Nations Industrial Development Organization.* The Draft Report[20] of this meeting, held in India, stated that:

> It is the women of the developing world who are most concerned with the problems of energy supply and use, because it is they who do the cooking and, in most countries, gather the fuel. Furthermore, it is usually the women who draw and carry the water for domestic use. Thus, although action programmes [are] undertaken to meet the energy level during planning and implementation, their impact on women must be taken into account and, indeed, should not be planned or implemented without the significant involvement of women at both the planning level and the village level.

However, when the Report of the Conference at the Ministerial Level[21] emerged, there was not one mention of the subject "women."

It is revealing to attend meetings, to follow the discussions closely, and then to read the reports and summaries of reports, agendas, and speeches. All too often important points are omitted, either by design or oversight. Constant monitoring and continuing personal contacts are necessary just to insure that the *words* remain in documents. For action to follow the words requires still another continuing, vigilant operation.

At the fourth session of the Preparatory Committee in April and May 1979, the Group of 77 was opposed to including any "sectoral" issues—women being one of them. However, working with NGOs through the NGO Forum's activities and seminars, as well as with the delegates, we were able to keep the issue alive. When one method of approach failed, we tried another.

As the format of the Programme of Action changed from six target areas to three (A/CONF.81/PC/28), so did our suggestions for change. The following was circulated to the delegates in April (changes italicized):

Target Area A

A.6. Each country should . . .

(b) Consider the establishment of a broadly based national council for science and technology (NCST) consisting of high-level representatives of different sectors, including the directors of all the research and development institutions in the country, members of the concerned departments of the Government, representatives of universities, professional associations, trade unions, entrepreneurs, non-governmental organizations, *end-users* and the like.

A.17. Developing countries should:

(a) Establish and strengthen a network of research and development institutions and link them more closely to the productive system so as to enable them to meet the actual demand created by the dynamics of the economy and by government action; such a network should include institutions with explicit responsibility for translating the results into commercial application; governments should promote basic research as well as applied research and development in a balanced mix; *existing UN regional training and research centres for women in Asia, West Asia, Africa, and Latin America should be strengthened and expanded to focus on development issues more specifically and their data should be integrated into plans nationally, regionally, and internationally. Those national institutions, including non-governmental organizations, should actively assess both indigenous and imported technology, and make appropriate information readily available to both women and men.*

(c) Closely co-ordinate research and development work between the State, industry, universities and other institutions, *as well as the village levels. National planning should proceed from the community level up, with women and men participating equally in the identification of priorities,* so as to achieve optimum utilization of the national resources and skills available in the interests of national development.

A.22. Developing countries should establish adequate machinery for the evaluation of the social and cultural aspects of science and technology and of the cost-benefit ratio in technological innovation. *A revised data base for national planning should be established to measure the needs and activities of women, as well as the impact of technology on women. Data is needed on women's work in the informal sector in both urban and rural areas.*

A.24. Developing countries should offer special incentives *to both women and men,* including taxation measures, to stimulate their enterprises, particularly the small and medium-sized ones, to undertake research and development activities consistent with their national science policy, either individually or collectively and to adopt more rational management and production methods.

A.26. Governments should give priority to enterprises *run by women and men* that either generate or use domestic technologies in awarding research and development contracts related to the specific needs of the Government or to sectors where the return on investment is uncertain or long delayed.

A.29. Developing countries, before concluding technology transfer transactions, should ascertain the nominal costs (payment for the right to use patents, processes, know-how, trademarks, technical services and the like) and the real costs (return on investment, price of raw materials, intermediate goods, technical assistance, management and the like) and ensure that adequate information is obtained to enable the proper technical and financial evaluation of the transactions. Developing countries should develop the capacity to unpackage transferred technologies so as to determine the costs of the different elements. *It is essential to think about technology in the context of the cultural and socio-economic environment in which it will operate, since this environment will influence the lives of women and men, and their families. Not enough attention is given to the link between technological choices and this environment; between specific economic goals, such as increasing agricultural export, promoting industrialization, or providing employment, and the consequences of these choices for people, especially on women and thereby also on the condition of children.*

Target Area B

B.17. The international community should promote personal contact between the scientists and technologists of developed and developing countries through such means as conferences, meetings, visits, and study tours, *through UN bodies, governments, and non-governmental organizations.*

B.24. Foreign and transnational corporations should play a constructive role in the economies of developing countries and contribute to the objective of achieving autonomous technological capabilities. To this effect, such enterprises should:

(a) Respect the social and cultural identity of the host country and refrain from encouraging undesirable patterns of consumption;

(b) Participate in promoting exports of manufactured goods;

(c) Participate in the process of domestic dissemination of imported technologies and stimulate research and development in their subsidiaries in developing countries;

(d) Enter into research and development contracts with host country institutions, preferably through specific provisions made in the budgets of their subsidiaries;

(e) Adapt their imported technologies to the social and economic needs of the host country in accordance with its stated requirements;

(f) Give preference to the use of local raw materials and subcontracting;

(g) Employ workers and technical personnel trained "in plant" or in local institutions;

(h) Strengthen the science and technology infrastructures of developing countries, particularly in relation to production and process innovation.

(i) If technology transfer is to be successfully implemented, transnational enterprises, as well as national enterprises should make available appropriate education and training to women and men on an equal basis.

Target Area C

C.4. The machinery for coordination and over-all policy making for science and technology in the United Nations system should have *five* essential components: One representing member states; one representing the specialized agencies and other organizations of the system; one representing independent scientific and technological expertise, one corresponding to a substantive secretariat, and *one representing non-governmental organizations.* The substantive secretariat should also have referral functions, identifying for Member States and other interested parties the most appropriate United Nations organization to perform required scientific and technological activities.

C.19. The United Nations system should give serious consideration to the need for identifying a certain number of action-oriented international research pilot projects or demonstration projects of an interdisciplinary and interagency nature, so as to illustrate the advantages of combining knowledge, resources and the political will of the member states. Such programmes should be consistent with the social and economic priorities of developing countries and should be chosen from subject areas identified by the Preparatory Committee at its second session. *Specific projects for women in rural and urban sectors could be developed and involve such UN agencies as UNITAR, UNIDO, ILO, FAO, UNESCO, UNDP, WHO and UN regional training and research centres for women, together with national governmental agencies and non-governmental organizations.*

There are terms, such as "manpower," "mandays", and "manyears," that are used to refer to both men and women. A problem arises in that to some people these terms are interpreted to refer to males only and to exclude females. This has serious adverse effects on the status of women in some situations. To avoid such consequences, the use of more precise language is needed; i.e., instead of "manpower" use "work force," "labour force," "personnel," "people," or "human resources."

Aware of the many conferences being held prior to UNCSTD, I read with surprise and dismay of a meeting in Mexico City, cosponsored by ACAST on Science and Technology in Development and Planning for which no woman had been invited to prepare papers or to participate and at which there was an agenda item on "Manpower." I wrote a letter to the chairman of ACAST making these points. He replied with an invitation to attend, which was graciously confirmed by the president of the Universidad de Mexico, who was chairing this ACAST symposium.

I was given the status of "observer," the only one so designated, but was able to participate in all the discussions. When I learned that the paper on "Manpower" had not arrived, I offered to present a paper on "Human Resources." The chairman agreed, but with the admonition not to talk only about women. This was easy. All I had to do was to add "men" after "women" in my address.

Included in what I said was that human resources meant not only highly skilled people, such as those present at the conference, but also – and predominantly – a labour force, often underemployed, existing in the industrial and rural sectors, in the formal and informal sectors. They had to be trained, and new forms of competency-related education had to be developed. For example, in rural areas women and men, girls and boys, should receive formal and informal training in agriculture and agricultural extension work through the use of agricultural technologies and machines, e.g., mills, pumps, and carts.

The majority of people in the developing world live in the rural areas, and they are the poorest of the poor – and the poorest of that lot are women. The problem is how to teach the poorest of the poor to be more productive, to gain not only income but also dignity, self-respect, and self-reliance. How can we develop plans without considering who will implement them?

A basic premise is that technology is human knowledge applied to human needs. It is not gender related, but affects all people and all needs, from the most humble to the most sophisticated. Social and economic development cannot be successful without the participation of women, who make up half of humankind. All elements of society must be involved in the choice of science and technology for development; all must understand its limitations; and all must enjoy its benefits.

At this meeting a specific project was suggested for UNCSTD regarding rural energy. This would include the coordination of past rural energy projects and the initiation of national and regional projects utilizing different forms of energies and technologies over a period of ten years. An example of this was the fuel-saving Lorena stove that was being built and used by women in Honduras. The issue was not women or men, but rather the better utilization of natural and human resources together with the application of technologies. The output can make available a variety of solutions drawn from the combination of: 1) centuries-old traditional models, and 2) application of modern technologies, affording a choice of technologies to the users and conservation of natural energy resources.

The report of the Symposium on Science and Technology in Development Planning,[22] delivered in Vienna, shows that we did have some impact. The suggested project on rural energy was alluded to in the following paragraph:

> In connection with rural energy development, considerable emphasis was laid on local sources, with the aid of new appropriate technologies, and on fuel-saving measures. There is need for a better utilization of natural and human resources together with the application of technologies; the role of women in rural areas was particularly underlined.

And the following excerpts are notable for the use of significant words, such as "people," and "human resources," and "personnel," rather than "men" or "manpower."

> Science and technology planning and even development planning must be people-oriented. New strategies which provide a decent livelihood, a capacity to participate in national development and a capacity to earn a satisfactory living are urgently called for. This implies provision of technologies for small producers and small farmers to improve their production, distribution, and marketing capabilities. The debate whether such technology should be intermediate or high is not relevant. It is a suitable adaptation of technology that is called for.

> The creation of high quality and broadly oriented scientific and technological human resources is the key to more successful development. But it is not enough to train "white collar" scientific and technological personnel. Experience in many countries shows that "blue collar" contributions to innovation at the industrial plant level may be very important, and programmes should be developed to encourage such inputs.

> There is a lack of adequately trained people, professional and non-professional, women and men, in the fields of science, technology and development planning. Greater attention to this particular area of education is urged as is the development of competency. The interna-

tionally recommended emphasis on science and technology policy formulation, which in the developing countries requires the actual training of highly skilled personnel in such policy matters, needs to be supplemented by much greater concern with criteria for decision-making and for policy implementation.

A further happy twist to this tale was that Mr. Chagula, the ACAST chairman, who supported and facilitated my participation in the Mexican conference, was the same delegate who introduced the Resolution on Women, Science and Technology that was adopted at the closing plenary session in Vienna.

In June 1979, for the fifth session of the Preparatory Committee, and bearing in mind the prior UNCSTD meeting held in Lomé, Togo, and the information gleaned from national papers, a list of specific areas for specific projects related to women was drawn up. It included:

1. Pure water for human use.
2. Reducing postharvest food losses.
3. Nutrition.
4. Soil and water management at the farm level.
5. Development of indigenous energy resources for local utilization.
6. Infrastructure for creating and using industrial technology.
7. Strengthening scientific and technological policymaking.
8. Education and training of scientific and technological personnel.

These are areas in which women are already working. Emphasizing this fact together with the need to improve the productivity of women's labour should–and could–be economically beneficial to both women and men in the development process. These suggested possibilities were discussed with the Task Force members, who were asked to develop more specific projects for distribution at the conference itself.

The following incident illustrates the offhand way in which women are often asked to participate at conferences. I received a telephone call from the UN asking me to suggest the name of a Pakistani woman journalist to participate in the UNCSTD journalists' encounter in Vienna. However, it was specified that the candidate had to be produced within twenty-four hours and that she be closer to Vienna than Pakistan. With the help of a Pakistani woman diplomat, three journalists were suggested. One was selected and did participate. This was a plus. The minus was the manner in which it was done.

From April until UNCSTD convened in Vienna, the NGO Subcommittee preparing for the NGO Forum was active in developing its program, which ran parallel in time with the intergovernmental conference. There was a deliberate and successful effort to include women in the opening-day session of the forum, as well as in all the other forum symposia. Dr. Bolanle Awe of Nigeria and Maaza Bekele of Ethiopia were invited to speak at the opening. Both chose to speak about women, the difficulties women encounter when science and technology are introduced into the development process, and the inequities women encounter in science.

We agreed that the Symposium on the Roles of Women in Science and Technology for Development would be held early in the NGO Forum to permit workshops to follow through on the issues raised. The following is a digest of the program of the symposium, which was held on August 22:

Dr. Bolanle Awe, Co-ordinator, who is a professor at the Institute of African Studies, University of Ibadan, Nigeria, opened the symposium by saying,

> The professional and non-professional contributions of women to development are often impeded by the unfavorable socio-economic environment in which they operate. Developmental progress will remain incomplete until women fully participate in the community. . . . There is a need to identify problems and to undertake serious research. . . . In Nigeria and other developing countries there are groups who are taking the study of women very seriously. The impetus for these comes from women, but they need help, expertise and funds. NGOs can help in this and in workshops, seminars and documentation centres. It is very important that NGOs should realize that responsibility for this research should come from the indigenous people who are more aware of their problems and have a better idea of what they want.

Ms. S. Chakravorty, Director, Women's Program, Ministry of Agriculture and Irrigation in India, and an economist, spoke first about the problems women in rural India face every day. Eighty percent of India's population live in villages (approximately 244 million out 264 million); women perform most of the agricultural work, but few play managerial roles. She spoke fervently about the need to overcome traditional and institutional obstacles and urged women to organize both at the national and local levels. Before any gains can be made, she said "women need to develop a sense of self-respect and respect for the valuable work they do in the community."

Dr. Irene Cousins, Director of Consumer Affairs, Ministry of Industry and Commerce in Jamaica, reported that at the International Colloquium just prior to the opening of the UNCSTD in Vienna, only 12 women were invited to participate out of a total of 244 invitees, or 4.9 percent, and the representatives of organizations of the UN system included 4 women out of 80 participants, for a total of 5 percent. She went on to say:

> Were things different, were we all equally represented or even reasonably represented, certainly there should not be the necessity to mention women specifically – but all is not well in the state of science and technology.
>
> If we therefore accept the premise that women are a real human resource, and that we need to use all available human resources to speed up development in a way which will improve the quality of life of our peoples (the true measure of development), and particularly in countries which contain the lion's share of its population – it then follows that the "other half" of the world's population *must* become actively involved in the process. If we accept that science and technology are the very necessary vehicles for development, then we must accept that at least some women become the drivers of these vehicles.

Waclaw Micuta, former United Nations Development Programme (UNDP) official from Poland and one of the organizers of the primary energy exhibit at the Messepalast, recounted some of his observations of the desperate living conditions of rural villagers in poor countries. He gave an impassioned appeal in which he stated that women today were the beasts of burden. He urged that the following resolution be passed:

> *Conscious of* the unnecessary hardship and drudgery suffered by people, largely women, in many countries of the world owing to the lack of appropriate agricultural and domestic tools and implements;
>
> *Aware that* their burden can be considerably lightened by the introduction of already available inexpensive and reliable equipment using primary sources of energy;
>
> [The NGO Forum] *strongly urges* that immediate steps be taken by governments and international organizations to make available to deprived communities the equipment needed to improve their agricultural production and living conditions;
>
> *Decides that* this resolution should be transmitted to UNCSTD for appropriate and urgent action.

Dr. Davidson Nicol, Executive Director, United Nations Institute for

Training and Research (UNITAR) and Under-Secretary-General, United Nations, reported on the four studies on women that UNITAR had commissioned for UNCSTD. A report, "The Implications of UNC-STD's 'Ascending Process' for the Exploitation of Women and Other Marginalized Social Groups," by Pamela M. D'Onofrio-Flores, UNITAR, was distributed. Dr. Nicol said that

> an increased participation of women in science and technology for development will depend on persistent and aggressive attempts on their part to gain more political power and equally important, to *use it*. It is unlikely that participation will increase through petitions and conferences only. Women are not disliked or ignored in a bureaucracy, they are simply placed low down on the list of priorities for change. It is much easier for those concerned to justify the status-quo or to make modifications which are either simply cosmetic or continue to confirm the inferior and supportive role of women.

In closing, I expressed the hope that specific projects related to women would emerge from the conference and that women would be recognized as equal partners with men in seeking solutions to the problems of development. I also said that any discussion of science and technology, especially the need for research and development, must begin with the end-user, who is often a woman. The more potential users are involved in the identification of their needs and the choice of technology, the more appropriate that technology is likely to be. Our basic premise is that technology is human knowledge applied to human needs.

Following the symposium, seven workshops were held. Carmen Lugo, professor and researcher at the University of Mexico, led the Spanish-language workshop on Science and Women; Farkhanda Hassan, head of the Engineering Department at the American University in Cairo shared the leadership with Sheila Pfafflin, president of the Association for Women in Science in the United States, of the English-language workshops on Science and Women; Irene Tinker of the Equality Policy Center in the United States and Jairam Ramesh of India, who is with the World Bank, cochaired the workshop on Energy, Technology and the World Poor; Bettina Corke of the United Kingdom, President of Decade Media, Inc., and Mrs. Soepadmi of Indonesia, senior officer of the Industrial Research and Development Institute, directed the workshop on Light Industry and Women; Dr. Bolanle Awe led the one on Water and Women; Professor Erna Hamburger of the Swiss Federal Institute of Technology and Nurmandsjuria Surdia of the Institute of Technology in Bandung, Indonesia, cochaired another workshop on Science and Women. B. Matl Hare of the Associated Country Women of the World in Botswana and H.I.S. Gunawardana, a teacher of agriculture in Sri Lanka, were the joint leaders of a workshop on Agriculture and Women; and Leah Janus of the Overseas Education Fund of the League of Women Voters in the United States presented an audiovisual program on "Village Home Technology."

One meeting was cancelled. It was to have been a discussion of reports of UN agencies and bodies related to the roles of women and development to see how their various report recommendations were being carried out. Excerpts from such reports had been part of the paper I prepared for the UNCSTD conference, "Women and the United Nations Family."[23] Unfortunately, no representative from any of the UN agencies invited was able to participate. Surely they must have had some affirmative action to report.

Having worked to organize the Symposium on Women and the eight workshops in Vienna, I was in a quandary when asked to be a member of the United States delegation. But when it was pointed out how much the Task Force had stressed the importance of women serving on delegations, I had no choice but to accept. And so, finally, after all the preliminary work for UNCSTD, working with so many delegations and NGOs, I found myself in Vienna in a dual capacity. But I was not alone. There were other women on other delegations who participated in the NGO Forum as well as in the intergovernmental conference. According to some male delegates, women delegates were there as a result of our pressure.

However, despite all the pressure, women at UNCSTD were not that visible. Of 128 national delegations, 4 were headed by women; 3 deputy heads of delegations were women; 4 delegations had two women each; 1 delegation has as many women as men; 90 delegations had no women; 2 delegations had six women; and 1 delegation had nine. At the NGO Forum there were 87 women and 1,082 men registered.

But numbers were not important. There was a strength and solidarity among the women. We had a common goal, and we were going to pursue it. And pursue it we did—in the different UNCSTD committees, in the corridors, in the NGO Forum, and in the press.

Initially, a resolution on rural energy and women was circulated, as was one on population; ultimately eleven other resolutions on women were developed. At the outset the delegates, though friendly, were reluctant even to consider a resolution. However, as the days went by and delegates were looking for areas of agreement, a resolution on women did not seem so threatening. Many delegates, particularly those from the Nordic countries, played an important role in drafting and circulating a general resolution on women. We were all grateful to Pamela D'Onofrio-Flores (UNITAR) for her contributions to this effort.

The resolution was introduced at the final plenary meeting of UNC-STD by Ambassador Chagula of Tanzania, who said:

> We all know that modern science and technology are to a large extent the domain of *men* and that the majority of the world's scientists and technologists, including engineers, are men. In addition, it is common knowledge that the aims and trends in the world's research and development in general have so far reflected men's values and aspirations, although women in our societies, both in developing and developed countries, do by tradition employ a lot of knowledge and skills which provide the various necessities of our daily life including some of our basic needs, a point which we have so far not given adequate attention. Thus, within the technological development process, it is essential that the improvement of these women's existing knowledge and skills should be given adequate attention and developed in parallel with the modern ways and means of production.

The resolution was cosponsored by sixteen countries: Australia, Austria, Denmark, Ethiopia, Finland, Hungary, Jamaica, Mongolia, Norway, Papua New Guinea, Sweden, Thailand, Tanzania, United States of America, and Vietnam. The preambular paragraphs cite prior resolutions and actions; the operative paragraphs "invited member states to facilitate: equal distribution of the benefits and application of science and technological development to men and women; the participation of women in the decision-making process; equal access for women and men to scientific and technological professional training"; "recommended that all UN organizations and bodies should continually review the impact of their programs on women and promote their full participation"; and, "invited the proposed Intergovernmental Committee on Science and Technology for Development to include in its annual reports a review on the progress made concerning the implementation of the tenets of the resolution." The resolution was unanimously adopted.[24]

One could say the delegates realized their oversight at the previous meetings. More likely, it was the result of many interventions over the preceding year, as well as crucial elements coming together at the conference itself. Representatives of NGOs and governmental delegates, supported by members of ACAST and the UN Secretariat, plus numerous daily articles on women in the conference newspapers, "Retort" and "Echo," working together, persistently and persuasively, contributed to the passage of the resolution – the only substantive resolution passed at the conference.

All issues were not resolved, but UNCSTD did result in a Programme of Action. Women are referred to, mentioned, and included in its preamble and in certain other sections, as well as in the statement on the future. Most particularly, the Nordic countries, Portugal, and the United States were active and effective in raising these points.

In the report of UNCSTD,[25] in the summary of the general debate, the following items appear:

89. Many representatives of both developed and developing countries recognized the importance of the role that could be played by women in planning and implementing the application of science and technology to development. It was noted by the representative of one developed country that, while new technologies implied economic advantages, they also changed social and cultural factors. In this connection this representative added that, in the transfer of technology, every effort should be made to respect the social and cultural values of the recipient country. Care had to be taken to ensure that the traditional role of women in agriculture should not be curtailed by the introduction of modern machinery and that home industries, which were often women's occupations, should not be adversely affected. It was suggested that guidelines should be drawn up for the participation of women in decision-making and development. Proposals to that end would be a valuable input to the World Conference of the United Nations Decade for Women to be held at Copenhagen in 1980.

90. The representatives of two developed market economy countries drew attention to the adverse social effects which could result from the introduction and application of technologies. The role of women was, for example, often radically altered by the utilization of modern agricultural technologies. They stressed, therefore, the need for integrating the use of science and technology in a strategy for social and economic development, giving all groups of society – women and men alike – equal influence on decisions relating to the introduction of new technologies and the use of new scientific methods.

In the same report, in the "Vienna Programme of Action on Science and Technology for Development," this first excerpt is from the preamble:

5. The ultimate goal of science and technology is to serve national development and to improve the well-being of humanity as a whole.

Men and women in all groups of society can contribute positively to enhance the impact of science and technology on the development process. However, modern technological developments do not automatically benefit all groups of society equally. Such developments, depending on the given economic, social and cultural context in which they take place, are often seen to affect various groups in society differently. They have had a negative impact on the conditions of women and their bases for economic, social, and cultural contributions to the development process. This is seen to happen in industrialized as well as in developing countries. Therefore, steps should be taken to ensure that all members of society be given real and equal access to and influence upon the choice of technology.

In Item "I. Strengthening the Science and Technology capacities of the Developing Countries," under "Recommendations," we find the following:

3. Measures and mechanisms for strengthening the scientific and technological capacities of developing countries . . .

> (g) To ensure the full participation of women in the science and technology development process;
> (h) To advise local education and training bodies and make projections for building up a capacity in human resources for science and technology development.

and in Item "II. Restructuring the Existing Pattern of International Scientific and Technological Relations – Recommendations,"

D. Development of Human Resources . . .
99. The organs, organizations and bodies of the United Nations System should . . .

> (g) Strengthen support for national efforts to promote the full participation of women in the mobilization of all groups for the application of science and technology for development.

In the same report, in the section on "Science and Technology and the Future," the following items appear:

21. Technological development often affects men and women differently and the introduction of new technologies has tended to have an adverse impact on the latter, thereby lessening their earnings and social status. It is therefore of the utmost interest to society that in future the

full participation of women be ensured in the planning and setting of priorities for research and development as well as in activities relating to the design, choice and application of science and technology for development. They should also be provided with equal access to scientific and technological training and professional career opportunities. In developing countries an adequate share of resources available for research and training should be allocated to the advancement of skills of women in the fields traditionally occupied by them as well as new fields. . . .

22. Rapid development of science and technology throughout the world will depend in part on the younger men and women who can be brought into these fields and involved in decision-making bodies and given full opportunity to use their intelligence and skills. In the bio-sciences, for example, three steps are essential to accomplish this: (a) improved education in the ideas and methods of modern biology including the necessary grounding in physics, mathematics and chemistry; (b) creation of well equipped research laboratories in many developing countries; and (c) a much greater exchange among young biological scientists and technologists of developed and developing countries. This approach should be equally applicable to all other fields.

It was the 34th UN General Assembly in the fall of 1979 that had to approve the findings of UNCSTD, including the Resolution on Women, Science and Technology. An experience I had had in 1978 with the passage of the Resolution on Women and Development and International Conferences forewarned me that all was not yet won. With that resolution, we discovered that the introductory paragraphs had to be changed *to ask ECOSOC specifically* to consider it. However, that was not the only change. The delegates who represented their countries at ECOSOC were not the same delegates who represented them at the UN Status of Women Commission. Here, as in all bureaucracies, communications are not the best. Fourteen countries had cosponsored the resolution, but every delegate looked leerily and warily at the document – even those whose countries had introduced it and even though no substantive changes had been made in its content. Some said they would have to wire their foreign offices for agreement; others declined altogether. Ten minutes before the item finally had to be tabled, one country agreed to sponsor it, and it was passed. That was in the spring of 1978.

To avoid a possible recurrence with the UNCSTD Resolution on Women, Science and Technology in the fall of 1979, letters were sent to all the heads of delegations, bringing the resolution to their attention and looking forward to their continued support. The General

Assembly Resolution on the 1979 United Nations Conference on Science and Technology for Development adopted at the 34th Session of the General Assembly includes the endorsement of the resolution, "Women, Science and Technology."

What can this resolution mean?

1. That the new Intergovernmental Committee on Science and Technology for Development (ICSTD) will include women;
2. That ICSTD programs will incorporate women into their design;
3. That out of UNDP funds money will be earmarked for women's programs;
4. That the UN family will increase the number of programs designed to integrate women into the development process and provide women with equal access to innovations in the application of science and technology;
5. That the design of the Development Decade will include women prominently in the design and planning of the decade program; and
6. That the consciousness-raising process will continue and will provide the awareness needed for both women and men to work effectively together.

What can women do?

1. Influence foreign offices and delegations at the United Nations and at all conferences;
2. Assess the reports of the UN family to ensure that programs do not have a negative impact on women, and that when programs are important to women, they are carried out;
3. Monitor the progress of women in appointments to ICSTD, as well as in the programs that will emerge from UNCSTD;
4. Develop projects for submission to concerned UN bodies and agencies regarding science, technology, and development;
5. Strengthen links with women and their organizations in the developing countries.

These actions toward the integration of women in development will move slowly—at times, imperceptibly.

National and international policies are formed in response to the pressures of national and international political forces. And these forces are people. An international conference brings people together, setting up international person-to-person communications systems. This networking of like-minded people promotes innovative thinking and gives support to new efforts. This is what happened with the Task Force on the Roles of Women for UNCSTD.

Persistence at learning how the bodies act, where and how the decisions are made, the significance of agenda items and resolutions, who the decision makers are, and how to become one – all are parts of the strategy. The ongoing tactics were many: networking, speaking, research, conference-going, political maneuvering. However, the strategy was to involve women actively and equally in the development process, utilizing science and technology.

Did we succeed? With the short-term, limited goal of raising the consciousness to the need for including women in considerations regarding science and technology in development, we could say yes. However, we are still just at the beginning stage of transforming words into action. As His Excellency Salim Ahmed Salim, the president of the General Assembly, said, "I am confident that, with the continued assistance and co-operation of a number of non-governmental organizations, the early attainment of the objectives of the Conference, particularly with respect to its decisions relating to the active role of women in all aspects of development, would further be enhanced."[26]

The conference process, with its one hundred regional, subregional, national, governmental, and intergovernmental meetings, provided ideal opportunities to state our case over and over again in different perspectives. They are the fora for the politics of consciousness. UNCSTD was an important conference. It could have a far-reaching impact on the roles of women in science and technology for development.

Notes

1. Mildred Robbins Leet (Chairperson), Elise Boulding, Judith Bruce, Mary P. Burke, Mary Cassidy, Kim Conroy, Esmerelda Arboleta Cuevas, Daisy George, Adrienne Germaine, Rosalind Harris, Hazel Henderson, Esther Hymer, Leah Janus, Valeriana Kallab, Marion Fennelly Levy, Edna McCallion, Margaret Mead (deceased), Kathleen Newland, Achola Pala, Mildred Persinger, Sheila Pfafflin, Jean Picker, Irene Pinkau, Priscilla Reining, Dao Spencer, Lyra Srinivason, Irene Tinker, Nancy Todd, Mallica Vajrathon, Nadia Youssef, Michaela Walsh, Barbara Walton (Rapporteur), and Mary Wolff.

2. "The Role of Women in African Development," report of the Economic Commission for Africa, UN Document E/Conf.66/BP.8; and "The Participation

of Women in the Development of Latin America," UN Document ESA/CSDHA/AC.10/4/Rev.1, February 1976.

3. "Development and International Cooperation: Effective Mobilization of Women in Development," report of the Secretary General, UN Document A/33/238, September 1978.

4. "A Study of the Interagency Programme for the United Nations Decade for Women: Equality, Development, and Peace," UN Document E/1978/106.

5. "Women, Technology and the Development Process," ILO Contribution to the African Regional Meeting on UNCSTD, Cairo, 24–29 July 1978.

6. "Draft Resolution of November 7, 1978 for an Additional Sub-Item for the UNCSTD Agenda," MRL/7 November 1978.

7. Excerpt from speech delivered at the NGO Forum on Science and Technology for Development at UN Headquarters, 25 September 1978.

8. "Women, Technology and the Development Process."

9. "Background Discussion Paper," prepared by the NGO Task Force on Roles of Women for UN Conference on Science and Technology for Development for presentation at the Third Preparatory Conference for UNCSTD, January 22–February 5, 1979, dated December 20, 1978.

10. "Recommendations for the UNCSTD World Programme of Action," sponsored by Non-Governmental Organizations in Consultative Status with ECOSOC for the Third Session of the Preparatory Committee for UNCSTD, sponsored by International Alliance of Women, International Council of Women, International Federation of Business and Professional Women, Associated Country Women of the World, Baha'i International Community, Baptist World Alliance, Cooperative for American Relief Everywhere, Inc., International Council of Jewish Women, International Humanist and Ethical Union, International League for Human Rights, International Society for Community Development, Pan Pacific and Southeast Asia Women's Association, World Federation of Christian Life Communities, World Federation of Mental Health, World's Women's Christian Temperance Union, World Union of Catholic Women's Organizations, and Zonta International. (Available from Mildred Robbins Leet, 54 Riverside Drive, New York, N.Y. 10024.)

11. UN Document E/CN.6/L.740/Rev.1, introduced by France, Indonesia, Mexico, Niger, Pakistan, Thailand, and the United States at the 27th Session of the Commission on the Status of Women, 20 March–5 April 1978.

12. UN Document E/Res/1978/34.

13. UN Document A/Conf.81/PC.12.

14. UN Document A/Conf.81/PC.21.

15. "Women and Development Recommendations," a report resulting from a Workshop conducted by the American Association for the Advancement of Science for the U.S. Department of State, as a contribution to U.S preparations for the United Nations Conference on Science and Technology for Development, March 26–27, 1979, Washington, D.C.

16. UN Document A/Conf.81/PC/L.15/Add.1.

17. Testimony prepared for the Joint Hearing on U.S. Policies and Initiatives for the U.N. Conference on Science and Technology for Development, held on

July 17, 1979, by Mildred Robbins Leet.

18. At the Aspen Institute for Humanistic Studies, Aspen, Colorado, 20–26 August 1978, ed. by Mary Wolff and Lloyd Slater.

19. UN Document A/Conf.81/PC.17, 12 December 1978, "Report of the African Regional Meeting – Preparatory Committee for the United Nations Conference on Science and Technology for Development."

20. Draft Report of the Technical/Official Level Meeting to the Ministerial Level Meeting at the International Forum on Appropriate Industrial Technology sponsored by the United Nations Industrial Development Organization in New Delhi/Anand, India, 20–30 November 1978.

21. "Report of the Ministerial Level Meeting," at the International Forum on Appropriate Industrial Technology sponsored by the United Nations Industrial Development Organization in New Delhi/Anand, India, from 28–30 November 1978.

22. UN Document ACAST/COLL/BP.2/16 July 1979.

23. Mildred Robbins Leet, "Women and the United Nations Family," paper prepared for the UN Conference on Science and Technology for Development/NGO Forum Symposium on the Roles of Women in Science and Technology for Development, Vienna, Austria, August 1979.

24. UN Document A/CONF.81/L.4/Rev.1.

25. "Report of the United Nations Conference on Science and Technology for Development, Vienna (20–31 August 1979)." UN Document A/CONF.81/16.

26. In a letter dated 12 November 1979 addressed to Mildred Robbins Leet, Chairperson, NGO Task Force on Roles of Women for UN Conference on Science and Technology for Development.

6

Some Reflections on Women in Science and Technology After UNCSTD

Sheila M. Pfafflin

Throughout all parts of the world, developed and developing, women participate in science and technology to a lesser extent than do men. Science and technology have traditionally been viewed as masculine fields. The extensive training requirements of a career in science raise barriers to the entry of women, as do many cultural attitudes and customs.[1] Women who do try to enter scientific fields frequently encounter discriminatory practices that discourage them from pursuing careers in science or lead them to settle for lesser accomplishments than their abilities warrant.[2]

Countries with well-developed scientific and technological establishments show considerable variation in the extent to which they utilize women. The Soviet Union has greatly increased the numbers of women who enter engineering and the sciences, especially since the Second World War.[3] The United States, on the other hand, showed essentially the same proportion of women entering the sciences over a fifty-year period and has only recently showed a significant change in the participation of women under the impact of the women's movement and antidiscriminatory legislation.[4]

However, the type of economy is not necessarily a determining factor. Finland, for example, is reported to have a relatively good record of encouraging the participation of women in scientific and technical professions, and countries with market economies appear to vary considerably in the numbers of women they have in such nontraditional areas.[5] Furthermore, even countries with substantial numbers of women at entry level have failed to achieve significant numbers of women at policymaking levels in the scientific establishment. The Soviet Union and other East European countries have far fewer women in high scientific positions than one would expect from the numbers of women working in scientific and technical areas. McGrath reported, for example, that in the Soviet Union, women make up nearly one-half of the scientific work force, and one-fourth of the scientific doctorates, but only one-tenth of senior professors are women, and only about 1 percent of academicians are women; Dodge reported similar figures.[6]

The factors that have operated to prevent women from playing a significant role in science and technology in those countries with highly developed scientific and technological establishments also appear likely to operate in the developing countries. Throughout the world, women have less access to education than men, and when they do have access to education beyond the primary level, they are likely to be channeled into traditional women's fields, such as domestic science or education, not into the more technologically oriented training programs.[7] The cultural traditions of different countries vary in their implications for the incorporation of women into science and technology, but most show some features with potentially negative impact. Scientific and technological employment in the developing countries already shows a strong trend towards male dominance. Statistics on the number of women now in science and technology in developing countries, for example, indicate that their numbers are frequently low relative to the participation of men, especially in many Islamic countries.[8]

However, the developing nations are still in the early stages of developing their scientific and technological work forces: It is not too late for action to change this trend. They can take steps to insure that women are incorporated into their scientific and technological work force as these are developed. But failure to do so will almost inevitably result in structures that systematically discriminate against women. There should be no misunderstanding about the need for specific action if women are to be allowed to participate equally in science and technology in developing countries. The view that this will take place naturally, once the resources are available to the developing nations, is simply unrealistic in view of the history of the developed nations and the known barriers that exist to the participation of women in science and technology. The refusal to recognize the need for positive action is, in effect, a decision to discriminate against women and perpetuate the practice of their exclusions from these areas.

Why should women be incorporated into the scientific and

technological work force and encouraged to participate fully in it at the highest levels? First, because it is right. Women make up half the human race. They should participate fully in all aspects of their societies. It would be wrong to limit their participation in so important a part of modern society as science and technology. And not only must they be permitted to engage in these activities, but they must be allowed to realize their potential fully and participate in science and technology at all levels, including those with important decision-making capability. The exclusion of women from the power structures of a society, including the scientific and technical power elites, is the sign of an unjust society. That women are now so excluded was very evident at the recent United Nations Conference on Science and Technology for Development (UNCSTD), where the delegations had few women.

Another consideration is that the developing countries can ill afford to disregard the talents of half of their people in such an important area. To fail to take advantage of many of their most able citizens is a waste of human resources that even most developed countries now recognize cannot continue to be tolerated. The developing nations have great human resource needs. If they allow artificial restrictions to prevent them from making the best use of the talents of all their population, they will place themselves at a serious disadvantage.

There is a third reason why the participation of women in science and technology is important, and that is because of their potential role in science policymaking. Technology is coming increasingly to dominate modern societies, and policy decisions regarding science and technology have enormous impact on every nation. As long as these decisions are made only by men, the interests of only half the nation will be reflected in them.

I am not talking here about such unlikely hypotheses as the idea that women have a special way of thinking that makes them particularly qualified for certain aspects of science. The available evidence indicates that the intellectual capabilities of men and women are very similar. Maccoby and Jacklin report, for example, that the sexes do not differ on tests of analytic cognitive style and are equally proficient on various learning tasks. Although some differences may exist between the sexes in the distribution of verbal and quantitative skills, they conclude that these are not sufficiently marked to determine occupational choice for the sexes.[9] Therefore, neither sex should have a special place within the scientific structure. Science, insofar as its purely technical content is concerned, is neutral with regard to the sex of the investigator.

However, the same is certainly not true as regards the allocation of scientific and technical resources and the uses to which research is put. As long as men and women occupy different roles within society, their needs will differ and must be considered equally in the allocation of resources. The ideal of complete equality of status between the sexes remains the goal of many, but it is not realistic at present to act as though this goal has been achieved. Active steps are necessary to insure that women's present needs are met and that progress is made toward the improvement of their status within their societies.

In view of the importance of science and technology and their potential impact on women, it is essential that all societies have trained women in science and technology and have them in the highest policymaking positions within the scientific hierarchy. It is difficult to believe, for example, that research on lung cancer, which affects men more often than women, would have received so much more support than research on breast cancer over the years in the United States[10] if the institutions making the decisions had not been run almost exclusively by men.

While in Vienna during UNCSTD, I had an opportunity to meet a number of women scientists from Third World countries and discuss these issues with them. During the meeting of the Caucus of Women Scientists for UNCSTD, they also expressed their concern over the need to explicitly address the role of women in planning for development and the lack of decision-making and research involvement of women. The caucus also discussed other problems relating to women in science in developing countries. Their views are formulated in a series of resolutions, which were subsequently presented to Mr. da Costa, the Secretary-General of the conference. I will try to summarize some of the other issues discussed; the full text of the resolutions can be found in Appendix A.

The concerns of these women regarding the status of women in science and technology in their societies mirrored in many ways those of women scientists in developed nations. However, they gave more emphasis to the importance of changing patterns of education for women and to elimination of cultural barriers that prevent them from fully utilizing such opportunities as are available. In most developed countries, although problems of access to training remain, the barriers are considerably lower than they were. Even institutions such as the Ecole Polytechnique and the Ecole des Mines in France and the Universities of Oxford and Cambridge in England, long regarded as male bastions, have opened their doors to women. The focus is now on working to insure that women receive the necessary early training, especially in mathematics, to enable them to take advantage of advanced training in the sciences and on procedures to insure that they have full opportunities to pursue their careers without discrimination once they have entered upon them.

But in many developing nations, present patterns of education discriminate heavily against women who might wish to enter the sciences. Female children are less likely to receive an education than are male children. When they do have access to education, they face more problems in taking advantage of it. They are more likely than boys to have home duties that interfere with their education and that may result in its abnormally early termination. Education beyond the primary level frequently must be paid for by the parents, and there is often reluctance to spend family resources on female children, especially if these resources are limited. Such attitudes may persist even in countries, such as China, that have attempted to establish equal opportunity for the sexes. It has been reported that in rural communes there is sometimes reluctance to give girls opportunities for advanced training for fear that their skills will be lost through marriage outside their communes.[11]

The caucus also felt that the practice common in many developing countries of separate schools for boys and girls, especially at the secondary level frequently results in girls not having access to the necessary prerequisites, such as good training in mathematics, necessary for future study in the sciences. Although this need not be an inevitable result of separate schools, it is happening at present because of the failure to make provisions for technical subjects in women's educational institutions. Partly as a result, those women who do manage to achieve advanced training are less likely than men to enter science and technology.

This trend has disquieting implications for the future social and economic status of women. As societies become increasingly technological, experience elsewhere suggests that the job opportunities for those without technical backgrounds will become increasingly restricted. They will be competing for an often shrinking pool of professional openings, and the nonprofessional jobs not requiring some technical training will be increasingly dull, repetitive, insecure, and poorly paid. Thus, the economic discrimination against women that already exists in most countries will be greatly aggravated by the failure to provide technical training for women.

When I refer to technical training, I mean not only opportunities for careers in science, engineering, and other professions. A very important part of the development process will be the increasing availability of technician and craft jobs requiring specialized skills. And there is evidence that women are being excluded from such training at present, in both developing and developed countries. Low percentages (less than 5 percent) of women are reported in vocational training for industry in France, the United States, Argentina, and Japan, among others. It is estimated that in developing countries, only 20 to 25 percent of the students receiving vocational training are female, and most of these are in domestic science courses that do not prepare them for earning a living.[12] If women are excluded from the training required to deal with an increasingly mechanized society, most of the new employment that comes with development, at whatever level, will exclude them.

That entry of women into science can be achieved is shown by the experience of such countries as the Soviet Union, which is presently reported to have equal numbers of women and men entering physics, a traditionally male field. However, as noted earlier, the problem of dealing with the achievement of equal career opportunities appears to have been solved nowhere. Even countries with relatively high numbers of women in the scientific work force show the same pattern found elsewhere: The higher one looks in the scientific and technical hierarchy, the fewer women are found.

Several reasons may exist for this, depending on the particular society. Discriminatory patterns may persist in job assignments, access to research funds and facilities, and promotions. Because these practices are often more subtle than those used to exclude women completely, they can be more difficult to combat. The experience of the United States in attempting to eliminate discriminatory patterns in science suggests that it is easier to eliminate discrimination in entry into science and related professions than it is to eliminate barriers to equal opportunity for professional achievement. Institutions, such as the colleges and universities, have been especially resistant to change.[13] In physics, for example, although the percentage of women at the assistant professor level increased slightly between the 1971-1972 and 1977-1978 academic years (from 3.3 percent to 4.5 percent), the percentage of women with the rank of full professor decreased from 2.4 percent to 1.4 percent. Although the percentages differ in other fields, the patterns are similar to that found in physics.

Even in the absence of active discrimination, the existence of "old boy's" networks, which substantially influence selections for higher positions, tends to work against women.[14] There was some feeling among the women scientists at UNCSTD that there might be fewer barriers to professional success for those women who did enter upon scientific careers in many developing countries. However, this may reflect simply the fact that the numbers of women are small at present, and that they are probably a highly select group. Certainly, experience to date would suggest that it is better to take steps to insure the absence of discriminatory patterns than to try to change them after they have become established.

Another barrier that deserves consideration is the double burden imposed on women by the fact that their entry into the work force has not been accompanied by an equivalent shift in their domestic responsibilities. Studies show that working women spend substantially more of their time on household duties and childcare than do their husbands. In one study, for example, the total workload of the wives who moved into paid employment rose by an average of thirteen hours a week, while that of the husband actually dropped an average of one and one-half hours.[15] Women, in effect, have two jobs, while their husbands, by and large, have only one, although they may help out in varying degrees.[16] Especially in such countries as the Soviet Union, where the resources allocated for domestic consumption have been limited, the burdens imposed by household responsibilities have been hypothesized to be a major factor in the relatively low numbers of women who achieve high positions in the sciences.[17] A similar double burden is known to exist for women in many developing countries.[18] Until the structures of societies are reformed to deal with this question, women will be limited in their contributions to science and technology, in both developed and developing countries.

The issues involved in such a fundamental reorganization go beyond the scope of this paper. There are two points of particular relevance to women in science and technology, however. One of these is that the very demanding nature of a career in the sciences can make it very difficult for women to achieve equally with men unless they have societal support. Most studies of women in science indicate that their productivity is equal to that of men (their failure to be found in high academic and administrative posts does not seem to be explainable by differences in accomplishment), but it is also clear that those women studied are a highly select group. They have achieved a great deal despite cultural pressures and special burdens; many other capable women have been excluded by these factors. If women are to enter the sciences on an equal basis, not only must the formal barriers be removed, but the cultural environment must cease to burden them with responsibilities and pressures that do not burden their male colleagues.

A second point is that this double burden has been used as a rationalization to deny technical training to women. Because they have been viewed as a marginal part of the labour force, societies have been reluctant to invest in the cost of technical education for them. This has been true despite the extensive participation of women in the work force in many countries. The effect of this pattern of discrimination, however, is to leave women lacking in the skills necessary to compete for the better jobs. The effective utilization of women's labor depends very greatly on whether they have received training appropriate to an increasingly technological world.

A number of studies have been done of factors that have limited the participation of women in science and technology.[19] Most of these have been done in developed countries, and further research is needed in the developing countries to identify specific problems and solutions. Some research, such as the series of studies done in Iran, suggests that many of the problems are similar. For example, it was found that women with traditional outlooks were less likely to be scientists, a finding that replicates the results of studies elsewhere.[20] Research in Kenya[21] on the other hand, suggests that the problems that may be found in cultures where women have had a relatively high degree of economic independence, but in spheres of activity where they do not normally compete directly with men, present some special features. Women raised in such cultures tend to have many of the characteristics associated with career orientation in women elsewhere. However, until they start upon their technical training, they have seldom competed directly with men, and such competition is openly resented by many males. There are conflicting views about whether the development of their skills under conditions that do not force them to face male antagonism until they have established some sense of security in their own abilities and the openness of the opposition that they later face will facilitate or deter achievement in women as compared with other cultural patterns, such as the covert discrimination faced by women in cultures that assert equality while practicing discrimination.

Each nation must deal with these problems in the context of its own culture. However, a number of steps can be suggested that have wide applicability. More funding for the technical education of women can be provided. Women scientists from developing nations can be provided with funds to attend scientific meetings and get additional training. The Netherlands government set an excellent example in providing funds for several women scientists from Third World nations to attend the Non-governmental Organizations (NGO) Forum accompanying UNCSTD. Laws prohibiting discrimination on the basis of sex can be passed and enforced. Programs to change cultural factors that limit the participation of women in science and technology can be initiated.

But active planning to provide women with the opportunities they need is vital. The view that one can simply bring in development, without planning for the participation of women in science and technology, and find that they do, in fact, benefit, is either an expression of wishful thinking or of an indifference to the fate of women that reflects the traditional view of women as chattel, not human beings with rights and responsibilities. Planning for the integration of women into the scientific and technological work force is a sign of a knowledgeable and responsible developmental effort. For this reason, the passage at UNCSTD of the Resolution on Women, Science, and Technology, which included a section on women as participants in the work of science and technology, was a welcome development. However, its implementation will require great efforts. For if there was one thing that the women scientists at UNCSTD felt above all, it was the great distance that all nations still have to go to give women true parity with men in the sciences and the need for full cooperation from the governments of all nations, as well as the efforts of concerned scientists, both men and women, throughout the world to achieve this goal.

Notes

1. H. S. Astin, *The Woman Doctorate in America* (New York: The Russell Sage Foundation, 1969); J. S. Giele and A. C. Smock (eds.), *Women: Roles and Status in Eight Countries* (New York: J. Wiley & Sons, 1977); M. S. Horner, "Toward an Understanding of Achievement-related Conflicts in Women," *Journal of Social Issues,* Vol. 28, 1972; M.T.M. Mednick, S. S. Tangri and L. W. Hoffman, (eds.), *Women and Achievement* (New York: J. Wiley & Sons, 1975).

2. A.M. Briscoe and S. M. Pfafflin (eds.), "Expanding the Role of Women in The Sciences," *Annals of the New York Academy of Sciences,* Vol. 323, 1979. J.A. Ramaley (ed.), *Covert Discrimination and Women in the Sciences* (Boulder, Colo.: Westview Press, 1978).

3. N. T. Dodge, *Women in the Soviet Economy* (Baltimore: Johns Hopkins University Press, 1966), p. 193; G. W. Lapidus, *Women in Soviet Society* (Berkeley: University of California Press, 1978), pp. 173–174.

4. A. M. Briscoe and S. M. Pfafflin (eds.), op. cit. See especially Part II.

5. C. Safilios-Rothschild, "A Cross-Cultural Examination of Women's Marital, Educational and Occupational Options," *Acta Sociologica,* Vol. 14, 1971, pp. 96–113; E. Haavio-Mannila, "Convergences between East and West: Tradition and Modernity in Sex Roles in Sweden, Finland and the Soviet

Union," *Acta Sociologica,* Vol. 14, 1971, pp. 114–125.

6. N. T. Dodge, op. cit., pp. 216–237; P. L. McGrath, *The Unfinished Assignment: Equal Education for Women,* Worldwatch Paper 7 (Washington, D.C.: Worldwatch Institute, 1976), p. 38.

7. P. L. McGrath, op. cit., p. 26; UNESCO, E/CN.6/498, *Access of Girls and Women to Technical and Vocational Education,* 1968; UNESCO, E/CN.6/557/ "Study on UNESCO Activities of Special Interest to Women," 1972, pp. 17–18; United Nations Document A/34/577, "Status and Role of Women in Education and in the Economic and Social Fields," Report of the Secretary-General, 1979, pp. 4–12.

8. UNESCO, *Statistical Yearbook 1977* (Paris: United Nations, 1978).

9. E.E. Maccoby and C. N. Jacklin, *The Psychology of Sex Differences* (Stanford: Stanford University Press, 1974), pp. 350, 370.

10. R. Kushner, *Breast Cancer* (New York: Harcourt-Brace Jovanovich, 1975).

11. P. L. McGrath, op. cit., p. 38.

12. P. L. McGrath, op. cit., pp. 25–26.

13. B. R. Sandler, "Women in Academe: Why It Still Hurts To Be a Woman in Labor," in A.M. Briscoe, and S. M. Pfafflin, op. cit., pp. 14–26.

14. N. T. Dodge, op. cit., p. 221; A. K. Daniels, "Development of Feminist Networks in the Professions," in A. M. Briscoe and S. M. Pfafflin (eds.), op. cit., pp. 215–227.

15. E. Boulding, *Women in the Twentieth Century World* (New York: J. Wiley & Sons, 1977), pp. 70–71; N. T. Dodge, op. cit., pp. 233, 240–241; Juanita M. Kreps and R. John Leaper, "Home Work, Market Work and the Allocation of Time," p. 74 in Juanita Kreps (ed.), *Women and the American Economy* (Englewood Cliffs, N.J.: Prentice-Hall, 1976), pp. 61–81.

16. E. Haavio-Mannila, op. cit.

17. N. T. Dodge, op. cit., pp. 233, 245; V. Kistiakowsky, "Women in Physics: Unnecessary, Injurious and Out of Place?" *Physics Today,* February 1980, pp. 32–40.

18. E. Boulding, op. cit., pp. 112–113.

19. J. Bernard, *Academic Women* (University Park: Pennsylvania State University Press, 1964); L. K. Epstein (ed.), *Women in the Professions* (Lexington, Mass.: D.C. Heath & Co., 1975); R. B. Kundsin (ed.) "Successful Women in the Sciences. An Analysis of Determinants," *Annals of the New York Academy of Sciences,* Vol. 203, 1973; Ramaley, J. A. (ed.), op. cit.; A. A. Yohalem, *The Careers of Professional Women* (New York: Universe Books, 1979).

20. F. Salili, "Determinants of Achievement Motivation for Women in Developing Countries," *Journal of Vocational Behavior,* Vol. 14, 1979, pp. 297–305.

21. B. B. Whiting, "The Kenyan Woman: Traditional and Modern," in R. B. Kundsin (ed.), op. cit., pp. 71–75.

APPENDIX A

These resolutions are presented as recommendations to increase the effectiveness of the UNCSTD Plan of Action.

Resolution on Women in Science

A scientific career requires appropriate education from an early age, access to advanced training and professional employment with the opportunity to utilize fully professional skills. Much evidence exists which shows that in many countries, developed and developing, girls receive less education than boys, and what they do receive has less technical or scientific content, and they frequently encounter barriers in obtaining advanced scientific training. Those women who do achieve professional training often face discrimination in hiring and advancement, and are seldom allowed to hold posts involving scientific and technical policy decisions.

Therefore, we urge the following:

1) That equal educational opportunities be provided to males and females including training in technical subjects, from the primary level up, and that advanced training be made equally available to men and women. Men and women from all economic levels should be encouraged to fulfill their potential in science and technology. This should be a prerequisite for support of educational programs proposed in this plan. For the promotion of equal opportunity for women in science and technology we urge UNCSTD to encourage that all educational institutions, primary, secondary, and advanced, be coeducational in all countries. Facilities in such institutions should take into account the cultural heritage of the country concerned.

2) That specific actions be taken to eliminate discrimination against women scientists in such areas as employment, promotion, and access to research support and facilities. Any new research institutions funded under the various proposals in this plan should be required to follow a policy of equal opportunity in the employment of women, and to have effective procedures for implementing this policy.

3) Every effort should be made to select women for scientific

review boards, international conference delegations, and government and private positions in scientific administration and policy making. The impact of science and technology upon women in their daily lives should be a matter of consideration in all planning.

Additional Recommendations

1. In the future at least 30% of the participants in the preparatory conference should be women. The role of women in development should be addressed explicitly in all areas of planning.

2. The UNCSTD should provide guidelines to nations on the code of conduct in the transfer of technology, particularly in forms of technologies which affect women (e.g., in medicine, pharmaceuticals, agriculture, handling of food, labour-saving devices). Products of technology are literally imposed upon women who are not involved in decision making and research, except when they play the role of guinea pigs.

3. We urge UNCSTD to encourage research and development on contraceptives for males to the same extent as is now done for contraceptives for females, so that a higher percentage of males are encouraged to take part in family planning.

APPENDIX B

Women, Science and Technology: A Resolution

The United Nations Conference on Science and Technology for Development,
  Mindful that the United Nations Decade for Women was proclaimed in order to draw attention to the problems faced by women in their daily lives and to stimulate recognition at the national and international levels of the loss experienced where women, accounting for half of the world's adult population, are not given equal opportunity to contribute fully to national development,
  Recalling General Assembly resolutions 3342 (XXIX) of 17 December 1974 and 3524 (XXX) of 15 December 1975 on the integration of women in development, in which the Assembly urged Governments to give sustained attention to the integration of women in the planning, formulation, design and implementation of development projects and programmes, as well as Assembly resolution 33/184 of 29 January 1979 on the importance of the improvement of the status and role of women in education and in the economic and social fields for the achievement of the equality of women with men,
  Recalling the relevant proposals of the World Plan of Action for the Implementation of the Objectives of the International Women's Year adopted at the Conference of the International Women's Year held at Mexico City,[16] the World Population Plan of Action[17] and the World Food Conference,[18] as well as the World Conference on Agrarian Reform and Rural Development[19] on the integration of women in development,
  Noting the importance accorded to the integration of women in development by the Governing Council of the United Nations Development Programme at its nineteenth session and by the Industrial Development Board of the United Nations Industrial Development Organization at its ninth session,
  Mindful that the Training and Research Centre for Women of the Economic Commission for Africa, the Economic and Social Commission for Asia and the Pacific, the United Nations Conference on Trade and Development, the United Nations Children's Fund, the International Labour Organisation, The United Nations Development Programme, the Food and Agriculture Organization of the United Nations, the United Nations Educational, Scientific and Cultural

Organizations and the World Bank have planned activities and studies concerning technological development in order to enhance women's contribution to economic life,

Recalling Economic and Social Council resolution 1978/34 of 5 May 1978 on women in development and international conferences, in which the Council urged all Governments to ensure that the topic of women and development be included within the substantive discussions of international conferences, including the United Nations Conference on Science and Technology for Development,

Recognizing the importance of the present quantity and quality of the contribution of women, and its potential value where fully and appropriately utilized and developed, for the well-being and wealth of their families and societies as a whole,

1. *Invites* Member States to facilitate:

(a) The equal distribution of the benefits of scientific and technological development and its application to men and women in society;

(b) The participation of women in the decision-making process related to science and technology, including planning and setting priorities for research and development and in the choice, acquisition, adaptation, innovation, and application of science and technology for development;

(c) The equal access for women and men to scientific and technological training and to the respective professional careers;

2. *Recommends* that all organs, organizations and other bodies of the United Nations system related to science and technology should:

(a) Continually review the impact of their programmes and activities on women;

(b) Promote the full participation of women in the planning and implementation of their programmes;

3. *Invites* the proposed Intergovernmental Committee on Science and Technology for Development:

(a) To give due regard to the perspectives and interests of women in all its recommendations, programmes and actions;

(b) To include in its annual reports a review on the progress made concerning the implementation of the tenets of the present resolution;

4. *Recommends* to the forthcoming World Conference of the United Nations Decade for Women: Equality, Development and Peace, to be held in 1980, to give due consideration to the relationships between

women, science, technology and development.

Notes

16. See *Report of the World Conference of the International Women's Year* (United Nations publication, Sales No. E.76.IV.1).
17. See E./CONF.60/19.
18. See E/CONF.65/20.
19. A/34/485.

Index